SURFING THE BLACK

WAVE

BRAND LEADERSHIP
in a Digital Age

DANIEL BRIAN COBB

SURFING THE BLACK WAVE: Brand Leadership in a Digital Age

For more information, please contact Daniel Brian Cobb by visiting **danielbrian.com** or write to:

222 South Main Street, Rochester, MI 48307

Printed in Canada

ISBN-13: 978-0-9980106-0-1
ISBN-10: 0-9980106-0-X

CONTENTS

ENDORSEMENTS

This is not only an important book for advertisers. It's a timely book for leaders. Dan offers a practical guide to the next decade of business. *Surfing the Black Wave* offers a tremendous metaphor for how leaders will rise and fall under the great innovation surge breaking through in digital marketing.

At Chick-fil-A, we believe our success in digital marketing will not be measured by the sales we can get, but rather how these changing tools can be used to create additional value for our customers. If we give generous value to our customers, we believe they will generously pay us back. Dan's book boldly proves out the science behind this belief. It outlines an exciting future where the greatest innovations will come from brands that add remarkable value rather than extracting it by using remarkable new platforms. He shows us practical solutions and real-world examples you can use today. Don't miss this wave!

– David Salyers, *V.P. of Marketing, Chick-fil-A*

Dan Cobb is one of the brilliant creative minds of our time. Having worked with him since he first set up shop in his basement 25 years ago, I am continually impressed by his quick grasp of the changing consumer landscape and his ability to create breakthrough messages that resonate in both form and function. *Surfing The Black Wave* is another bold step in the evolution of marketing.

– Liz Schnell, *V.P. of Brand Strategy, Henry Ford Health System*

Today's leaders are silently frozen, directionless in navigating the trendy waves of digital marketing. Dan came alongside our teams at Microsoft and provided prescriptive guidance through uncharted waters. *Surfing the Black Wave* establishes a vision of the future for building the brands that will lead the world. Don't traverse the next business decade without this book.

– **Frank Riviera,** *Director Productivity Sales, Microsoft*

The global consumer landscape is changing at near the speed of light, creating unforeseen challenges for every business. This complex environment makes this book a "must read" for a broad audience, including every C-suite executive and entrepreneur.

– **Brad Fogleman,** *SVP, Huntington Bank*

Dan Cobb delivers a compelling how-to for anyone who is looking for strategic counsel on how to ride the wave of turbulence we are all experiencing in the Participation Age. He describes in detail what we need to do to move customers from passive observers to adoring fans. In atypical "Mad Men" fashion, he speaks to authenticity, values and bold reinvention to successfully navigate the next generation of the digital revolution.

– **Rose Glenn,** *SVP, Communications & Chief Marketing Officer, Henry Ford Health System*

With Dan by our side, my colleagues and I did remarkable marketing work that was far beyond what others imagined they could do. I have known Dan for years, and through those years, he has taught me to think distinctively in terms of marketing. Dan's ideas were far-reaching and amazing, and that is why I am not surprised that Surfing the Black Wave is challenging and forward-thinking. As marketers, it is imperative to stay ahead of the wave, and that is what Dan always challenged me to do. Through this book, he is now teaching the world of marketers to be bold. Thank you, Dan, for being a good friend, colleague and adviser, but mostly thank you for being ahead of the wave and writing this book for us. Congratulations to you! *Surfing the Black Wave* was an incredible read.

– **Denise Beaudoin,** *Director Consumer Engagement, Trinity Health*

ACKNOWLEGMENTS

It takes a village to write a book. At least this book did. I'd like to acknowledge the researchers, marketing gurus, creative-concept thinkers, tech-heads, fact-checkers, content filters, editors, proofreaders and friends who made this book possible (in alphabetical order):

- Phil Borel
- Matt Bunk
- Dale Buss
- Denise Charen
- Carey Chesney
- John Lewis
- Rosario Molina
- Josh Schneider
- Stefanie Shuttari
- Stephen Thomas
- Alyssa Webb
- Cindy Wickersham
- Michael Wilberding

Most of all, I'd like to thank the co-founder of Daniel Brian Advertising (*and my beautiful wife*),

Krista Cobb

In the mid-1500s, Martin Luther, a German professor of theology, arrived at the biblical revelation that man was intended to have direct access to God. This was an idea dramatically contrary to all previous dogma, which dictated that man could only speak to or be heard by God through the good offices of the Church.

Luther's proclamation ushered in the Age Of Enlightenment: That inflection point in history, where the Western world moved from a general feudal system, where a royal few ruled over the vast masses — to an age where all men were enabled to engage in commerce and trade. An age that took the average man from a life of toil in honor of his feudal lord to a life of opportunity and self-sufficiency.

It could be fairly argued that the greatest gift of Martin Luther and of The Enlightenment was enabling and calling on all to participate in the making of their own lives. To become active participants in their own success. The Enlightenment ushered in the earliest stages of the earliest participation age. In that light, I see Dan Cobb's book as a wonderful gift to us all, and to every endeavor. *Surfing The Black Wave* is an insightful and enlightening guide to the Participation Age — for business, and for us as individuals — in finding a path to a future of sustainable growth and success.

– Michael J. Wilberding
Founder of Traverse Bay Strategy Group and
former executive with Ogilvy Advertising

> **❝** I know at least half of my advertising budget works; I just don't know which half.
>
> *– Often attributed to Henry Ford, among others*

Often as I sit for conversations with seasoned CMOs, media executives and "mad men" from the previous generation, we discuss the state of the digital revolution in media. By the time we become completely honest with ourselves, somebody will look around the room as if to avoid being caught by a Millennial, and in a transparent whisper someone will finally say, "Advertising is broken." At least that's what a 40-year veteran from a multinational advertising agency said to me recently.

After the awkward silence which follows a statement like that, we can finally start a real conversation. So that's what we did. This book is a gathering of conversations about the current state of advertising and, more important, its future.

Consumerism is the latest buzzword in marketing. It simply means the consumer is in charge, and we, as marketers, are not. Madison Avenue and the media elite have lost their grip, and mass media have come under the control of the masses. All social structures including government, business, family and religious institutions now face the same disruption.

Digital and social media have rendered a generation immune to any influence, except their own. It's not that they don't trust authority. They think they are the authority. On everything. If you doubt it, just try to challenge them in social media. Then watch for the wave. This is dangerous territory for brands.

With the greatest access to knowledge in human history, we lack only one thing: wisdom.

As previous institutions of influence fall and totally new institutions rise to take their place, we face a crisis of leadership. In the midst of this crisis, a select few will take action and be chosen by a power greater than themselves to rise up and lead the next golden age of social influence.

These are the *black wave riders* ...

INTRO

THE THIRD WAVE

LESSONS FROM THE TSUNAMI THAT ROCKED THE WORLD

> ❝ No problem is so big or so complicated that it can't be run away from.

> – *Miki Dora, Professional Surfer*
> *a.k.a., "The Black Knight"*

On March 11, 2011, at 2:46 p.m., the city of Kamaishi was hit by the largest tsunami in the history of Japan. The Tōhoku quake that triggered the wave was so strong that it threw the entire planet off its axis; following this great event, our days are now 1.8 microseconds shorter.[1]

Dark with sediment from the sea floor, the black wave created by the tsunami towered more than 30 feet high as it approached the bay. After the initial warning signs in Kamaishi, there was just enough time for the locals to run inland for more than a mile. And, for many that wasn't far enough.

In the aftermath of the disaster, one story emerged that defied reason. As a devastated country searched for meaning, the attention of the nation was turned to Kamaishi East, a small school that was destroyed by the disaster, but surprisingly did not experience one casualty. Our assumption is that the children of Kamaishi East had prepared for this. We presume they saw the signs. But, regardless of what happened, we know they acted quickly, and every child and every teacher in the school experienced what was officially deemed a miracle.[2]

Today, these children are national heroes. But, only a select few understand what actually happened that day.

There is another tsunami coming. The next one will hit your business. The signs of change in digital consumerism are sirens to alert vigilant CEOs, CMOs and all marketing professionals. The survivors of this tsunami in Japan can inspire us. In fact, learning from these children and the saga of the black wave can help us not only survive the tumult ahead, but even ride the waves of disruption to create epic impact in our world.

If we take the time to understand the "Miracle of Kamaishi," we will discover an insight into a powerful form of leadership for this new age.

THE WALL

When the sirens sounded in Kamaishi, the people turned their focus toward the world's largest sea wall, which stood 227 feet above the sea floor. Rising 20 feet above the surface, the wall was a three-decade project heralded as the national plan to stop such a tsunami. Some even referred to it as the Great Wall of Japan.[3]

From the shore, some people gathered to watch fish flopping on wet sand as the ocean waters quickly receded toward the horizon. This was the first visible sign.

Ominous video footage shows the first wave was not the big one. Again, it was just a warning. The second wave flooded the local businesses. The second surge of water might have seemed to be the end of the frightening event, but after a short lull, it was the third wave that darkened the shoreline and crashed through the city. As this powerful wave towered over the wall and rushed into the streets, carrying cars and houses many kilometers inland, anyone unprepared was caught helpless in its path.

Many who stood gazing at the wall — thinking they were safe — were never seen again. However, none of the 3,000 students of Kamaishi East were complacent. While others stood waiting for instructions, they had other plans. And, what they did confounded a nation.[4]

Laced with oil and dark sediment extracted from the sea floor, the black wave destroyed almost the entire eastern seaboard of Japan. The only ships that survived were the ones that had sailed out to sea. A few hundred meters out in the ocean, ships barely felt the quick rise in water levels as the tsunami waves built strength under the surface. Yet, when they reached the shore, these same waves blackened the sky, and vessels that had been harbored by their owners — presuming their endless safety — tumbled into the city like bathtub toys. Some of these massive ships remain on shore or perched on top of the remaining buildings — to this day.

Not unlike this wave, disruptive changes are upon us who work in the marketing and advertising industries. How do we sail our corporate ship out to sea before a black wave can crush our brand? How do we get our children to safety before the disruption overtakes our community? Can we find the courage to face this wave of change or possibly ride it?

The black wave is the third great wave of consumerism. The first wave brought us an Industrial Age that democratized access to products through innovation. The second wave powered the Information Age, bringing us the internet, blogs and the democratization of self-publishing. But, that was just a sign of what is coming.

Now the Third Wave casts its shadow on our industry with the towering influence of social media, but soon it will hit like a tsunami of cultural disruption, making everything else open, interactive and free.

The new black wave of marketing, this Third Wave, really is about the democratization of influence. Connected tech has defined a new culture of consumer engagement and empowerment. Each consumer wants his own voice. Each wants her own social newsfeed, her own blog, his own broadcasting station. They want to tell their own stories, build their own worlds and run their own companies. They want to be heroes in their own, virtually gamified adventures. And all that is free to anyone — in exchange for their email address and a password.

Social media is just the beginning. With the freedom of unlimited self-expression at our fingertips, consumers have tasted the power of influence, and they want more.

No longer spectators of media, but registered "members," these consumers boldly join in, and even lead, the social debate. If citizens disagree with political bias in the news, they post against it. If buyers don't like a product, they deploy the influence of a tweet to change it.

It's about being free from regular programming schedules and advertising, so they can binge watch the latest TV series — without interruption.

Don't be like the townspeople of Kamaishi, who watched the sea recede into the horizon and stepped closer to the edge, sealing their fate. When you finally see the fish flopping in your sales reports, it will be too late. And, most of all, beware of your confidence in your wall. If you think you already have digital media under control, you are probably one of the ships harbored at bay.

The more experience you have in digital or social media, the more it will work against you. In this age of disruptive change, paranoia will be the only productive motivator. Some industries have already been hit, and they don't even know it. If you work in the retail, banking, health care or entertainment industries, don't bother to run behind your wall of safety.

There is no safe harbor. If you are navigating a large corporate ship, now is not the time to anchor in the formerly safe cove of last year's core strategy. Last year's business plan won't work next year. Now is the time to leave the safety of your wall and go out to sea. It's time to explore new innovation.

The black wave is lifting your new competition, powered by a force of nature: millions of digitally engaged users. These are the customers you didn't know you lost. They are no longer loyal to your brand. They put their trust in community posts that your advertising budget has no control over.

Beyond social media, the wave brings digital media technology and branded content techniques that your marketing team has never seen before. Your brand won't be able to buy space on these new consumer networks, because your competition invented them.

Marketing is not just about advertising anymore. Heads up — it never was. It's about creating platforms of influence for your brand.

FACING THIS GREAT WAVE

How can marketers stay ahead of the innovation curve and even cruise safely into a leadership position while the waters roil around them? By facing our new reality and answering five important questions:

1   What is brand management in a world controlled
     by the consumer voice?

2   What will be the moral consequences for the
     brands that pick sides in social debates?

3   How will brands communicate with elusive
     consumers — as they shift to advertising-free TV?

4   How can we make digital media more accountable
     for branding and gross sales results?

5   What will be the opportunity cost for the brands
     that don't participate?

It's time to change. Everything. Because the black wave is coming.

"THE MIRACLE OF KAMAISHI" THAT WASN'T

After the tsunami, the nation celebrated the surviving school children as *The Miracle of Kamaishi.* They became a symbol of hope during a dark time for the country. Songs were written, poetry was authored and documentary films were made about the heroic actions of these unlikely heroes of a nation.[5]

But do we really believe blind chance saved them? It's a nice thought. The idea of this story about helpless children saved by chance makes people feel better after such a tragedy, but how is it possible that one school district would rise up and create such a flawless escape when so many others were lost? Other school districts employed regular tsunami drills, but failed to get these results. Was it a miracle, or was it something else?

Researchers have been studying this event for years. Interestingly, so have philosophers. Even religious leaders have studied this story to find inspiration and meaning. The reason 3,000 students survived the tsunami of 2011 was years of preparation for such a disaster by just one man: Toshitaka Katada, professor of civil engineering at Gunma University.

"No matter how big the tsunami is, there is always something you can do," Katada told anyone who would listen to his quixotic efforts. He was driven by a deep purpose to get residents of the seaside city to take seriously the effects of the tsunami that surely, some day, would come.

Before Katada's influence, they would have hesitated. The children were passive about the threat because of overconfidence seated deep in the culture of this city. Most people believed nothing could happen to them.

So he took it upon himself to develop the "three principles of evacuation" that were drilled into the reflexes of these students.[6] We will explore these three principles later in this book.

But could it be that simple? Could there be three principles that are so powerful? Katada's model scored almost perfect results against the greatest tsunami in Japanese history. Imagine if we applied these three principles to other disruptive forces in our lives, or in our business leadership?

Katada made more effective leaders out of children than were found among the adults that day. If we are to survive, and even thrive amid the disruptive wave of social change engulfing our world, we will need to become better leaders, too. If we wait to follow others, we will face the devastation that will be common to those who remain behind. However, if we disregard old assumptions and refuse to hesitate, we can create our own miracle.

Katada's message was to warn about the risks of being passive. We, as marketers and brand managers, cannot afford to be passive either. As Katada often said, "What's important is your attitude," so we need to be prepared to step into the future without fear.

Researchers who studied the aftermath of the Tōhoku Tsunami were so impressed by the results of Katada's children that they didn't accept the simplicity of Katada's three principles alone. They believed there must be more to this story. My colleagues and I join them in their curiosity. Leadership models are proven in crisis. We believe something special happened that March of 2011. Something worthy of further exploration.

If we study the pending waves of change like Katada did, we just might discover the secret to developing better leaders to help us survive times of great change. We might even become better leaders ourselves. Specifically, if we can unpack these three principles and predict the greatest waves of change in digital marketing, we can find a way to higher ground for our brands.

You may ask, why study the waves? Every once in a generation, a great wave of social change arises. The brand that catches such a wave transcends its category to a place of dominion in culture. These brands make us curious. Think about brands that were established by riding the waves of great social change. Ford Motor Company was established in a wave of industrial automation. Nike was established during a national health and fitness revolution in America. Apple was founded during a wave of technology innovation. And Amazon rode out the first surge of the World Wide Web. There is almost a rhythm to these waves. Just when we thought the internet revolution was over, Facebook ushered in a second surge of online consumerism.

Each brand that was created by a movement eventually went on to define that movement. Ford defined the automation of industry. Nike defined a generation motivated by fitness. Apple defined personal computing. Amazon defined eCommerce. Facebook defined social media, and so on.

Branded movements like these make us wonder, "How do their leaders foresee the future?" "How does the marketing team engage social change?" These brands inspire us. They show the way.

> ❝ Winds in the east, mist coming in, like somethin' is brewin' and 'bout to begin. Can't put me finger on what lies in store, but I fear what's to happen all happened before. ...
>
> – Bert (Dick Van Dyke) in the movie Mary Poppins, Walt Disney Studios, 1964

On our journey, these brands will guide us to discover the three key principles for effective leadership in this new age of digital consumerism.

TSUNAMI ON MADISON AVENUE

The Golden Age of Advertising is coming to an end. And, I'm not just talking about the deterioration of print. We are seeing the same chilling trends in social and digital media. The average consumer sees 1,700 social and digital ads every month.[7] How many do you remember?

How will brands grow in the face of a digital consumer with a highly developed condition of banner blindness? The radio is being replaced by advertising-free MP3 playlists, and there is a surge of "Netflix Millennials" who are cuttting their cable TV and may never see another television commercial again.

Leadership is losing its footing in the undertow. How will brands communicate with consumers? How will leaders of governments, religion or even families maintain any influence as they face the wave of social conflict arising against every premise of central leadership and control?

The tide is receding on the previous model. It feels dry when the ways of the past recede over the horizon of ineffectiveness. But, that is merely the last sign before what comes next.

The following pages explore a thesis on the disruptive change happening in the marketing industry. It's a compilation of the studies and experiences of a team of marketing professionals with a vested interest in the future of advertising and media. Much of the research was developed in a partnership with Daniel Brian Advertising and Traverse Bay Strategy Group along with leading national brand partnerships, many of which will be identified in the stories contained in the pages ahead.

Our *big hairy audacious goal* was to answer the age-old question:

> ❝ I know at least half of my advertising budget works; I just don't know which half.[8]

Commonly attributed to several retail marketers including John Wanamaker and J.C. Penney, as well as my personal favorite, Henry Ford, the question has been lingering for more than 100 years. With new digital analytics, we may finally find the answer. Drawing from consumer psychology and new findings from cognitive neuroscience, our conclusions contained in this book represent almost five years of focus groups and case studies that reveal the best practices in real world digital marketing.

Some of our fundamental models of consumer behavior have changed, and others have been proven false. From our study, we have uncovered three key principles for predictable success in business during the shift toward digital consumerism. These principles are each rooted in Katada's three principles for surviving a tsunami. Not surprisingly, the answer was found in leadership.

Focused on mega-patterns, our discoveries led us to construct a model, or a representative picture, of a great wave. The word picture of this wave offers a source code to envision the future of advertising and to help marketing professionals lead their brands toward true digital media integration.

The raw truth is that marketers might know something about what worked in the past; they just don't always know why. Although digital metrics offer new insights, advertising involves human decisions that are extremely complex. When science becomes too complex to understand within the cognitive process of our brain, we tend to label it "art," "philosophy" or "religion."

Few people would call advertising a religion, but the practice is still far from science. Our objective of this thesis was to close this gap. In our conclusion, we have discovered there is a science to marketing after all, but we had it all wrong for years. As we unfold our findings, we will provide case studies for dozens of the current leaders in digital marketing — all of which navigated in their leadership roles from the same three principles that we will eventually reveal.

Throughout this study, I used my personal blog as a way to process what we were learning. Given that this process was a journey for me and my team, we decided to simply include some of them, unedited, between chapters of the book, so our readers could take this journey along with us.

Our study starts in the early 1900s. ...

SELLING BUGGIES IN FACEBOOK

BLOG POST | FEBRUARY 13, 2017 – Being a Detroiter, I am enamored with how the Industrial Age was born in my hometown. I'm especially drawn to the legend of Billy Durant[9], the spring-suspension innovator of the horse-and-buggy industry. In the late 1800s, Flint, close to Detroit, was flourishing — as was the Durant-Dort Carriage Company. That is, until Henry Ford introduced the Model-T.

Almost a decade after the automotive industry was taking over Detroit, Durant saw sales decreasing each month, but he was reluctant to change. His carriage company was still No. 1 in the world. He was a famous man in his town. Why retool? Why change things? After a series of layoffs, the unemployed buggy workers of Flint came to Durant with one desperate request: *Save this town!*

He joined with David Buick and used his buggy distribution network to sell automobiles built by Oldsmobile, Cadillac and Oakland (which eventually became Pontiac). He joined with the famous race driver Louis Chevrolet to form General Motors.

The reluctant innovator became a national hero, and Flint became the epicenter of the automotive "roar" in the "Roaring '20s."

As our team was doing some work with the bank that gave Durant his first loan (Citizens Bank), we took the opportunity to tap into the local history. The marketing director there described Durant's legendary role in building the bank itself. We learned how GM survived the Great Depression: Billy bet it all by putting his personal wealth into his company to save his town. He died penniless, but Durant made his mark on mankind — leaving behind banks, hospitals, universities and one of the world's largest companies.

Today, a new industrial revolution is taking place. This time, the communications industry is being disrupted, and it will be a great time of impact on mankind — for both good and bad. Forgotten names who led the Industrial Age like Durant and Ford were replaced by newly memorable names like Jobs and Gates, who led the Information Age.

But our kids won't aspire to become like any of those legends of industry. The new gold rush is social media apps and the gamification of everything. Enter the age of Zuckerberg and Bezos.

The Participation Age has begun. Like all organic movements, this one is not being defined by its leaders, but by the people who empower them. And, the people have true power this time. All broadcast media as we know it will become digital and interactive over the next decade. Print media is being replaced by social media. Newswriters are being replaced by bloggers. And, our digitally connected neighbors will be the trusted sources of news. Broadcast TV, radio and home video will follow this same trend, becoming digitized and socialized. Next, all linear commercial messaging — like the interruptive TV spots we love — will eventually go the way of the horse and buggy.

It's not too late to join the digital revolution as a leader. Consider this: Billy Durant incorporated General Motors on September 16, 1908. That was five years after the Packard Motor Company built the "world's most advanced factory," as touted by the media at the time. Only two weeks after GM was issued their certificate of incorporation, an unknown wannabe named Henry Ford introduced an awkward little vehicle named the Model-T. By the time Henry Ford was pulling down $100 million in car sales, GM was still a tiny startup trying to find its way.

Durant was not satisfied to end his life as a washed up horse-and-buggy innovator. In a relentless push to ride the new wave of automation, he drove GM toward the next innovation, sporty automotive design and powerful V-8 engines. Although Billy himself went broke investing in this future, GM built on his legacy with cars like the '57 Chevy and the Cadillac Eldorado, surpassing Ford in vehicle sales. Even the great Packard Motor Company with its stylish Studebaker could not compete with the innovative changes introduced by GM.

No, it's not too late to catch the next wave. And, if you are already ahead of this wave, don't get cocky. Most people don't even know who Packard is anymore. Today, the Packard Motor Company building has become a tourist destination for photojournalists who take the pilgrimage to Detroit, just to capture the essence of the world's largest abandoned factory. And it's a favorite set for post-apocalyptic movies.

What drives such radical market change in times of disruptive innovation? What was the secret of GM? How does this caliber of leadership arise and maintain such a culture of sustainable innovation? A man saw the wave coming.

You can try to market your buggy on Facebook. You can even add social media links to your horseless-carriage blog. But, if your business doesn't continually innovate and digitally "participate" with your consumers, you won't be relevant very long. If your business is losing ground already, now is the time to make the change. If your business is a booming buggy-works, it's time to innovate. It's going to be hard. You might not even experience all the benefits in the current marketing cycle, but the world will eventually thank you.

[Based on the first blog post that initiated our journey four years ago.]

1

THE PARTICIPATION AGE

THE NEXT AGE OF ENLIGHTENMENT

> **ff** Category creators are 13% of the Fortune 100, but they create 74% of the growth.[1]
>
> – *Harvard Business Review*

Great waves of change often come in patterns of three. I once had the opportunity to learn to surf with some seasoned pros. They taught me how to look for sets of waves. Often these came as three or more. Nature reveals mega-patterns like this so often, that society actually have a term for it — Rules of Three.[2]

Decades of study of tsunamis in Hawaii have revealed a similar pattern. The first tsunami studied hit the Big Island on April 1, 1946.[3] A tsunami generated by a 7.4 earthquake in the Aleutian Islands arrived in Hilo without warning. As students and teachers at a school in Laupahoehoe watched the two first sets of waves recede, they were actually drawn to the ocean by the fish flopping on the wet sand. Then suddenly, a violent third wave rose up as tall as the palm trees, engulfed the students, devastated the shoreline and destroyed the school, as well as downtown Hilo.

The loss of these students served as inspiration for international researchers including Japan's Toshitaka Katada, the man responsible for the drills and education that saved the students of Kamaishi East.

RULES OF THREE

Since the tragic third wave of Hawaii in 1946, scientists studied[4] this repeating pattern of threes years later in Hawaii, among other places in the world. Some scientists believe this observed pattern of three is generated at the molecular level. In the 1970s, Soviet nuclear physicists began a study of a trio of cesium atoms forming a consistent pattern of Borromean rings.[5] They found that these threesomes exhibited a surprising feature: They had the ability to scale in a predictively consistent pattern from infinitely small at the atomic level to infinitely large beyond the scale of the universe.

In art, the rule of three is used to create balance. In the ancient Jewish study of numbers called gematria, three is a sacred number that represents divine completion or resurrection that leads to an enlightened "blooming age."[6]

This presents an interesting philosophical hypothesis. Could the rule of three apply to waves of social change? As we explore mega-patterns, it's difficult to ignore the two previous revolutions of consumerism. After thousands of years as an agricultural society, the first wave struck society as the Industrial Age slightly more than a hundred years ago. The second wave defined the Information Age, introduced only 50 years ago. Although it was an impressive shift in consumerism, the Information Age may not be the last word in social progress. In fact, it probably isn't. Could there be a third wave coming? Could it be even greater than the first two?

Now is the time we should be looking over the horizon for the inevitable third wave of consumerism: the Participation Age. Recently named by business and social thought leaders, experts expect the Participation Age to be the most disruptive shift since the Age of Enlightenment.[7] Not unlike when the peasants rose up against their feudal Lords during the first Age of Enlightenment, some even describe the current shift toward consumer-driven culture as a revolution.

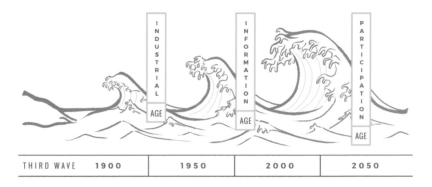

| THIRD WAVE | 1900 | 1950 | 2000 | 2050 |

THE SIGNS OF REVOLUTION

Revolutions occur when people want more freedom. Inevitably, passionate leaders arise with self-abandon to give it to them. Social media has given a powerful voice to these leaders.

This power was demonstrated in the 2016 military coup in Turkey that played out on social media. The surrender by the Turkish commander ultimately telling his unit to lay down arms was broadcast to the population in the form of a Facebook post.[8]

Media used to be under control of the state or big business. Today, the media is controlled by the people, and they have a say in the revolution.

Revolutions are not only taking place in countries. Revolutions are taking place in the business arena, too. The revolutionaries were college students like Mark Zuckerberg, who led his revolt from a Harvard dormitory room. Who knew that Facebook would eventually play a role in toppling governments? Similar to government revolutions, business revolutions are driven by a passion for new forms of freedom. People want freedom to express themselves, freedom to own things or change things. To make things better. As leaders rise to provide these new freedoms, they establish brands that help people explore and change the world. History can teach us the patterns that will help us detect these watershed moments.

Consider the automotive revolution led by Henry Ford, who passionately proclaimed, "Every man should be free to enjoy God's green earth."[9] Brands like Ford Motor Company contributed to the Industrial Age, and drove new freedom to travel nations.

The next wave that followed the Industrial Age didn't bring more of the same thing. It was new. Revolutionaries like Steve Jobs and Bill Gates brought us a computer revolution that freely connected us to information previously unknown. In the next era, don't look for more mass manufactured products you can buy or more access to information. The third wave won't look anything like the first two. In this age of consumer engagement, we are witnessing the end of using computers merely for information, and the beginning of using them for influence.

All this power of influence feeds our desire to participate in politics. New workers expect to participate in office policy and profits. And, the participation in hotly contested social and political debates has flown off the chart.

Pioneering brands are gaining *direct* access to their consumers. We've removed the network middleman, and brands are becoming the new broadcasters. As news and commentary become controlled by brands, this creates a new discourse on corporate values. Branded content is powerful. Do we really want brands to tell people what to think and believe?

Some brands are picking sides on social issues, including GMO foods, human rights, global warming, religion, gay marriage and cross-gender bathroom use. Many brands still avoid participation, merely to save marketing budgets or hoping to avoid the risks involved in the debate.

Meanwhile, consumers continue to polarize ideologically, reducing their tolerance for any entity — including brands — that won't choose sides in the various culture wars.

RUN FOR THE HIGH GROUND

When people face great forces of change, they don't always make good choices. Facing their fear of the unknown, they tend to hesitate. They question sound judgment. Katada studied fear. He understood fear can paralyze rational thought, rendering people helpless when danger approaches.

"In general, people don't evacuate even though they know they should," said Katada. "It's natural to be reluctant to escape when no one else is escaping. So I told the students that they must be brave and be the first ones to evacuate. If you do, others will follow you, and you can save their lives, too," he said. "And that is exactly what happened."

Katada's three principles were established from an old saying[10] from the Sanriku region of Japan, "Tsunami tendenko," which is translated as, "In a tsunami, flee separately." Normally, children would wait for instructions from adults, but Katada taught the children that followers and

> " I told the students that they must be brave and be the first ones to evacuate. If you do, others will follow you, and you can save their lives, too. ...
>
> – Toshikata Katada

those who hesitate are the ones who die. They were not taught to follow orders, but to save themselves and others around them.

When the earthquake hit, the intercom at Kamaishi East school was damaged by the shock, so there was no way for officials to warn the students. The students took it upon themselves to shout, "Tsunami!" "It was scary," one child survivor recalled. "I ran desperately ... I kept chanting to myself, just do it like you did in the evacuation drills and everything will be okay."

And when the children arrived at the designated evacuation center, with Katada's warnings echoing in their heads, they didn't stop there. One boy imagined that the cliff they had ascended to could collapse and urged the children to continue on to still higher ground. Junior high students holding the hands of kindergarteners and pushing strollers arrived at the higher ground just in time.

Looking back on where the road once was, they witnessed a cloud of dust climb high into the air from the very spot where they had just come. The tsunami had engulfed the designated evacuation center shortly after they escaped it.

As predicted by Katada, there never was time to wait for the teachers to decide what to do. Nearly 1,000 people died in their town, but none were lost who attended school that day.[11] When media interviewers came to document the story, Katada would always explain the same three principles.

In these principles, the children were taught to ignore what seemed popular. They were taught to see beyond what the crowd was doing. Similarly, we as marketers need to look beyond the trends. Early on, social media was about earning likes, views and comments on popular portals. Today, the rules have changed, and the social media platforms have begun to monetize their models. Now, we have to pay to boost our message to the fans and communities we worked so hard to engage. This raises the stakes on social engagement, and could cause marketers to hesitate.

When we pay for media, we tend to revert back to the old models, pushing promotions and sales gimmicks. Don't stop at this designated evacuation center. Facebook and Instagram might seem like safe platforms upon which to build your brand, but these platforms are more unstable than they appear. You don't own the platform. You don't even own your fan database. Facebook does. So, the rules can change.

Social media networks are merely a foreshadowing of a whole new way of engaging consumers through media. When we take our focus off its shadow and look up to recognize the movement that inspired social media, we will begin to understand the power of something much greater: *Participation Media*.

During this transformation of all media as we know it, brands that want to succeed can't simply push outdated messages into this new space. The once-powerful advertising monologue with the consumer now has become a dialog, and those of the Participation Generation who have grown up in this new dynamic are enjoying their power.

If your customers feel your advertising imposes an interruption on their freedom, they'll simply turn your ads off in their user preferences. More than one-quarter of Millennials already have cut their cable TV and satellite services in exchange for advertising-free TV services, such as Netflix and Apple TV.[12] And, the shift is moving quickly.

Beyond participation in social media websites, these new networks will soon provide Participation TV, Participation Radio, Participation News and a new breed of Participation Mobile Apps.

If you are a brand manager, don't hesitate. When you see the white crest of the black wave coming, don't simply relaunch last year's media plan, adding incremental digital ad placements and social media monitoring services. That wall is coming down. These tactics may have kept us safe during the previous wave, but they won't protect us from the power of the third wave. Instead of waiting to sponsor the next big thing after it reaches critical media mass, we must begin exploring and even creating whole new media channels to reach our consumers.

This might sound foreign, but tomorrow's successful brands will no longer rent their voices from the media. They will invest in their own media platforms. They will eventually own the media ... and the voice of culture.

You don't have to look far to see this wave of disruption transforming entire industries.

For example, the app store isn't just for angry birds anymore. With more than half of all consumer digital time spent in apps, branded apps are the new advertising.[13] Quick-serve restaurants are building connected relationships with consumers through online ordering apps. Starbucks now collects more than 21% of its revenue from mobile app orders.[14]

Announcing an option to "Bypass the Line," the Chick-fil-A One™ app was the No. 1 download in the App Store during its launch in 2016.[15] And, now more than half of all orders for leading pizza brands happen online. Retailers are accelerating this trend as they learn buyers spend 30% more per transaction when using some of these apps.[16]

More importantly, these mobile buyers are staying loyal. Independent retailers are dying without a corporately sponsored app. For example, the leaders in the pizza industry are growing by 5% to 10% per year with most of the new revenue coming from app sales, while the independent pizza shops who have no online ordering apps are losing 1% or more in gross revenue annually. That's because app users visit 67% more frequently than non-users.[17]

The banking industry was disrupted when Quicken Loans launched Rocket Mortgage, promoting "Push Button, Get Mortgage."[18] Suddenly, less advanced mortgage companies became obsolete. The empowered consumer believes the best service is self service in the Participation Age, and many new home buyers have never met a banker.

As bankers become replaced by bots, health systems are automating health care. Under the headline of telehealth, Kaiser Permanente has grown a media network of five million participating members.[19] This managed health community is only to be surpassed by Nike, which has 28 million users of its fitness app. While others would have invested in posting "Just Do It" memes in Facebook, Nike built its own social network instead. Marketers were left scratching their heads as Nike dominated the shoe industry after reducing its traditional and social media spending by 40% to pay for its own social media network.[20]

In one of the most disruptive changes, nontraditional movie producers are emerging, including Netflix, Amazon, Xbox and even Red Bull, with their own film studios that make movies to compete with Hollywood. Investing billions of dollars into original TV series and made-for-digital movies, these streaming studio budgets could soon eclipse those of the home video and TV industries.[21]

After Amazon Prime achieved 69 million members on its own home video channel, Amazon cut its TV advertising budget to relatively nothing at all.[22] Now, this former broadcast advertiser has more paid TV subscribers than the entire cable TV industry.[23] Perhaps the brands Amazon sells will eventually pay to advertise on the Amazon channel. Our concept of media is about to flip.

Brands including Blockbuster, Borders and many local newspapers were blown into oblivion by some of the industry newcomers during the second wave. More brands will face this same demise in the next transition. Winning brands won't stand behind their walls of safety, watching and waiting to see how others do it first. By then, it will be too late.

In the aftermath of the tsunami in Japan, the mayor of Kamaishi, Takenori Noda, said that although the loudspeakers warned people to escape the city, many did not. He said, "I do believe that, unconsciously, the breakwater did give people a false sense of security."[24] It was strong enough to stand up to almost 30 years of waves. However, we cannot afford to believe our future is secure because of the past success we have experienced. We need to build our marketing plans as if there were no wall of safety.

PARTICIPATION IS A NEW WAY OF THINKING

Of course, it's time for innovation. But, before we all run off to build a TV studio or launch our own social network, let's back up to consider the forces that are driving marketing innovation in the Participation Age. For starters, breakthrough marketing is no longer about posting innovative content on Instagram or Snapchat. It's not about what we say to consumers at all.

It's about what we do, and consequently, what our consumers say about us. Of course, everybody knows that in concept by now, but how does that affect the daily duties of a marketing director, CMO or CEO? How do we empower the right behaviors to extend beyond our daily mandates to thousands of micro-actions we cannot control within the workforce and social community? It's about communicating the vision and values that exude from the brand's core purpose.

Yes, you've probably heard a lot about "corporate purpose." If you've been to a leadership seminar in the last decade, you've heard the grand prescription: People don't care about what you sell until they believe in what you stand for, blah, blah, blah.

It's all true, but after you get your corporate life-coach to help you deep-dive into your inner corporate child, after all of the falling exercises and group hugs, what then? How do we activate our core purpose in the marketing department?

Let's explore how purpose connects with employees and consumers in the Participation Age.

POWERED BY PURPOSE

In the Industrial Age, there emerged a passionate pursuit of mass production to make the world better. In the Information Age, pioneers improved how technology could inform our lives.

To be sure, the industrialization of nations has improved the human condition, providing almost all of the food and shelter we could ever want. If you doubt it, visit a Third World country, where they don't even have dirty water to complain about. And following the rise of industry, the rise of access to information has reduced unlimited knowledge down to a keyword search. As a result, our unending quest for knowledge has provided a free worldwide network that has nearly commoditized education itself.

So, what is the third wave of corporate history that will transform the human condition again?

Now that consumers have almost all of the goods and information they need, their internal demand for something more meaningful drives them. Each person has a very personal need to understand his or her purpose, and to give something back in a way most meaningful to them. Beyond making things, a new corporate product has become paramount: making meaning.

This journey from finding success to contributing significance can be mapped in social movements as expressed in three waves in the history of consumerism. In each wave, marketing progressively offers more value beyond selling a product that meets physical needs to selling a cause that provides personal fulfillment.

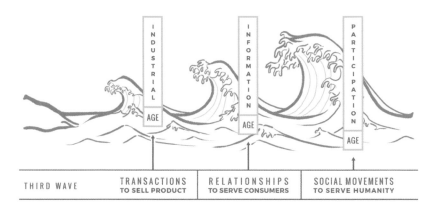

THIRD WAVE	TRANSACTIONS TO SELL PRODUCT	RELATIONSHIPS TO SERVE CONSUMERS	SOCIAL MOVEMENTS TO SERVE HUMANITY

In the first wave, created by marketers to address the needs of the Industrial Age, advertising promoted transactions to sell products. All we needed to do was label the cup "coffee," and the consumer had all the information needed to make an informed purchase. A simple gas station coffee would cost as little as 50 cents. Differentiation was irrelevant.

In the second wave, advertising built relationships to serve the consumer.[25] We crafted a logo to differentiate a brand based on a better service experience. Brands like Starbucks evolved to provide an environment with music and community. We could charge obscene amounts for a cup of joe, with a new wave of choices and exclusive flavors. Branding experts thought we had arrived at marketing nirvana.

Now, as the third wave propels the consumer economy, individuals have more than their needs met — at several competing coffee shops. Now, individuals want to give back to society with every purchase. They want to be assured that the coffee is grown by a brand that provides good working conditions for the coffee growers and brewers. Self-actualized consumers want to know that the product is organically grown or that a percentage of each purchase will support sustainable causes around the world or even prevent global warming ... and create world peace. Don't laugh. Just look around the room next time you visit a Starbucks.

THE MASLOW EFFECT AND THE CONSUMER BRAIN

In recent studies, neuroscientists have discovered that we spend 80 to 90 percent of our brain function processing social interaction.[26] Apparently, our brains obsess about social needs, social status and how we will contribute to society. As the brain achieves dominion over each new measure of social need, it progresses to achieve something greater: Social Purpose.

These findings take me back to my Consumer Psychology 101 classroom at Michigan State University. Remember Maslow's Hierarchy of Needs?[27]

Abraham Maslow developed a pyramid to model the influences that drive human behavior. At the base of the pyramid, we visualize the base needs of every human being — to have food, water, shelter and a sense of safety. Once these base needs are met, new needs become relevant, unconsciously driving us up the pyramid toward fulfilling our need to belong in a community. The bottom of the pyramid is focused on self, but as needs of self are met, the brain becomes aware of and concerned about the needs of our family, our tribes and the greater needs of society.

After we as humans get each successive need met, we become aware of deeper desires that ascend up Maslow's proverbial chart until we finally reach the zenith: Self-Actualization, or Purpose. Perhaps this could be the reason most billionaires actually give away most of their wealth before they die. Self-Actualization is when we finally realize it's not about self at all.

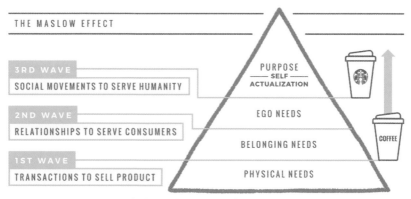

Abraham Maslow, "A Theory of Human Motivation." Psychological Review, 1943.

All of these forces give us insights to the consumer brain, or the parts of our gray matter that drive consumer decision-making for our brands. Cognitive scientists have studied the behaviors of split-brain patients to determine the locations in the brain that focus on these basic human needs. They have discovered very specific regional differences in brain processing. With few exceptions, the decisions made at the base of Maslow's pyramid, including fulfilling self-sustaining needs for food and shelter, are processed in the left hemisphere of the brain.

Interestingly, the selfless part of the brain is most often found in the right hemisphere, where we are able to understand spatial relationships such as the greater context of the world, outside of self. In short, scientists have learned that the left brain projects a perpetual need for more food and a bigger house, while the right brain pauses to consider the fact that other people are homeless and starving.

According to leading cognitive neuroscientist Michael Gazzaniga, in this study of split-brain patients, he found the right brain generally tends to be the emotional hemisphere that might even write a song or cry over the plight of others.

As opposed to the conscious awareness in our left brain, we are not consciously aware of our right brain's needs or desires. The emotional side of the brain is dark to us. However, right brain passions tend to be unlocked from our unconscious as we ascend the chart. In addition to unconscious thought, the right hemisphere is also responsible for creativity, art, music and emotions, including love. Perhaps this is why during times of great prosperity and emotional safety, we discover enlightenment driven by human empathy, peaceful civilization and artistic renaissance.

This is a logical outcome if we look at society as a community of human brains. When any large group becomes enlightened to selflessness, a unified movement to improve the human condition makes sense. In other words, if we are all unknowingly designed to find self-fulfillment in serving others, awakening this desire to do good can be the secret to building movements.

The same holds true for branded movements. Brand advocates are inspired when brands do good.

APPEAL TO SELF-ACTUALIZATION, NOT SELF-INTEREST

This new paradigm is being simultaneously studied in multiple disciplines. It answers questions that previously baffled cognitive neuroscientists. Questions like, "If our brains are wired for self-interest, why would a soldier fall on a grenade for his friends?" Researchers in the fields of science, sociology and economics are beginning to discover what many religions have always known: the answer to the question, "Am I designed to be my brother's keeper?"

The previous theory of self-interest has misled an entire society to become defined by selfishness. The relentless quest to fulfill self-interest has produced some of the most unfulfilled and unhappy societies in the world. This is evidenced by the fact that some of the wealthiest countries in the world, including Korea and Japan rank among the highest in the world for suicide rates.[28] In America, the suicide rate hit a 30-year high by 2016, passing the worldwide average for men.

It seems we should remove economic factors from the happiness index. In the comparative analysis of the prosperity index, we've found that many Third World countries have much happier societies. Of the 25 countries deemed to be the most depressed, 11 are ranked among the wealthiest societies on the globe, based on Gross National Income per capita.[29]

These trends have confounded experts. Sociologists and psychologists — including Abraham Maslow himself — have even questioned his famous hierarchy. In Maslow's later years, the study of mental hopelessness revealed that his pyramid could be upside down. Without purpose, the human brain will actually neglect its base need for food and shelter. It seems that hope is truly more important than food. This crushes Maslow's pyramid into one consumer influence that drives all others: Social Purpose.

This means that prosperity has been ill-defined. We have come to the proverbial end of ourselves, after the endless chase after physical things. Our industrialized and information-rich society has made this possible. It's as if we each live today as kings of our own castles. In the land of designer-labeled toilet brushes, what further substance can we who live in an advanced society "consume," except a great mission by which to live our lives?

These influences make for an exciting possibility. An entire society of brains have become fulfilled in the quest for the obvious physical needs of life, but they remain starved for something they cannot understand. The need for a greater social purpose arises at such a time as this.

FLIP THE PYRAMID

Influence in the Participation Age manifests in a very different leadership style. Modern leaders don't merely attract followers; they inspire other leaders. This new breed of leader doesn't pay people to do a job with mere money. They pay them in delegated authority.

So, if you plan to lead in the Participation Age, don't entice employees with more money only. Don't attract consumers with mere discounts, either. You can't buy loyalty with financial incentives. Loyalty and trust are empowered by purpose.

A 2017 *Harvard Business Review* article titled, "The Neuroscience of Trust"[30] explains why employees would work longer hours and even reject up to a 20% salary increase in exchange for the opportunity to have more personal influence on the company's purpose. Consumers show a similar behavior in their purchasing patterns in relation to purpose-driven companies.

Researchers in the lab of Vernon Smith, a Nobel laureate in economics, focused on a brain chemical named oxytocin and its impact on building movements by building trust. The HBR study concluded, "Trust and purpose then mutually reinforce each other, providing a mechanism for extended oxytocin release, which produces joy." Oxytocin also increases empathy, which can unify a movement. In fact, it's the very chemical that is released during childbirth that mysteriously bonds a mother to her child.

Perhaps this is what makes Coke taste better with the label on the can. The associated sense of trust associated with the Coke brand can actually change the perceived flavor of the beverage in your brain.

This represents a change in how brands will engage people at every level. As marketers, we must stop appealing to base human needs and start appealing to the highest human expectations.

In the subconscious brain, prosperity is not defined by what we get, but by what we give. We had it all upside down. New study of the unconscious side of the brain reveals the deepest and most powerful of human forces: the need to be needed — to provide value within the society in which we identify ourselves. This is why the previous model of behavioral economics is being replaced with identity economics.[31] Ego and belonging are not merely the pathway toward progress, but the destination itself. Our self-worth is defined by our relationship with others.

Consider Maslow's pyramid upside down. If self-actualization and social influence are base human needs in our society, then how would our consumers want us to engage them?

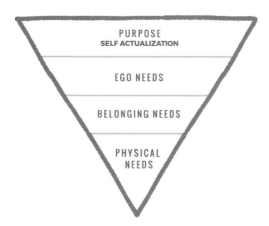

Consider ourselves and our own desires. At the highest level, we want to have influence in society. That's what motivates us to have children. Life is a journey starting as a disciple, but finding fulfillment as the teacher; from being hungry to feeding others; from feeling needy to living generously. We enter this world as followers, but we are all restless and driven to self-actualize as leaders of society.

At our very core, what we all desire most is to become leaders. I've met with dozens of CEOs and CMOs to discuss corporate objectives, and I've never met one who would be happy to be second best at anything. Customers and employees are no different. They don't want to be used or taken for granted as followers, either. Like CEOs and CMOs, these consumers of your leadership are hard-wired with the same desires: to become leaders, too.

Resist the temptation to tell leaders how to do their job. Even worse, don't do their jobs for them. They will be the first to call you a micromanager. Like a child who who desires to grow up, they are telling you that they want to do it themselves. Embrace listening instead. This is a powerful leadership discipline for influencing the participation generation. Give them vision and actually use their ideas. If you refuse to listen, you will be surrounded by useless minions who refuse to speak or think for themselves.

> ❝ Don't fear failure. Embrace it as the pathway toward progress.

Even allow them room to fail. This is how you will teach them. They don't cognitively learn lessons from books alone, but from experience. So, don't fear failure. Embrace it as the pathway toward progress. If you don't trust your followers to lead, they will leave you and lead on the behalf of others who will. That is the black wave coming from your competition.

Brands are enlisting consumers and employees to become self-actualized because this generation wants to have a voice. They want the opportunity to lead. Don't give them a task to do. Don't sell them a product to buy. Provide them with a worthy cause to join. They will lead change in your industry with you.

This is precisely how Katada inspired the students of Kamaishi East to rise up as leaders and save their entire student body, as well as the people they met along the way. Katada couldn't depend on followers to find adults to show them the way. He had to inspire children to become leaders, and create a movement.

Now, let's examine the first of the three principles for surviving a tsunami and how it will apply to the next surge in marketing. ...

KEY PRINCIPLE NO. 1:

TRAIN LEADERS TO FOLLOW PRINCIPLES, NOT PATHWAYS.

Disregarding the traditional model of teaching children obedience to a set of rules, Katada told the school kids they should distrust outdated assumptions, and rise up as leaders. They were taught to be protectors rather than wait to follow or be protected. Katada inspired the children to lead in the spirit of "going from one helped by people to one who helps people."

Most importantly, Katada taught the children to distrust guidelines, official pathways and hazard maps. Like he told them, "Those maps are based on past tsunamis and there is no telling that the next one will be exactly the same."

In the same way, the old model of marketing no longer applies. The fundamental consumer psychology model built on self-interest has been turned on its ear. In our conclusion, the first principle for surviving the black wave can be summed up by one phrase:

Like Katada, we must flip Maslow's pyramid in our brand management model and turn followers into leaders. Let's review our findings:

Leadership is powered by purpose: Move your brand to higher ground. Similar to how people self-actualize, we've found that a fully developed brand will not end its quest for differentiation until it finds its greater calling, with its own movement to lead.

Appeal to self-actualization, not self-interest: Consumers aren't inspired by consuming products for themselves, but for a greater purpose. This is what happened to the children at Kamaishi Bay. Instead of escaping with only their own physical and safety needs in mind, they self-actualized and turned their focus toward the needs of others.

Don't attract followers; inspire leaders: Don't treat consumers like children, followers or sheep. If our core purpose is worthy, we will develop our staff and empower our customers to join our movement as leaders in our cause.

This makes up the first of three principles. Now that we've *flipped the pyramid*, let's seek out the remaining two principles that will turn followers into leaders among our consumers, in our organizations and on our teams.

PURPOSE BEFORE PROFITS

BLOG: JANUARY 15, 2017 – It's no coincidence that purpose is arising in the dialog of corporate motivational circles. It's a sign of the times. Purpose has always been a key indicator of human change. Today, more than ever, purpose powers a new breed of corporate leaders. Just consider the mission statements of some leaders of the Participation Age:

> *Facebook:* "To give people the power to share and make the world more open and connected."[32]
>
> *Amazon:* "To be Earth's most customer-centric company."[33]

If you think about it, media can no longer be bought with money alone. If our aim is to earn media by becoming remark-worthy in the social-media space, what is more worthy of remark than a world-changing corporate purpose? Nothing is more shareable about a brand. And, shareable purpose is less costly than paying for every media impression through advertising.

Some marketers wonder, "Will this encouraging trend toward purpose-driven brands last? Or is this just an enduring principle of business that simply has been magnified by the power of social media?" Many experts believe the latter is true.

In fact, a litany of new marketing textbooks features purpose, debunking the previous doctrine of business success, "making money and maximizing shareholder value." As Henry Ford said, "A business that makes nothing but money is a poor business."

Another legendary personality of purpose-driven leadership, Walt Disney was neither interested in fame or fortune, nor was he inhibited by lack of resources. He once said, "Money, or the lack of it, does not excite me. Ideas excite me." He was often cited for his driving purpose to put smiles on every guest at his parks, which he built to bring children and parents together.

> " Money, or the lack of it, does not excite me. Ideas excite me.
>
> – Walt Disney

The whole concept seems to be counterintuitive. Isn't the primary purpose of business to maximize shareholder value? Aren't businesses supposed to be concerned with making money, not fixing societal problems?

Even Harvard and Cornell now admit they had it all wrong for years. Nobody saw it coming when professors at these top business schools published a shocking white paper which concluded that the shareholder value dogma is "a myth." As corporate law expert Lynn Stout put it, "Prioritization of shareholder value harms returns in the long run."[34]

Obviously, a business cannot survive very long without profits. But, as has been proven time and time again, businesses that don't provide adequate value to their customers won't survive very long either — and the bar to meet consumer expectations is rising.

Brands that want to become market leaders need to do more than create ads. They need to be bold enough to create a movement.

They need to lead in measurable results by doing remark-worthy things — not only for their company, but for their industry. And their world.

When a brand stands for something greater than its features and benefits, its best advertising will come from its fans, who will promote the brand better than any advertising campaign can.

2

PRINCIPLES BEFORE PATHWAYS

HOW PURPOSE-DRIVEN BRANDS WIN

> **❝ Companies with ideals of improving people's lives at the center of all they do outperform the market [by 400%].**
>
> *– Jim Stengel, former Global*
> *Marketing Officer of P&G*

As young Kawasaki Aki[1] ran from school with the tsunami closing in on that fateful day in March 2011, she kept her focus on her purpose, telling herself, "With our hearts and souls, we will cherish having normal lives. We won't be beaten. We will laugh a lot, have many amazing experiences, and we will all support one another."

A third-grade girl began hyperventilating. Another became unable to speak. "It's OK," first-grader Dai Dote told the older girls while encouraging them to continue running up the hill. Other children joined them in the hills, running from their homes, leading their grandmothers and siblings.

One boy who witnessed the surge[2] recounted, "A dark, black wave came at us from behind." The wave was dark because it was laced with oil and debris unearthed from diesel reservoirs and various industrial structures it already had swept away. A teenager picked up a crippled boy and put him on his shoulders. Later, the crippled boy told reporters he was embarrassed to be carried to safety, but thankful to be alive.

Another, Konno, was only in junior high, but assisted children from the neighboring elementary school. "I kept telling the students, 'It's okay, everything is going to be okay,' while I gathered up my emotions," he recalled. "I have to protect the elementary school students. I have to be strong, I thought. This is what galvanized me against a fear that had me on the verge of tears."

After the tragedy, tsunami researchers generated a digital re-enactment map that was animated to visualize the children's various escape routes. Their goal was to find a pattern for how 3,000 students survived against all odds. Surprisingly, there was no pattern found in the routes the children chose to safety. The movement of the children seemed to be random.

But researchers noted one anomaly. Some children moved much more slowly than the others. Taking a closer look at the data, these were found to be the children who were assisting elderly residents or younger children. The students of Kamaishi East became leaders in preserving life that day because they were focused on their driving purpose. Katada had effectively inspired the students to *"Flip the Pyramid."*

In the study of social behaviors, researchers have found that among large social groups, purpose-based leadership drives the greatest propensity for success. Rather than creating one-off success stories, purpose unites communities with a common cause to create movements. For the children, their purpose was clear: They were taught not only to save themselves, but also to save others.

Cognitive neuroscientists have recently mapped a specific part of the brain that can project itself to feel the pain of others. This function located in the unconscious right hemisphere is so powerful, it can actually take over the brain and direct it to reject its own natural tendency toward self-interest. Is it possible that the children were saved by this neurological phenomenon? Were they pulled together by a common concern for others?

In alignment with this scientific finding, great philosophers and religious leaders have historically taught that if we put others before ourselves, our outward compassion can help us overcome our own inward fears and anxiety.

OF PURPOSE AND PRINCIPLES

So it seems that where science, philosophy and religion come together is where we may find truth. Heroes are born of selfless acts on the battlefield. Religious saints and saviors are defined by their selfless acts of sacrifice. Selfless purpose has been discovered as a common psychological link for how great leaders have overcome their own pain to turn their focus on the task at hand, while everyone else becomes frozen from shock or fear during great disruptions in life. And many eagerly follow leaders who are driven by such powerful purpose.

Under Katada, the children of Kamaishi studied up to 15 hours per year so they would rise to leadership and take initiative in a crisis. They were taught to get to high ground and bring others with them. By taking their thoughts off themselves alone, their purpose drove them to brave acts of leadership and selflessness.

The young students actually encouraged their teachers to go beyond the restrictions imposed by their elders' own training. In fact, if the kids had followed the strict instructions of their teachers, they would have stopped at the designated evacuation zone, where they all would have been washed away.

Katada believed that teaching the children principles would prove more important than teaching them pathways. He was right. After an earthquake, routes could become blocked. High ground could become low ground, and pathways could become unrecognizable. This is why the children were taught purpose and principles rather than routes and rules.

Once the purpose was completely understood, they were free to use their own minds. They could become creative with the principles that guided each decision toward a cause greater than themselves. That's why they became so innovative to save their lives, and the lives of others. That's why their routes were so seemingly random, yet effective.

Katada didn't merely train the minds of these students. He trained their emotions. While many adults hesitated or cowered in fear, the children rose up and took action.

An estimated 18% of the adults who were in the bay area that day were counted killed or missing after the tsunami, but all of the students who went to school that day survived. What were the odds of 3,000 students all escaping the strike zone of Japan's most life-threatening tsunami?

These school-aged children were the most unlikely of the population to survive. The youngest were slow. They had no cars as adults had. They hadn't lived an adult lifetime in the city to know the best routes. They had no experience with existential threats. They were children, after all.

Yet this impossibly young group, coaxing grandparents, carrying invalids and holding the hands of even-younger children, showed the highest survival rate by a significant margin. Why? Is it possible that their childlike faith worked in their favor?

Just like the children, most adults knew that high ground would be safe. Going to high ground was in their self-interest. Yet many adults ignored this basic human instinct. Is it also possible that self-interest isn't the highest form of human motivation? Could our tendency to depend on intelligence actually work against us?

We as marketers often make the same mistake these adults did. In business, we depend on the wrong human motivation. Then, we wonder why it doesn't work. We assume people behave rationally. We depend on logic or our education. We are taught to suppress our childlike emotions in the development and evaluation of business strategy. We typically believe consumers are most effectively motivated by self-interest, so we push price, value or convenience, assuming product features and benefits matter most.

Likewise, we also assume that the greatest capitalists and corporations are motivated by money. So we fall into the same trap. Is it possible that the reverse is true? Is it possible that we have it all wrong?

In his first principle, Katada taught the children to ignore the hazard maps. He said, "When people look at hazard maps and see their houses are outside the affected zone, they're often relieved. But those maps are based on previous tsunamis." Experience can create complacency. Instead of maps, Katada gave the children a greater purpose to guide their faith, and taught them to toss their maps into the wind.

By the very definition of leadership, leaders go first. There are no maps to guide your team to places nobody has ever been. So, as we explore new ways to build our brands, we will need to toss our old maps to the wind, as well.

A LEGACY OF PURPOSE-DRIVEN LEADERS

As we enter the Participation Age, there will be a new rage at the center of this debate: Purpose-Driven Leadership. Just as the students of Kamaishi East were guided by purpose, many businesses are finding that a social cause has become the primary determinant of successful branding, too.

In this purpose-driven movement, the currency will not be sales volumes or profit margins. The new currency is social capital, born of business leaders who are driven by a passion greater than their own corporate self-interest.

Purpose-driven brands are not new. The greatest movements in corporate history were driven by an awakening by men and women of great purpose, who intended to change the world through business. Consider the corporate giants who have *Flipped the Pyramid* throughout history:

Conrad Hilton, for instance, established a company of purpose with the motto, "World peace through international trade and travel."[3] At the time, it may have seemed like an absurd religious

quest to some, but eventually, the London Hilton became the first structure to rise higher than St. Paul's Cathedral.[4]

Another titan of the Industrial Age, Henry Ford, was a common man frustrated with the wealthy elitism that drove the early automobile industry.[5] This frustration awoke Ford's passion, driving his mission statement to "Democratize the Automobile." Ford expressed his passion often in his favorite statement, "Do the most good for the most people," which he manifested in many things he did. Consider his impact on doubling worker salaries, inventing the five-day work week with no more than eight hours per day, and providing health care benefits — not to mention, a car every Ford employee could afford. Thanks to Henry Ford, many of us will drive home at 5:30 today.

When the Information Age dawned, new purpose-driven leaders arose. Steve Jobs recognized digital technology as a way for man to transcend himself. Jobs was frustrated by the mainframe computers of his youth, which were complicated and out of reach for most people. Driven by his unveiled religious fervor, he established a purpose statement that called for a revolution: "Man is the creator of change in this world." This statement became the vision for Apple as it set out to build what he called "the computer for the rest of us."[6]

The academic naysayers among Apple jeered at the lofty and unrefined use of passion in Jobs' mission and vision. Such ridicule came from some of the same pompous critics who actually fired Jobs from his own company, then nearly destroyed it.

EMOTIONAL THOUGHT LEADERSHIP

Academia and corporate establishment types have always been frustrated by people like Jobs, the college dropout, and Ford, the blue-collar tycoon. But the passion that drives great purpose doesn't bow a knee to pedigree. In fact, like intelligence, passion can't be taught or certified. It arises from a deep human need to make things better. It's a power that exudes from our very God-breathed DNA. It transcends education and protocol. It derives from a higher dimension that science doesn't yet explain. For lack of a better word, we simply call this primal instinct "emotion."

Before you snicker, consider this: Emotional thought is not the opposite of rational thought. Recent study[7] has proven that it's actually much more powerful for influencing unconscious bias such as brand loyalty, so don't overlook the role of emotion in the development of your Brand Purpose.

Several years ago, the debate raged between the so-called "feelers" and "thinkers" over the subject of emotionalism in marketing. Studies were conducted by Daniel Brian Advertising in collaboration with Traverse Bay Strategy Group.[8] We tested the importance of emotional decision-making in contrast to rational decision-making for the most important financial, health and medical decisions that affect the lives of the subjects we tested.

Our research team employed the conjoint methodology. That means in each case, we tested analytical content in a matched-pair analysis against emotional content, isolated from the noise of outside influences. Our findings were both consistent and unexpected.

PASSION BEATS PROOF POINTS

In one health system brand study[9] for CHI St. Vincent Health System based in Little Rock, Ark., we explored dozens of hypothetical advertising value propositions to determine the impact of emotional persuasion in contrast to rational persuasion in consumer advertising. The study was divided into two components:

First, we tested the impact of various proof points that might persuade patients to prefer the health system over other local options. In this test, we used text ads only, void of creative artistry or any emotional context. This test held potential bias as text-based analysis has been shown to be processed primarily by the conscious left brain.

Second, we tested these same proof points, but placed them within the context of various creative executions, complete with music and emotional imagery. This test was designed to study both the unconscious right brain and conscious left brain in a real-world advertising concept.

In the test of advertising devoid of emotion, we discovered that the sample was most impressed by the hospital being described as having a neurosurgeon ranked among the top 1% in the country.

We call this "the halo effect." In this case, this consumer belief states, "If your hospital is good enough for the best brain surgeon, you are good enough for me." This proof point ranked higher in importance among the sample than did proof points about the health system's top rankings by patients and clinical outcomes.

The hospital's top 1% neurosurgeon ranking also showed significantly more impact than promoting the brand's core values as a faith-based institution. Although founded by nuns with a profound vision for "spiritual, emotional and physical treatment," this aspect ranked only third in importance among prospective patients.

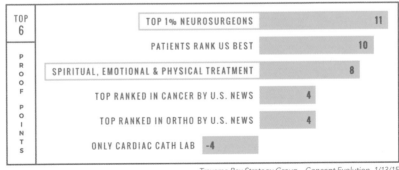

Traverse Bay Strategy Group – Concept Evolution, 1/13/15

From an analytical perspective, the outcome of the first component of the study was not shocking. After all, we are all aware of our left brain cognition. However, when we tested these same proof points within the context of a creative experience, enhanced by music and emotional imagery, the results actually flipped. The test designed to understand the reaction of the unconscious right brain revealed a very different result.

The second concept that focused on a unique health system founded by visionary nuns, offering "spiritual, emotional and physical treatment," showed significant impact. In fact, faith-based values of the health system rose to the top position in the second study, blowing away all other tested value propositions. Further testing showed us that it wasn't just the emotional appeal of the faith-based message but also the communication of CHI St. Vincent's underlying purpose that also shined through and clinched this approach as the most influential on viewers. In the study, multiple creative concepts were narrowed to a winning matched-pair analysis: Concept A versus Concept B.

C O N C E P T S	A "VISION"	SPIRITUAL, EMOTIONAL & PHYSICAL TREATMENT	73*
		TOP 1% NEUROSURGEONS	74
		ONLY CARDIAC CATH LAB	70
	B "RANKINGS"	PATIENTS RANK US BEST	36*
		TOP 1% NEUROSURGEONS	41
		ONLY CARDIAC CATH LAB	33

*Average campaign score   Traverse Bay Strategy Group – Concept Evolution, 1/13/15

Concept A we called "Vision" because the series focused on the passion of the visionary nuns who built the faith-based health system.

We called Concept B "Rankings" because the series focused on the top rankings and patient outcomes that set the health system apart.

We then tested each concept with the highest performing proof point ("top 1% neurosurgeon"), followed by a test of that same creative execution, but including the lowest performing proof point ("only cardiac cath lab"). We did this to help determine if it were the creative concepts, or the proof points contained within them, that drove greater preference.

We found that the faith-based message of the "Vision" concept tested with twice the impact of the "Rankings" and outcomes message. The spiritually resonant message of a founding nun speaking with passion about the future was more convincing than the ads about the hospital having top-quality rankings and a top 1% neurosurgeon. Respondents actually indicated they would rather have a physician who prayed instead of a top 1% neurosurgeon who did not.

We can't make this stuff up.

Furthermore, we found that adding the proof point about the top 1% neurosurgeon into the spot with spiritual overtones added no significant impact to the overall message. Most surprisingly, what took us off guard was this: When we put the lowest-ranking proof point in the spiritual concept, and put the highest-ranking proof point in any other concept, the spiritual concept with the visionary nuns would always beat the alternative ad.

Ultimately, we found that when we tested real-world creative, the visionary passion demonstrated by the brand was more persuasive than any or even all of the proof points combined. This reaffirms the commonly held marketing belief that more proof points are not better, but only distract from the job of advertising.

It's important to understand that consumers will never properly evaluate a brand based on an analytically written value proposition. That's why testing proof points proved to be a futile exercise. People experience brands through the product, the service or through advertising. Those experiences require processing by the whole brain. Text-based information is only processed by our rational left hemisphere.[10] That is why we should always use creative art and music in focus groups. It appeals to the whole brain, including the powerful unconscious right brain, which is arising as a critical factor in modern branding.

It wasn't the rational knowledge and awareness of pathways that saved the children and teachers of Kamaishi, but instead it was the guidance of children who bypassed their cognitive knowledge with unconscious decision-making that led them to safety.

SO, WE "FLIPPED THE PYRAMID"

We removed all references to proof points and produced the CHI St. Vincent campaign materials around the "mind, body and spirit" purpose of the visionary nuns. Before the launch of the ad campaign, our team was almost as cautious as we were excited. After all, a focus group and a conjoint study aren't the real world. Would brand purpose translate to consumer results?

Less than a year later, it was time to gauge how we'd done through our NRC scores, an awareness and preference study that annually is performed for health-provider brands in each metro market. Typically, a great branding campaign could only hope to deliver up to lower double-digit increases in awareness scores after a couple years, and that's if we had done everything just right.

However, the results were ten times better than we could have expected. The CHI St. Vincent Health System experienced an unprecedented increase of 305% in year-over-year top-of-mind awareness before the year had even ended.

Often, we look for ideas to break the 10x ceiling to motivate consumers, but we are looking in all the wrong places. Our campaign garnered ten times the normal results without mentioning the hospital's top surgeons, rankings, or even the fact that they performed medical procedures whatsoever. The brand tripled in awareness by passionately presenting their purpose and emotionally connecting to the values of the community it served.

Importantly, CHI St. Vincent is headquartered in the Bible Belt, where a faith-based purpose is considered a powerful brand promise. We actually found the opposite to be true of health systems that we tested in other parts of the country. For example, in St. Louis, a health system that promoted its religious values actually turned off its market sample by doing so. Obviously, it's always important to understand the target community before we assume our brand purpose will emotionally connect with a particular consumer (or, in this case, a patient base). This is the importance of using a new consumer testing process.

Associative communities are built on core values that draw much stronger ties than can your brand's features and benefits. Studies like this one have shown us that passionate communities are emotion-driven. They are more interested in your brand's passion than they are in your proof points.

After countless studies like these, it has become apparent to us that purpose-driven emotion is what influences people to choose a brand — even for their most important life-and-death decisions.

Reaffirming our findings about the power of emotion, Gallup conducted a poll that produced similar results. The poll found that even in the most critical decision-making, such as personal health-care choices, 70% of all tested consumer decisions were driven by emotion. Only 30% of these life-and-death decisions were found to be driven by rational thought. This study was announced as part of a report presented by the leading health care marketing minds in America at the Society for Healthcare Strategy and Market Development convention of 2014.

Remember young Kawasaki Aki, who ran from school with the tsunami closing in on that fateful day in March 2011? She kept her focus on her purpose, telling herself, "With our hearts and souls, we will cherish having normal lives. We won't be beaten. We will laugh a lot, have many amazing experiences, and we will all support one another."

The reason the children engaged emotionally when the tsunami struck that day was because they had contemplated and prepared their answers to the question, "Why?"

Likewise, the best way to discover your brand purpose and avoid a senseless outcome in your brand campaign is to ask simple, childlike questions like that. Ask your team, "Why?" Ask, "Why does this brand position matter?" Ask, "Why should consumers care?" When you get the answer to those questions, ask "Why?" again. When you start to run out of answers to the question, "Why?" — only then are you getting close to a brand purpose that can engage consumers and employees emotionally with passion.

THE HEART OF THE "CONSUMER BRAIN"

Consumer psychology is strange science. The above exercise may take you hours with your team. Especially if you want to get to an emotionally engaging answer. However, an even more difficult exercise is to ask consumers the same question. Researchers struggle to find out why they buy; consumers don't even know their own reasons for choosing a particular brand. Most purchase decisions happen at the unconscious level.

As Pascal said, "The heart has its reasons which reason knows nothing of ... We know the truth not only by the reason, but by the heart."

We have built the following model so that we can attempt to describe the two major drivers we discovered as influencers of the two sides of the consumer brain: competency and character.

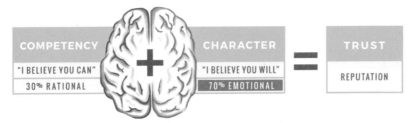

John H. Fleming, Ph.D. & James K. Harter, Ph.D., "The Next Discipline: Applying Behavioral Economics to Drive Growth and Profitability." Gallup, Inc., 2013.

Competency: First, your brand must meet a minimum threshold of competency required for consideration before a consumer will believe a brand can meet their needs. It's generally accepted that an evaluation of competency is assigned to rational or analytical left-brain decision-making. Therefore, this creates a conscious conclusion.

Character: In the second component of brand evaluation, the consumer brain will analyze your brand character to determine if it believes your brand will actually care enough to deliver on your promise. Cognitive scientists understand this as a right-brain function. The right side of the brain is known for its ability to subconsciously read between the lines into the complex nuances of emotion and motivations.

> 💬 We know the truth not only by the reason, but by the heart.
>
> – *Blaise Pascal*

If both components, competency and character, meet the criteria of both sides of the consumer brain, something powerful happens. There exists a yet-to-be-understood algorithm that takes place in the gray matter of a consumer's brain, but somehow this combination of forces can align neurons to assign trust to your brand.

In our findings, we also have discovered the bar for competency is much lower than the bar for character in the consumer brain. Referencing the Gallup findings,[11] 30% of the evaluation of your brand is based on rational persuasion and 70% of the evaluation of your brand is based on emotional persuasion. Mike Wilberding, lead research partner on the study from Traverse Bay Strategy Group, modeled the belief structure above to visualize our discovery: After the left brain of your consumer rationally concludes that "I believe you can," the right brain of your consumer must also conclude that "I believe you will" deliver on your brand promise. The left brain delivers the rational evaluation. The right brain delivers the emotional evaluation. When these two components come together just right, this builds high trust for brands in reputation-driven industries.

This is how the faith-based respondents in Arkansas were driven to override their initial reaction to top-ranked physicians in exchange for the passion of faith-based care at CHI St. Vincent. Even many Baptist respondents trusted a Catholic hospital more, primarily because they understood the passion that faith provides, and they apparently trusted the intent of the visionary nuns to deliver on their promise.

Keep these findings in mind as you build your next advertising campaign. Use analytics to measure the most effective hypothesis, but don't expect the message-benefit breakthrough to come from the analytics department. Brand character and emotional connections are usually best understood in the creative department. Why? Creativity comes from people with a highly developed right brain, and it always connects most effectively to the right brain of your consumer. This reaffirms Albert Einstein's stated belief in creativity: "Imagination is more important than knowledge."[12]

These consumer behaviors are not confined to health care. We have tested and found the same results in banking, food, vehicles and retail consumer purchases. Emotion drives critical decision-making for some of our most important human choices.

QUESTION:

Does this data about passion and emotionalism in business sound far-fetched? Perhaps you don't trust our consumer sample. Consider this if you are married, or if you are planning to be married. You can be your own sample of one in answering the following question: Did you use critical thinking to choose your spouse, or do you attribute the most important decision of your life to a feeling?

Select one answer below:

A   I used a rational process to evaluate various candidates for my spouse

B   I was emotionally driven in choosing my spouse

Unless you used a spreadsheet to compare the correlating advantages of the dating relationships in your life, you are probably driven by emotion. Emotion drives other, less important decisions the same way. When we find common purpose between any two human touchpoints, emotion is the output.

Just because we don't understand the power of emotion, it doesn't mean that the phenomenon doesn't exist. As Einstein said, "I am satisfied with the mystery ..."[13]

Advertising is an entire industry built to capitalize on the mystery of emotion. Leading agencies have long associated emotional commercials with sales volumes — but with mixed results. As the one version of the saying goes, "half of our advertising budget is wasted," but we don't always know which half. New digital tools and testing methodology are helping us understand why the other half hasn't worked for us in the past, and we are just beginning to crack the code on the influence of emotion to fill this gap.

Analytical thought and emotional thought are constantly at battle within a creative firm. We have discovered this battle is at the center stage of our mixed results. One emotional campaign is a winner, but the next fails. One analytical campaign creates sales, and the next flops. This is because the use of emotional intelligence is often at odds with cognitive intelligence behind the scenes; it's a constant battle over each brand's message-benefit. What proof points should advertising executives write into the creative brief? The analytical minds drive to talk about brand features while the creative minds want to produce passion. The marketing manager usually breaks the tie, from an analytical point of view or from a creative perspective, depending on their particular bias.

We try to remove bias through research and testing, but that model is flawed, as well. Although few marketing experts disagree that emotion is the most powerful factor in marketing, it has rarely tested well in the development of advertising campaigns. How do we test an emotional concept before we produce it?

This is why emotion is so difficult to sell to the C-suite. Executives expect to review proven evidence to justify the production budget before we spend it. (They are funny that way.) This contributes to the many reasons why so many ads lack emotion and effectiveness. It's easier (and less costly) to sell studies of text-based research programs than to produce full-scale creative concepts for testing. After the study of stale, text-based content, we never get the answer the creative team wants or needs, and that's why they typically fight the research findings. Perhaps this is why the process is so exhausting.

Due to the opposing forces of creativity and analytical study, there exists a passive-aggressive relationship between the creative department and the strategy department. I remember being an art director at a large advertising agency. When the creative brief came to me dictating a boring message-benefit, I was really good at ignoring the hours of research that the strategist plopped on my desk. Every good creative thinker knows how to interpret the strategic findings without letting facts and mandated product feature inclusions put them in an emotional box.

Creativity is not an analytical process that can be driven by a rational strategy. Like David Ogilvy said, "Big ideas come from the unconscious." That's why the output from an overly process-driven team can be so inconsistent. That's why every once in a while, a great creative agency breaks through with a success that science will never understand. I got it wrong for years, until I understood the balance between strategy and creative. It's a lifelong study, and we must all be lifelong students.

This analytical bias over message-benefit analysis is why a lot of our advertising from the automotive industry focuses on uninspiring features such as power windows and ABS brakes. This is also why most car advertising is forgettable. Built on a culture of engineering, research and academic thinking, the auto industry unfortunately forgets to study the emotional thought patterns of its consumers.

PASSION, 'IMPORTED FROM DETROIT'

Every once in awhile, advertisers get it right, in spite of all the factors working against them. And that's what Chrysler did in

2011 with its now-iconic Super Bowl ad that ran on marketing's biggest stage just as the company, and the country, were only starting to climb out of the meat grinder that was the Great Recession. Imagine if Chrysler had asked consumers if they would be influenced to purchase a car by a rap artist or a Hollywood movie star. Surely a focus group would have told them, "No way."

Consumers under the pressure of a survey question will proudly insist that they evaluate vehicles rationally based on features and price. They would never admit to being fooled by mere emotional appeals. Yet, those same consumers could be found the very next day after the Super Bowl, standing by the office water cooler discussing commercials including the Chrysler spot featuring Detroit rap artist Eminem and a humble car known as the Chrysler 200. The coverage the commercial received was as powerful as the spot itself. It lit up a movement that drove followers to YouTube with 17 million other emotionally involved viewers.[14]

"What does a town that's been to hell and back know about the finer things in life?" The Big Game spot asked viewers to consider that question as it toured Detroit landmarks against the lilting chorus of a gospel choir, ending at the legendary Fox Theatre. The commercial associated Chrysler with the hard work and artistry that embodied a brand that was "Imported From Detroit."

Chrysler's "Born of Fire" campaign[15] was delivered with great poetry and emotion, but it delivered more than that. It rebirthed great purpose for a brand that shared the plight of a city hanging on for its very life. Chrysler caught the wave of public purpose that arose from the American automotive industry fallout of 2009. As the Los Angeles *Times* reported, the ad "was an editorial in defense of a beleaguered Detroit and, perhaps, a withering philosophy of what America is about."[16] People in the U.S. were all recovering from a recession, and Detroit became a national symbol of the comeback. This passionate purpose established emotional connections with previously untouched consumers — the import buyers.

The irony behind this commercial is that Fiat Chrysler CMO Olivier Francois couldn't have selected a worse vehicle to carry the fortunes of his company that Super Bowl Sunday. The Chrysler 200 was what in Detroit they call a "reskinned" version of an older model, in this case the Chrysler Sebring, one of many bad small cars in a long line of bad small cars produced by Chrysler. In fact, the 200 was so bad that within three years, Chrysler felt compelled to replace it with an all-new version of the car just to be competitive in its segment.

But viewers of the 2011 Super Bowl spot, titled "Born of Fire" by the automaker and its ad agency, simply didn't care what car was being mentioned. When a Detroit automotive brand finally found its passion and broke its habit of engineering messages around features and benefits, something magical happened. After the launch, the market research company YouGov announced, "The motivational TV spots seem to have struck a strong chord with adults planning to purchase a car in the next 12 months. Reflecting the ad's 'comeback' tone, Chrysler not only achieved its best scores with that demo, but actually cracked the average for the domestic auto sector" for the first time in years.

It's not a stretch to say that CMO Francois and his purpose-based message to American consumers made all the difference for Fiat Chrysler's ability to survive the Great Recession, emerge from bankruptcy, pay off its debts to the U.S. taxpayer, and be left with a fighting chance to survive for whatever new era comes next. And in so doing, the company helped rally the entire City of Detroit to a similar renaissance.

There's still no way to measure any direct correlation from a single brand campaign to the rebirth of an entire city. But experts and analysts have awarded "Born of Fire" more than any other auto commercial for a reason.[17] Only a passionate purpose could power such a movement.

THE PRINCIPLE OF PURPOSE VS. THE PATHWAY OF PRICE

Arguably, price is the No. 1 analytical driver of consumer purchasing behavior; although, the lowest price doesn't always win. Why? We've found in consumer testing that coupons and money offers rarely generate the necessary level of emotional motivation to compete with a strong brand purpose.

This impact of passionate purpose has been measured among employees, too. You can't ever pay your employees enough to generate passion for a job they hate. If you ask employees why they hate their jobs, most often they'll tell you their job lacks purpose. Alternatively, if you enter a workplace that has a great culture and highly engaged employees and ask them why they love their jobs, they will most often give an answer saturated with purpose. Rarely will purpose-driven employees discuss their pay level, except to mention how they could make more money somewhere else.

Just consider the children of Kamaishi East. They were motivated by something greater than their own personal enrichment. It would be silly to think the kids would have been motivated better by money. As much as it's difficult for some people to understand, there are critical moments in the human condition when we all realize that money is not going to fix anything that really matters.

Yes, there is a principle of purpose that is more important than the pathway of money to motivate emotional loyalty among both your employees and customers. As author/researcher Jim Collins concludes, "True greatness comes in direct proportion to a passionate pursuit of a purpose beyond money."

Does all of this new focus on purpose mean you should never discuss your brand's performance, price or features in advertising? No. Promotional advertising still exists in the Participation Age, but those critical promotions won't be effective without first stemming from a passionate core purpose. As International House of Prayer leader Bill Johnson said, "Your heart will take you where your head won't fit."

Although, these findings don't eliminate all previous marketing models, this dramatically changes the age-old marketing funnel. Instead of placing "share of mind" near the top of the funnel, we have replaced it with "share of heart." Instead of "share of wallet" at the bottom, we measure "share of fans."

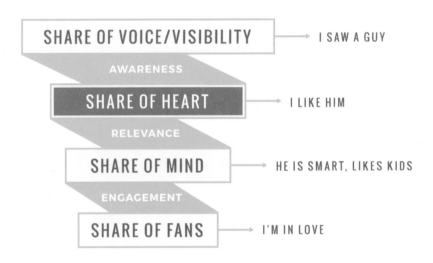

Going back to the way the consumer brain shops for a spouse, consider how this applies to the new marketing funnel. Let's call our shopper "CB," for short. If CB is shopping for a man in her life, she will need to see one first. We call the brand visibility of our man, "share of voice." A better name might be "share of visibility."

After meeting several brands of men, one stands out as

somebody she likes. We don't know why she likes him. In fact, most studies of human mating rituals prove that she doesn't know why, either. She just feels something for him. We call this "share of heart." This emotional connection relates to her identification with our brand's purpose and values or the common tribe they both belong to, but the processing takes place at an unconscious level.

When she gets excited to learn that he is smart and likes kids, we call this, "share of mind." This correlates to the features and benefits of our brand that are easy for consumers to articulate because they are processed at the conscious level. However, in studies of spouse selection, people often tell researchers they want certain characteristics at a share-of-mind level, but usually choose a spouse with completely opposite characteristics, defaulting to the decision made at the share-of-heart level.[18] However, certain minimum characteristics must be present in order to pass this filter in the mind of CB. After she falls in love, she tells her friends about her wonderful new brand. We call this "share of fans." Posting positive comments about her new man to friends socially shows love. This is how brand loyalty becomes a marriage.

Like a marriage, the emotional engagement with a brand has more to do with share of heart than it has to do with share of mind. In fact, this is the first filter in any human choice. It's not arbitrary that our consumer example is a woman. Women make 80% of most consumer purchases.[19] Women are also generally moved by social causes more than men. This is why purpose-driven brands that serve authentic causes of the heart so effectively engage the modern consumer.

GROW YOUR DOUBLE BOTTOM LINE

Brands that lead by heart and are socially responsible have been proven to reap many rewards. Following the principle of reciprocity, brands that are generous to social needs create a virtuous cycle with the modern consumer. Studies show generous brands attract generous consumers. In fact, 69% of Millennials tell us they choose brands according to the causes they support.[20]

Consider Warby Parker's contribution of "one pair of glasses for each one sold" under its "Buy a Pair, Give a Pair" positioning.[21] Missions like this are being inspired by the success story of TOMS Shoes, which freely distributes millions of shoes in the jungles of Third World countries.[22]

By associating with a worthy social cause, your brand can ride a wave of positive consumer sentiment and create a so-called double bottom line: making a positive contribution to society while increasing sales.

Is your brand facing a commoditized industry? Cause marketing could be your win-win option. Here are a few advantages of building your brand around a meaningful cause:

Cause drives choice: When quality and price are equal, 90% of consumers are likely to switch to a cause-branded product, one study says.[23]

Cause demands a premium: In a Nielsen study, 42% of consumers say they would pay extra if the company is committed to positive social or environmental impact.[24]

Consumers seek out cause brands: 88% of Americans want to hear about corporate social responsibility efforts — and the most preferred place to hear about these efforts is on the product's packaging or label, according to a Cone Communications study.[25]

Social good attracts investors, too: Social capital is cashing in among the investor community. Recently, socially responsible investments nearly doubled to $6.6 trillion in a single year.[26] Millennials are leading the charge to do well by doing good through their investments. TOMS Shoes, under its "One for One" donation concept, has distributed 60 million shoes around the world.[27] And, its founder Blake Mycoskie was rewarded with a buyout by Bain Capital for $625 million, in which he retained 50-percent ownership, along with a fund to create more cause-driven brands.[28]

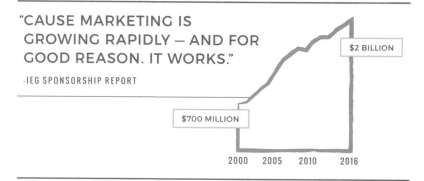

"CAUSE MARKETING IS GROWING RAPIDLY — AND FOR GOOD REASON. IT WORKS."

-IEG SPONSORSHIP REPORT

$2 BILLION

$700 MILLION

2000   2005   2010   2016

IEG Sponsorship Report/Cause Marketing Forum

MEET THE ASPIRATIONALS

In a study[29] of banking customers, a new consumer behavior is arising among Millennials. We call them the "Aspirationals." This group is demonstrating purchasing behaviors that are moving away from cash offers, cost savings and personal service toward bank brands that can offer social responsibility, integrity and investment into good causes that make a difference in their community.

In fact, the percentage of the sample we tested who was most likely to change banks for free checking was equal to the percentage of customers who would switch banks for demonstrated social responsibility.

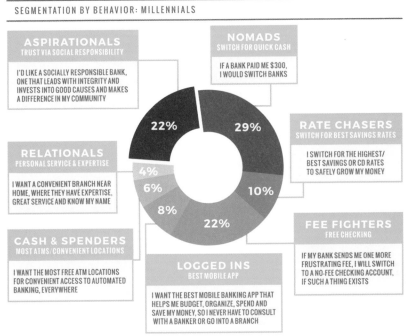

SEGMENTATION BY BEHAVIOR: MILLENNIALS

ASPIRATIONALS
TRUST VIA SOCIAL RESPONSIBILITY

I'D LIKE A SOCIALLY RESPONSIBLE BANK, ONE THAT LEADS WITH INTEGRITY AND INVESTS INTO GOOD CAUSES AND MAKES A DIFFERENCE IN MY COMMUNITY

NOMADS
SWITCH FOR QUICK CASH

IF A BANK PAID ME $300, I WOULD SWITCH BANKS

RATE CHASERS
SWITCH FOR BEST SAVINGS RATES

I SWITCH FOR THE HIGHEST/ BEST SAVINGS OR CD RATES TO SAFELY GROW MY MONEY

RELATIONALS
PERSONAL SERVICE & EXPERTISE

I WANT A CONVENIENT BRANCH NEAR HOME, WHERE THEY HAVE EXPERTISE, GREAT SERVICE AND KNOW MY NAME

CASH & SPENDERS
MOST ATMS/CONVENIENT LOCATIONS

I WANT THE MOST FREE ATM LOCATIONS FOR CONVENIENT ACCESS TO AUTOMATED BANKING, EVERYWHERE

FEE FIGHTERS
FREE CHECKING

IF MY BANK SENDS ME ONE MORE FRUSTRATING FEE, I WILL SWITCH TO A NO-FEE CHECKING ACCOUNT, IF SUCH A THING EXISTS

LOGGED INS
BEST MOBILE APP

I WANT THE BEST MOBILE BANKING APP THAT HELPS ME BUDGET, ORGANIZE, SPEND AND SAVE MY MONEY, SO I NEVER HAVE TO CONSULT WITH A BANKER OR GO INTO A BRANCH

22% 29% 4% 6% 10% 8% 22%

Traverse Bay Strategy Group, 10/8/15

It's important to note that most consumers want to see a tangible impact from their investment in a brand's purpose. Simply giving money to a popular charity isn't enough. A promise to take corporate responsibility for a specific social impact is more important than a philanthropic donation to a well-known foundation.

For example, Warby Parker started as an unknown newcomer in a commodity category: online eyewear. Their altruistic matching offer became a tangible and effective differentiator. Now, the brand has emerged as an eyewear leader with millions of passionate followers online, and the media loves to tell their "feel-good" story.

Another company that decided to create good in the world *and* profit from it is a growing Midwestern pizza chain. Consider the case of Hungry Howie's Flavored Crust® Pizza.

Hungry Howie's, a top 10 pizza chain in the U.S., is dedicated to supporting their communities while "adding flavor to life." Under their purpose-driven culture, the brand has printed more than 50 million pink pizza boxes and donated $1.5 million[30] to breast cancer research. To recognize Breast Cancer Awareness month each October, Hungry Howie's equipped all of their employees with T-shirt apparel and pink pizza boxes to highlight the cause through their Love, Hope & Pizza™ campaign.

And embracing purpose didn't disappoint the brand. It delivered a bigger slice of pie, with the following results:[31]

Consumer loyalty: By simply printing the pizza boxes pink in October, Hungry Howie's Pizza drove sales increases of 23% in the first year powered by a quarter-million new Facebook fans, who come back annually to support Howie's for their cause.

Higher price point: While the competition was reducing its price to $5 for a large "pie," Howie's was able to increase sales and maintain an average price of $7 for its quality, cause-based pizzas. Howie's found that the consumer makes room for margin when the brand provides them with more meaning.

Increased awareness: Today, this previously little-known regional brand, Hungry Howie's, has become the leader in brand awareness, statistically tied with Little Caesars and Domino's for first place in preference in their primary service area. The National Breast Cancer Foundation originally gave credibility to the message, but today, consumers in the primary service area have more recall of Hungry Howie's as a brand supporting the fight against breast cancer than they do of the National Breast Cancer Foundation itself.

Sales and revenue growth: As a result of rebranding and several purpose-based initiatives such as the Love, Hope & Pizza™ campaign, Howie's has enjoyed six years of year-over-year growth for more than a 50% increase in sales at the average store. The franchisees have now celebrated 27 consecutive quarters of sales increases. This has made Hungry Howie's the fastest-growing pizza franchise store among the top 10 chains nationally, passing the other celebrated digital leader, Domino's. Love Hope & Pizza wasn't the only initiative that made the difference. It takes a lot of good decisions to get such outstanding results, but in one study about the reasons people love Hungry Howie's, the pink pizza box and the brand's commitment to fight breast cancer were named as the primary value driver.

Improved lives: Not only did the Hungry Howie's cause raise money and drive sales results for the brand, it also made a difference in the lives of more than 1,500 women who were able to get a breast-cancer screening[32] as a result of the money raised. Early projections estimated that 67 lives will be saved as a result of this campaign.

Some might ask, "What does pizza have to do with the cause of breast cancer?" but it's hard to ignore the fan loyalty generated from the brand's commitment to help solve problems that consumers care about. When brands take the time to care, grow their double bottom line and bring authentic value to their communities, consumers return the favor.

GENEROSITY WINS

Brands like Hungry Howie's are leading us toward a new way of thinking: The brand that contributes the most value to society wins. This brand contribution must be sincere and real. We must have faith in the process of giving, or we might fall trap to using this approach as another gimmick to trick consumers into ways we can extract value from them. That can do more damage than good.

Generosity must be sincere at the executive level. A selfless purpose cannot be delegated. Let's explore a model to formalize the process of development to support your benevolent marketing model. Consider the following core components that can be used to build or evaluate a purpose-driven marketing plan:

THE CME GENEROSITY CYCLE

Here are the three legs of this self-perpetuating virtuous cycle:

Contribute: The first step of purpose-driven branding involves contributing remark-worthy value. Give something free, funny, surprising, inspiring or socially redeemable to invest in the consumer relationship before making the pitch.

Motivate: Don't just push features and benefits in advertising. Consumers will self-actualize as influencers and leaders when you provide them an emotionally inspiring, authentic and generous cause to participate in.

Empower: Once we've created a community of raving fans, it's not enough to hope they will find a way to mobilize without our help. Supercharge storytelling with social channels that will help motivate influencers, enlist a movement and tell your story for you.

BEST PRACTICES OF PURPOSE-DRIVEN BRANDS

The children of Kamaishi were not only taught tactics. Katada *flipped the pyramid.* Katada taught the children leadership through dedication to a purpose greater than themselves, so they gave of themselves and, ultimately, they inspired a nation. In branding, we must focus on certain best practices as we navigate disruptive change:

1 **Passion beats proof points:** In the spirit of Katada, brand leadership should be built on a passionate purpose that will be more effective for connecting with consumers than using proof points or even price.

2 **Earn share of heart:** Emotion is the most powerful of all intellectual capacities of the brain. Instead of attempting to grab share of wallet, we will build better relationships by earning share of fans.

3 **Grow your double bottom line:** When a generous company contributes authentic value to society, it will motivate fans and empower them to return generous purchase patterns, loyalty and referral to its brand.

As we employ these best practices, we will find that the consumer voice is the wave that moves our brands. It's a powerful wave, but just as in surfing, we don't control it. We simply find our groove and hold on for the ride.

WHY SO ANGRY?

BLOG POST | JANUARY 8, 2015 – Having an emotionally compelling purpose is exciting, meaningful and even spiritual to some of us. But, keep in mind, no matter how much we drive toward the purpose and values of a brand, old habits die hard. Product- and service-oriented organizations tend to lean back toward the traditional features and benefits discussion. Keeping your brand purpose-driven will take a firm commitment by the branding team.

After all of the books, blogs and research, there is yet another voice in the market calling our purpose-driven approach a "do-gooder" movement that has no marketing value at all. And, they are strangely angry about it.

Just consider the violent reaction to this seemingly benign Seth Godin blog repost:

> **❝** Our job is to connect to people, to interact with them in a way that leaves them better than we found them, more able to get where they'd like to go.
>
> – *Seth Godin, Author, Entrepreneur and Marketer*[33]

One online responder said, "What crap! Marketing's job is to sell stuff. In a nice way. Without pissing people off."

A cynical commenter protested, "Among the most pompous statements I've heard to date. Seth forgot to add ... so that marketing can save the world."

One retired marketing exec thanked the cynical commenter with, "... A wise voice in the wilderness of today's 'CMOOOOOOHS.'"

And, this telling comment summed up the angry forum for me: "I viewed my fellow man not as a fallen angel, but as a risen ape."

I couldn't help but notice these responders were seasoned pros. Some had been in the business very long. Maybe too long. They seemed a little jaded about the industry. Even a little hopeless about our potential contribution to a brand's value. I couldn't hold back my comment. My response to the debate included the following excerpt:

"It's an age-old debate. Does marketing provide inherent value, or is it merely used as a temporary strategy to trick people into buying our brand? When TOMS Shoes marketed a generous brand, many of us paid double for shoes, so one pair will be given to others in need. When marketing contributes value beyond the product, the product itself becomes more valuable to us. Coke proves this in blind taste tests every year. People like the flavor better with the label on. This is not a theory to debate anymore. We now have case studies for evidence."

Most agreed with my comment, but many still jeered. As I find myself debating this issue online, I'm realizing this is no small matter. Marketing is in search of new meaning in the post-Golden Age of mass media advertising. As the CPM rate of media increases and results of old media options are deteriorating, the old guard is holding to what remains of traditional advertising and sales models. Others are arising with new solutions and almost religious fervor — and they are getting results.

Ultimately, the angry bloggers proved my point. After the smoke cleared from this post mob, I noticed an important outcome from it all. This online debate that I participated in had more than double the average comments of other marketing blog posts, plus exponentially more views. That is content marketing at its best. People get excited to have conversations about their passionate purpose, and the debate has just begun.

3

NORTH STAR VALUES

YOUR COMPASS IN THE MAELSTROM OF SOCIAL CONFLICT

> 66 It's easy to make
> decisions when you know
> what your values are
>
> – *Roy Disney*

Here I am, off the coast of Hatteras Island, North Carolina,
on a retreat with a bunch of surfer pros and trainers so I can learn
kiteboarding. I'm sitting at a kitchen table, looking out the window
over some of the roughest water I've ever seen. The gray sky is
broken by dark, ominous clouds, and 8-foot waves reach out like
massive hands falling upon the beach as if to tear it apart.

So, why kiteboarding? I grew up with a skateboard attached to
my feet, and I flew kites as a kid. So, I figured, how hard could this
kiteboarding thing be? Then I looked online. I viewed video after
video of people flying 50 feet off big waves, then smacking into
electrical towers, bridges and hotels.

Instead of launching a 12-meter kite by myself, I decided to get
lessons from a pro. It was like going to aviation school. I learned
wind windows, line rigging, upwind, downwind and toeside
navigation. The most critical lesson of all was gauging wind
direction to find the safest place to launch a kite.

If you are pulled out to sea by an outbound wind, you are swimming home against the current. That's just one of several terrifying ways to court death out there. I was even taught an unsettling lesson on how to spend the night at sea by using my kite as a flotation device.

But of course, it's one thing to learn about surviving great waves. It's a whole 'nother experience to actually surf them. As I ponder these huge new waves, I'm still recovering from waves only half the size that battered me yesterday. After being hit by one wave, I came up in time to be hit by another, then another, with barely a break between each massive swell.

I can still feel the burning in my lungs. And I think about the courage it would take to pick up my kiteboard and navigate that storm I see today. I'm asking myself, "Is it possible to surf a tsunami?" Then the thought passes. "Silly!" I mumble under my breath.

Even after all of this, it's still hard to imagine waves many times the size and strength of the Atlantic swells I'm contemplating today, tearing into houses as the Pacific Ocean pours through the streets of Japan. The YouTube videos of a wave like that don't do it justice. Think about how slow a jetliner looks in the sky; up close, 500 miles per hour looks much faster.

The waves that are challenging me to a duel on my kiteboard also seem safer than the media maelstrom that is taking place back at the office every day.

Advertising has become a hot mess of political sensitivity. One client wants to kill an advertisement that features an "ethnic-looking angry man, who looks like a terrorist." Oops, did I say, "Kill?" Strike that from the record. Anyway, the bigger crisis is that we can't find any stock photos of a family that is ambiguously diverse. The ads feature "too many white males," then "too many black women." Don't forget about global warming, religious sensitivities and gender orientation. And, that's all before we run the concepts through the gauntlet of corporate ethics and compliance departments.

If a brand takes a political stand on a liberal issue, the people on the right won't buy it. If the brand stands for a conservative issue, the boycott comes from the left. Everybody's boycotting each other now. Hopefully, not all at once. A CEO in my town recently was fired because of a socially unacceptable post that was sent by a person who worked for him in another state. His ad agency lost several clients and almost a half-billion dollars of business in a single day. Do you know what your staff is posting today? But, I digress.

Back to the ocean view. The pros have told us to sit this one out. The water is too rough, and the wind would blow us and our kites to who knows where. I'm not going to question that wisdom.

But I don't have the choice to sit out the gales that are continually being whipped up by the Participation Age in marketing, and neither do you. As you navigate the complexities of brand management in this new era, consider the following object lessons that I learned from kiteboarding:

1   *Set a moral true north:* Establish brand values that guide everything your company and its employees do.

2   *Look around at your environment:* Figure out how these brand values will play in today's socially charged marketing landscape.

3   *Avoid unpredictable winds:* There are areas of marketing discourse that just aren't worth risking your brand values to explore.

4   *From a safe place, go for it:* Power your brand with universally shared values.

Let's look at these lessons one by one.

LESSON ONE: SET A MORAL TRUE NORTH

It takes a lot of preparation to go out into the erratic current of today's media environment. The best way to navigate the winds and waves of social conflict is to establish your true north. Like

a compass, brand values will be your guide, showing the way. If we don't create some ground rules, who knows what kind of rogue social post might get out into the ether?

Some of you are asking, "What do all these values and ground rules have to do with marketing? Whatever happened to the good old days when we just told the consumer what to do?"

In the first Golden Age of advertising, pushy salesmen had very little use for ground rules or values. Remember Lucky Strike's smoking Santa Claus[1] and the famous advertisement, "More doctors smoke Camels"?[2] Today, we wouldn't get away with this. Nor should we.

Today, truth is true north. If we fib, even slightly, consumers can set the record straight with hard evidence sourced from a quick Google search. And, they will post the truth just to keep your brand honest. Once that happens, all of the dollars you spent to advertise a lie will work against you.

Just consider this statement by Don Draper, the iconic ad-agency creative guru on the *Mad Men* TV series, that epitomizes the values of the previous generation of advertisers:

> ❝ What you call love was invented by guys like me ... to sell nylons.[3]
>
> – *"Don Draper" (Jon Hamm), Mad Men TV series, AMC*

Imagine if a modern CEO of a nylon company saw this sentiment in the form of a tweet from his advertising executive. Even Don Draper wouldn't be able to hold a job down in the Participation Age. Yes, values matter.

The Participation Age is an era of values marketing. Consumers are not evaluating your product only. They are evaluating your commitment to your brand purpose. Consumers don't want to be sold. They want you to prove your value. They're testing you to see if you share their values before they buy.

People don't post much on social media about the household goods at Target or the quality fabrics sold at Hobby Lobby; just do a quick Facebook search, and you'll see. Instead, consumers post about the values of these socially polarizing organizations.

Corporate responsibility is the new religion of Millennials.[4] During the social media revolution of 2011, the number of people who considered themselves social activists almost doubled to 7 in 10 young adults. Nearly 4 in 5 consumers are rewarding brands for their support for various social causes. That's double the number of people who went to church last Sunday.[5] Consumers are using social media and their purchasing power to reinforce brand values.

This new consumer expectation comes with a demand that corporations create economic value by addressing the greater needs of society. What stands out as concerning is the finding that up to 1 in 3 consumers admit they boycott business based on the causes they care about.[6] Brand controversy is the subject of the day, and social media feeds it. Some brands will be flogged for trying to use social media to manipulate cultural values, yet others will lead the world by being authentic and consistent about a noble brand purpose that resonates with consumers. It's critical to support that purpose with your brand values.

I know what you're thinking. I'm sure your brand already has well-documented core values. They might have been presented at your most recent rah-rah leadership retreat. You may ask yourself, "How are brand values different from our core values?" or "How do we prevent brand values from becoming lost in the dusty closet of company mantras, mission statements and vision-casting?" Many company efforts to build culture have failed before; so don't model failure.

Model success. The brands that lead the world always have rich cultural slogans and "isms." These are not generic or intangible one-word aspirations, such as "integrity," "excellence" or "quality." Brand values are your unchanging core values, rewritten in actionable, plain English to offer more specific and measurable guidelines for daily operations and marketing efforts.

It's not about what these statements say, but what they demonstrate or expect you to do. For example, if your core value is "service," it might be time to update. Perhaps service was a differentiator when your company was founded, but it's table stakes today. The consumer brain has evolved, and it expects more accountability from today's brands.

THE CONSUMER BRAIN AND BRAND VALUES

More and more, what used to be considered spiritual pursuits are becoming scientific pursuits. One of the current frontiers in science is the discovery of social morality. Leading cognitive neuroscientist Michael S. Gazzaniga, for example, recently reported findings that link moral values to a profound and tangible scientific impact on human behavior. In fact, we as humans create what neuroscientists call a "theory of mind" as a construct in our brain to judge and predict the intentions of others.[7]

> We as humans create what neuroscientists call a "theory of mind" as a construct in our brain to judge and predict the intentions of others.

We do the same for brands. When a person or a brand expresses similar values to ours or to those of the particular tribe we belong to, we assign good intent to that person or brand. When their values are different, we fear them. This is why we mimic people we like, and we like people we mimic. We feel safest among those who are most like ourselves. We assume people who look and act like us also share the same values. It's a simple way for our brain to assign trust.

Leading brands do the same. If our core consumer values service, quality and results, we design our core value list of one-word aspirations about service, quality and results. But, what happens when all of our competitors share the same values? How will our consumers feel any different about us?

If all brands assert the same values, they cancel each other out. Next, the evolved consumer brain seeks out new evidence that demonstrates intent. Recent studies have found that the consumer brain is more likely to accept your brand values if they are specific and measurable rather than simply stated without accountability. The evolved consumer brain has become cynical. Its built-in defense mechanism tells the consumer, "Just because the brand says it values 'service' doesn't mean they will actually provide service."

The consumer brain[8] looks for other signs or cues that will indicate intent. We also apply this logic toward any social being and even animals. This is why the human brain looks at a small animal with big eyes and has a different expectation of intention than it does for those animals with small, dark, beady eyes. Consumers fall for big-eyed dogs every time.

Of course the "size of a brand's eyes" offers no proof of intent, but the consumer brain has to come up with some conclusion even when the input is limited. We call this function "belief attribution," and this processing creates a permanent model for reference about your brand in the right hemisphere of the consumer brain. This is the emotional hemisphere of the consumer brain, where connections become more difficult to break.

Values assertion without an emotional connection is commonplace, and therefore most core values are meaningless to consumers. For example, if the consumer brain has no way to differentiate your claim of "service" versus your competitor's claim of "service," how will you disrupt the consumer expectation with something meaningful? How will you create an emotional connection?

Don't just state a value. Disrupt the definition of that value. Make it specific and measurable or even emotionally engaging. Make the right brain take notice. For example, it might be time to update your core value of "service" to something like, "Serve our guests like family" or "Service in seven minutes or less." That might be a more authentic value for your brand that can make you accountable to the consumer.

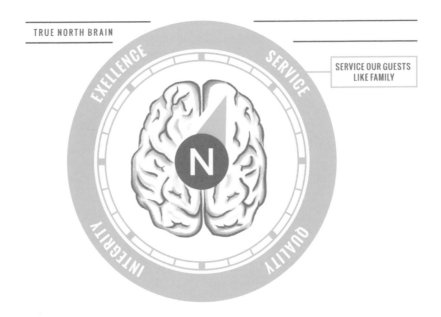

Once a tangible and measurable brand value becomes part of your culture, it becomes the true north of everything you do for your customers. That is how your customers become your "guests." This is why Ritz-Carlton, the gold standard of service, inspires employees to "build strong relationships and create Ritz-Carlton guests for life."[9] This clarity helps establish true north in the midst of the bustling winds of generic service.

Here are some parameters that can be used as filters for developing strong brand values:

1   Will they drive passion?

2   Are they aspirational?

3   Is there evidence that you mean business?

4   Do they make a promise?

5   Will they inspire moral conviction?

6   Do they hold you accountable?

7   Are some of them measurable?

FROST BANK'S BRAND VALUES – AND CULTURE

There's a bank in Texas that unapologetically uses its brand values to lead its industry. "Few banks have performed as well for as long as Frost, which consistently ranks among the industry's leaders in all key measures," according to *American Banker*. By June 30, 2015, Frost had a 1.24% return on assets, compared with the industry average of 0.86%, and a 10.32% return on equity, compared with 7.65% for the rest of the industry."[10]

The bank's CEO told *American Banker* he credited Frost's success to a 15-page handbook.[11] "What we call the Blue Book, or our philosophy, is really the answer," said Richard Evans, "and it's a way to guide us as we go forward."

The booklet begins, "At Frost, everything we do begins with this book. ..." It includes the company mission statement and a summary of the organization's values, which have an ethos rooted in strong customer relationships. Note the fact that the bank's 140-year-old values were recently updated to address relevant technology.

Here are Frost Bank's brand values:

- We believe in using technology to serve our customers. Not avoid them.

- Bankers should know their customers by name and vice versa.

- Courtesy should not be based upon the size of one's nest egg.

- The Golden Rule is more valuable than a free toaster.

- When a customer calls, an actual person should answer the phone.

- We believe in doing what's right, even when no one is looking.

- We'd never do anything with a customer's money that we wouldn't do with our own.

- We wouldn't say anything in this size print that we wouldn't say IN THIS SIZE.

- You get what you pay for.

- If it sounds too good to be true, it is.

- Slow. And. Steady. Wins. The. Race.

- All the ATMs in the world are no substitute for customer service.

These simple statements drive the organization, but there is much more detail to back them up. For example, Frost's value on diversity is a page long.

Evans often quotes from the Blue Book when speaking to employees and officers of the company. "People can have good philosophies and good culture, but the real trick is living it every day," said Evans. "That's what we try to do. We're far from perfect, and we never will be perfect."

ALIGNING EMPLOYEES

In any event, banks like Frost are teaching us that marketing is not a job that is exclusive to the marketing department anymore. Your brand will not only be evaluated by what you say, but what you do. This means marketing is the responsibility of the C-suite. It's about how we organize the behaviors of hundreds of employees to act in a consistent and authentic way.

Now that the Participation Workforce makes stories and tells your brand story for you, it's important to give them values parameters for these stories. That's why brand values must be written down, administered and held accountable throughout the organization. Each employee should be scored against these brand values in every review that routes its way through human resources.

Employee alignment is hard work, but it's critical. For leaders, it's about consistency and authenticity of a brand promise. If each individual employee is guided by his or her own personal compass, disregarding the company's "true north," the organization looks schizophrenic. It only takes one public comment by one employee to undermine the brand values of the organization. In contrast, if the values are consistent through each consumer experience, that builds trust.

LESSON TWO: LOOK AT YOUR ENVIRONMENT

Before launching a massive kite into 30-mph winds, I was taught it's important to look around. Do you see any electrical wires above you? Any trees? Any piers? The environment is not a variable you can control, so you should be aware of its dangers when kiteboarding.

Navigating the current social environment can be a tricky thing, as well. Like a political candidate running for office, our brand can appeal to consumer values, but we can't change them. When we connect with the values of our consumers, our brand can truly earn their trust, but we must be careful how we play on these emotions.

Especially if our brands enter the political arena. Building trust with one community can destroy the trust we have built with the opposers of that community. That's why it's important to understand the politics of the communities we serve.

Look at it this way: Of course, we all know it presents great risk for a company to endorse any political candidate, but we can make the same mistake by picking sides in a political conflict. Consider this example: Should a university hospital advertise to its students that it performs abortions? Should a Catholic hospital advertise to local churches that it refuses to perform them?

Before you wager to answer either question, let's look at the political landscape of our media environment. Remember, even professional kiteboarders don't try to control the waves or wind, and marketing experts know better than to attempt to control the political opinions of the communities we serve. What matters most is that we understand how to navigate or even ride them.

In the development of our study on brand values, our research team was well represented by members of each political party, so coming to a consensus became quite controversial — and even heated. But our debate underscored the real passions that exist around the concept of brand values. Politics have become unavoidable in the social space, so we determined to plow through our bias toward a belief structure that our brands can use to navigate these troubled waters.

NAVIGATING POLITICS

Since the inception of democracy, media and politics have been co-dependent forces. Furthermore, since the rise of the media elite, democracy itself has become a mechanism of their control. As the renowned progressive academic and cognitive-science expert Noam Chomsky[12] has put it, "The public relations industry, which essentially runs the elections, is applying certain principles to undermine democracy. ... It wants to construct elections in which uninformed voters will make irrational choices."

This power of traditional media was overthrown during the U.S. presidential primary election of 2016. From the beginning of that election season, most news anchors clearly didn't seem to want Donald Trump in the race. Strangely, the liberal media establishment and the conservative media establishment appeared to agree that he was unpresidential. Even Megyn Kelly of Fox News almost ruined Trump's run for president as a Republican by ambushing him with a debate question about his misogynistic rhetoric.

In spite of their best efforts, most political pundits were shocked to watch how the media elite from both camps couldn't stop the social media tsunami that powered Trump. In post analysis, the negative broadcast coverage against Trump was actually credited for driving the positive social media buzz in his favor.

While candidates, including Hillary Clinton, Jeb Bush and Ben Carson, each spent three to six times as many dollars on media advertising,[13] Trump managed to control a 40% share of total online engagement during the primary season — more than all the other candidates from either party, combined.[14]

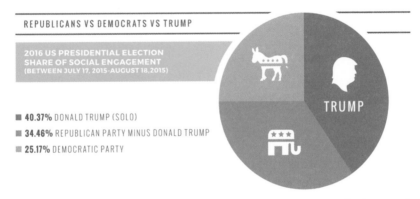

REPUBLICANS VS DEMOCRATS VS TRUMP

2016 US PRESIDENTIAL ELECTION
SHARE OF SOCIAL ENGAGEMENT
(BETWEEN JULY 17, 2015-AUGUST 18, 2015)

TRUMP

■ **40.37%** DONALD TRUMP (SOLO)
■ **34.46%** REPUBLICAN PARTY MINUS DONALD TRUMP
■ **25.17%** DEMOCRATIC PARTY

www.digitalcontact.co.uk

Although it was heated and ugly, the Participation Generation led the debate this time. The forum for the debate would not be held on Fox News or CNN. The "major news networks" of the Participation Age had emerged: Facebook, Instagram and Twitter.

The losers were the candidates who played politics as they had been trained. Polite and thoughtful language was ignored, and off-the-cuff controversy was rewarded by the online banter. Even after all experts said Trump clearly lost the first debate against Clinton, he moved up in the polls again.[15]

Candidates and media pundits denying Trump's rise apparently had forgotten that the voting population grew up watching Jerry Springer. Trump's arrogant persona had been well established during multiple seasons of *The Apprentice*, and the masses loved him for it. Like a mirror to the media culture that created him, Trump's nomination exposed a brash and independent nation to itself.

The carnage of the politically polite candidates reminded our team of what happened to the boats anchored in the harbor of Japan during the tsunami. By the time these presidential hopefuls started making remark-worthy comments, it was too late. The black wave of Trump's distinctly unpresidential social media had consumed them.

Ultimately, the least-likely candidate in our generation was named the standard-bearer for conservatives and the United States of America. The media elite in both camps were left scratching their heads during the entire election season. Something in the electorate had changed.

No, social media didn't completely work in Trump's favor. Nor did it always work in favor of his opponent, Hillary Clinton. Always-on digital recordings captured the reprehensible side of Trump's sexist attitudes and divisive commentary. Fake news exploded on both sides of the social media battle, as well as disturbing true news that soiled both candidates. The battle became so messy, some people watched the election asking themselves, "What happens when both sides lose? Who wins?"

Marketing professional Joe Kefauver captured what many of us felt in an article he wrote for the Nation's Restaurant News. Referring to the conservatives, he stated, "When did the 'family values' party lose its values?" Kefauver concluded, "It's time for the adults in the country to put the children running for president in a time out."

Is this behavior the new norm for presidential politics? We must understand the forces that caused such a tsunami to overthrow a history of civility connected to the presidential election process.

WHY SOCIAL MEDIA "TRUMPED" THE ESTABLISHMENT

On Election Day, CNN polls[16] reported the most important factor that rose up among voters was a desire for a candidate who would bring change. And, for good or bad, change is the message Trump delivered. Much of the change he promoted was directed at what he called "the system," which included those in power among the media elite.

Trump didn't create the perception of biased media or corrupt news reporting. More interested in persuasion than truth, the major news networks earned this reputation all on their own. Trump simply played on the existing wave of negative public sentiment toward pushy media coverage. Calling it a "rigged system," Trump tapped a nerve that pumped up his base.

Although I follow social media sentiment and statistics, I didn't have to be an expert to observe the obvious in this regard. I remember rotating channels between CNN, Fox News and MSNBC as a strategy to compile some semblance of the truth. Frustrated by that process, I like many other Americans, turned to social media to see what my insider friends had to say or repost. Social media made a mockery of traditional news, where — under the guise of unbiased reporting — bombastic sound bites and conflict supplanted rational debate. Whether it was the "angry" conservatives or the "smug" liberals, voters had heard enough.

I once heard an inspiring perspective on how Walt Disney approached conflict. According to his philosophy of unity, he believed the only reason people ever fought with each other was because they didn't understand each other, therefore a good marketer and promoter of a unifying movement must first seek to understand. Unfortunately, Disney wasn't running for president in 2016. Neither candidate demonstrated such wisdom. In my attempt to understand the mystery of the Trump voter, the following is my conclusion:

THE ELECTION WAS A VALUES-BASED MOVEMENT

Trump's election was a result of a movement of the people based on values, but not the values that were being discussed on mainstream TV. These elusive values were mostly discussed online, where political correctness could be disregarded.

The complex values of middle America had been long ignored by mainstream media on both sides of the political aisles. Even the conservative media pundits didn't get it. Large groups of unrelated and previously silent voters from both parties rose up and turned against the establishment with a great wave of frustration, and Trump simply rode this black wave.

Previously centric or left-leaning blue collar workers, coal miners, hunters, military and security workers, as well as conflicted pro-life liberals, pro-union conservatives or deeply committed and traditional religious voters found their advocate in an unlikely candidate. These disenfranchised groups felt bullied by both establishment parties, and they wanted to have their own bully to fight back. Brashly confronting emotionally charged issues that were either overlooked or considered taboo by other politicians, Trump often offended leaders of his own party, yet voters cheered him on.

RUNNING A "TRA-DIGITAL" CAMPAIGN

While Clinton attended fundraisers and spent more money on advertising, Trump hosted rallies and spent more time with people. Trump's random tweets were not random at all, but very calculated. Like a businessman approaching a foreign market, Trump met with people unlike himself. He meticulously studied the values of these constituents, then tweeted or retweeted on the subjects that fired them up.

Misquoting the Bible or misrepresenting what so many people were emotional about, his sincerity was questioned by many. But supporters strangely gave him the benefit of the doubt. He allowed their pastors to awkwardly pray over him. He entered their communities as a stranger, but left as one of their own tribe. Ditching his previous position, or lack of one on abortion, Trump emerged with sloppy and extreme rhetoric about punishing the women. Even his supporters thought he went too far.

Thinking these gaffes would cost him the election, the mainstream media repeated his abrasive statements in loops. That coverage only reminded Trump's followers he was clearly making an effort to understand them, albeit misguided. The mainstream media, being coastal enterprises with mostly urban values, were blindsided by the emotional tsunami Trump stumbled onto. Ultimately, all of the media polls were wrong. That's because their surveys were asking the wrong questions.

Overly focused on trendy metropolitan issues, the mainstream media lost touch with a large group of people who were sick of being called "the rust belt" or worse, "flyover territory." Featured news stories on racism, sexism and environmentalism being covered 24/7 by the mainstream media were issues that did not show promise to help anybody in middle America put food on the table for their children. None of those hotly contested urban issues were relevant to middle America's need to secure their religious freedom or family safety.

Media executives never had a family member who lost a job from a factory that moved to Mexico or China. They didn't compete for jobs with illegal immigrants being paid under the table, but many Trump supporters did.

Gun enthusiast bloggers were freely persuading masses of hunters and collectors to get out and vote for a man who was nothing like them. And, even previously "true-blue" Democrats from blue-collar industries were posting and blogging about a change in the way a nation should negotiate with Mexico and China — tipping the union vote toward the ultimate white-collar tycoon.

The vast majority of Americans want the same things. The problem with values is that we cannot all prioritize them equally. If we value everything equally, we value nothing specifically. For example, traditional religious women value their faith above their own gender. That doesn't mean they hate women's rights, but they might not necessarily vote on behalf of women. Likewise, pro-choice voters don't hate unborn babies. They simply believe the rights of a woman should be placed higher. But, good luck explaining these rational concepts to either party after emotions take control.

Values-based movements are not defined by rational thinking or self-interest. Because emotional and unconscious decisions are involved, values-based movements create strange bed-fellows. Case and point: Why would 42% of women vote for Trump after he was clearly documented calling women fat, ugly or worse? Did they forget? Were they all naive? Of course not. Why didn't they all vote to have America's first woman president? After Trump began to name conservative judges for the Supreme Court and once he began to speak out on the values of religious and pro-life women, the debate took a sharp turn. Driven by the power of a selfless call to duty, these women looked past Trump's undeniable sexist persona, and saw a champion for faith and unborn babies.

Many nice, church-going women even attempted to justify Trump's sexist behaviors that were caught on tape. Like a dirty-minded, loose cannon hero from a gunslinger movie, somehow Trump's flawed character and arrogant swagger actually awoke an emotional, values-based movement among these women. Tired of being told their religion was wrong, these religious women felt marginalized and threatened by a media culture that often ignored or attacked their values.

Because of Trump's awkward, but seemingly sincere attempts to understand their values, church groups were actively posting support for Trump to millions of faithful followers, who previously abhorred the man for his anti-Christian rhetoric and lifestyle. A vote for Trump became a vote against the media, and the movement was afoot.

No, Trump was not articulate, but his new friends and followers in social media were. And, they were more effective than the vastly disconnected news reporting industry.

Even several highly influential African American church leaders began to speak on behalf of Trump. The social buzz from these groups went off the charts. Perhaps this is why more African Americans voted for Trump than Romney in the previous election.

With nearly all projecting Trump could not possibly win, it was difficult for the mainstream media pundits to understand what was happening.[17] Failing to engage the values of more than half of its constituents, the media instead judged those they didn't understand, stubbornly describing the world in categories of old media demographics divided by male and female, black and white. These broad categories defined by old media mindsets were not longer as relevant. The hazard maps had changed. Social communities were driven by values instead.

Touting its most watched program in election history, election night reached 13 million viewers on CNN. However, in all this celebration of viewership and polling expertise, one poll was overlooked. Trump's channel of choice wasn't CNN or Fox. With almost 19 million Twitter followers, his own channel held more influence. The Trump Facebook follower count reached almost 17 million, with double that number of followers coming from the dozens of fan pages — while Clinton barely cracked 10 million followers on her Facebook page and never quite reached 12 million Twitter followers.

SOCIAL MEDIA FOLLOWERS

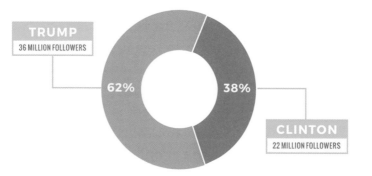

TRUMP
36 MILLION FOLLOWERS

62%   38%

CLINTON
22 MILLION FOLLOWERS

The social revolution had become a media revolution and a political revolution in a single night. But this social media tsunami wasn't built overnight. Many of these Trump followers were leveraged from his years of celebrity appearances on his widely distributed TV series, *The Apprentice*. Clinton had no such content marketing platform to build on. She and the media had been both anchored at bay for years, trusting in the powerful media wall they had built in newspapers and on TV.

After Trump won the presidency, in his first interview with *60 Minutes*, he clearly credited social media. Referencing the much larger advertising budgets and traditional media support of his competitors, he said "I think social media has more power than the money I spent, and I think that's why I won."

Following the election, the mainstream media became concerned about their loss of power. On January 1, 2017, in Trump's first year of his term, the first CNN story that led in the New Year was titled, "Trump tries to bypass media with

> ❝ I think social media has more power than the money I spent, and I think that's why I won.

tweets..." This presumptuous position was revealing. It became clear that the media was struggling to find its role in this new order of things.

The media channels of the future won't have to embrace Trump voter values in order to remain relevant. They will simply need to face the new realities. Instead of doing all of the talking, casting people as "bad" or "good," "enlightened" or "backward," we in the media should be taking the time to understand these diverse and complex values, considering tolerance and inclusion not only in our tone, but in our actions — taking the time to listen before we speak. Or, those of us in power could lose our voice altogether.

In one such attempt to have a conversation, after the election was over, CNN's Van Jones led the way by traveling to the Rust Belt to meet an Ohio family to discuss why a traditionally Democrat-voting group would switch to vote Republican. In the interview, the man of the house showed little interest in metropolitan issues or environmentalism. He didn't live in a place where gun violence was an apparent problem. Racial conflict wasn't an apparent problem in his neighborhood either. He was offended to be labeled a racist. He previously voted for President Obama after all. In fact, the vast majority of swing voters did.

Whether he lost his factory job as a result of environmental regulation or international trade policies didn't matter anymore. The jobs in his community were gone. The man became fearful of losing his gun because he was out of work, and he needed his gun to hunt for food. Formerly a Bill Clinton voter, the man said about Hillary, "She hurt us!" The compassion shown on Van Jones' face lit up a community who had felt forsaken by his class of media influencers.

Whether this populist movement will be a good or bad thing for history remains to be seen. My point is not to support or defend any political position or candidate. I personally wasn't a fan of the options that year, but I was raised to respect the process and the office itself. I have no idea how this particular transition of power will impact America, but what we can be sure of is that the media no longer controls its democracy. The media itself have been largely democratized. Sink or swim, "We The People" can take responsibility for our own destiny. Like a small child first learning to ride a bike, we will likely lean right, then left in the decades ahead as we wobble under the powerful new mechanism we have created.

A WARNING FROM HISTORY

It turns out, history predicted that the presidential candidates of 2016 might act like children. Like children with a new toy, powerful new media tools were being tested in our democracy for the very first time. This unlimited power of the common man seems to be a prophetic fulfillment of predictions by Alexis de Tocqueville. He was the French political pundit in the early Nineteenth century who tried to encourage America about the future of our particular democracy, with a strong warning about the pitfalls of giving all the power to the people.

> ❝ The people has consequently been abandoned to its wild propensities," de Tocqueville wrote in *Democracy in America*, "and it has grown up like those outcasts who receive their education in the public streets ... it was worshipped as the idol of strength; until, when it was enfeebled by its own excesses ... We have gotten a democracy, but without the conditions which lessen its vices and render its natural advantages more prominent; and although we already perceive the evils it brings, we are ignorant of the benefits it may confer.[18]

As much as de Tocqueville was concerned about the democratization of government, many communications professionals are concerned about the democratization of media. De Tocqueville concluded that the people would rule well in America as long as the people maintained their own moral society. However, once that society would become corrupt in any way, democracy would be the worst form of all governments.

What happens when immoral people become the majority voice or the majority vote? The people would vote upon themselves whatever they could lust for. The masses would extract from society more than they invest, and the people would become their own pestilence. This is why those who lead democracies should "Flip The Pyramid" for better results. Leaders in this environment will need to focus on selfless contributions to a greater society, rather than appealing to the self-interest of regional populations. Otherwise, the base human instincts that politicians appeal to may ultimately work against us.

We are naive to think democracy itself is good. It merely augments the power of the people. We see this in the Middle East, where Westerners encouraged democracy, but now the democracies they nurtured threaten to elect members of ISIS and the Taliban. Is a democracy truly better than a secularist tyrant in light of this potential outcome?

There is a moral responsibility we must consider in this great revolution. We who have a role in media will have a role in our own demise if we don't moderate our ambitions. With great influence comes responsibility to even greater ethics. We can manipulate the values of consumers for temporary wins, or we can use the power of new media for social good, but like the media elite, advertisers no longer hold the microphone unchallenged. And we will be called on the carpet if we say or do the wrong thing.

What is the wrong thing? That is the important question. And in determining the answer, we won't be judged by *our narrow* values. We will be judged by the complex values of the people we serve. This is the unpredictable environment that marketing decision-makers must navigate, so beware of the forces that we no longer control. Surfers don't tell the wave what to do.

In the end, it is debatable who was more arrogant: Trump? Or, the media who rejected him?

In the aftermath of the election, Advertising Age and Hollywood Reporter among others featured articles about the media industry being out of touch with the values of middle America. Madison Avenue advertising agencies and Hollywood producers began aggressively recruiting talent that would bring a perspective on the values from places like Indiana and Tennessee. Even Greta Van Susteren left Fox News, later to join MSNBC, while NBC made an aggressive move toward balancing its media team by recruiting popular conservative anchor Megyn Kelly.

Who knows what comes next, but in the end of the initial Star Wars trilogy, it was indeed Darth Vader who brought balance to the Force. As Edward Snowden said, "If we want to have a better world, we can't hope for an Obama. We should not fear a Donald Trump. Rather we should build it ourselves."[19]

> 66 Nothing is more wonderful than the art of being free, but nothing is harder to learn how to use than Freedom.
>
> – *Alexis de Tocqueville*

LESSON THREE: AVOID UNPREDICTABLE WINDS

What I learned in kiteboarding is that not all wind is good wind. An untimely gust could launch you 50 feet into the air, or drag you out to sea.

It's the same in social-media marketing. If the Trump campaign proved anything, it's that some conflict can be effective, but too much conflict can be impossible to navigate. The wrong wind can pull your brand into a political maelstrom.

It's always a good reality check to experience an election season. When we look at the "red" and "blue" regions on the American political map, the divides are clear and stark. In social conflict, we should always remain humble enough to realize that our "side" typically represents less than 50% of the population, regardless of the side we are on. Consequently, brands that pick sides in political battles can create a chasm between the brand and half of its potential consumers. The Participation Age will widen this gap.

"UNITED WE STAND. DIVIDED WE FALL."

-QUOTED BY U.S. FOUNDING FATHER PATRICK HENRY

Map Source: Adam Kole, NPR (Web)

This great divide creates unpredictable situations that could trap any brand between two major consumer groups. Here are just a few danger zones to look out for in the Participation Age:

• Religion	• Gender
• Economic policy	• Military action
• Race	• Abortion
• Marriage	• Sex

Do you think you can easily avoid these subjects? Think again. Social media is politically charged, and a battle is being waged online. If you have a large, visible brand, chances are that your company is already being listed on one side of the battle line, or the other.

By the way, it doesn't matter which position you take on any of these subjects. In the minds of half or more of your potential customers, you are already wrong. And, getting this wrong is not like missing one question out of 100. Think of it as getting half of the questions wrong on a test. And, this isn't elementary school: When you fail this test, angry activists will "grade" your company with boycotts, lawsuits or bankruptcy.

Like all tribal societies, modern cultures still have turf wars. In the U.S., one group is fired up by the "Black Protestant" view of racism. Other groups are fired up by either the "Secular" or "Religious Right" view of sexism. But, according to the Osher Lifelong Learning Institute, no single "tribe" represents more than 13% of the consumer population. Because of this fragmented social structure, it's challenging to find common values that align to create a critical mass for a major brand platform.

THE TWELVE TRIBES OF AMERICAN POLITICS

RELIGIOUS LEFT		HEARTLAND CULTURE WARRIORS		SECULARS	CONVERTIBLE CATHOLICS		WHITE BREAD PROTESTANTS		MUSLIMS & OTHERS		
12.6%	12.6%	11.4%	10.8%	10.7%	9.6%	8.1%	7.3%	7%	5.3%	2.7%	1.9%
	RELIGIOUS RIGHT		MODERATE EVANGELICALS		BLACK PROTESTANTS		LATINO CHRISTIANS		SPIRITUAL BUT NOT RELIGIOUS	JEWS	

Osher Lifelong Learning Institute, 2012

Be careful out there. An ocean of debate is raging over seemingly benign words, even "diversity." For example, who gets affirmed or protected under the term "diversity"? All philosophical views? All political agendas? Both liberals and conservatives? All religions? What about atheism, Christianity, Judaism ... ISIS? Can we really be inclusive of all their values at once? How? Don't some of them hate each other? Won't siding with one only cause you to side against the other?

Before we use our brands to take a stand for or against an entire religion or political position, we must always remember: A business is not a social-engineering platform. Beyond our personal convictions, we also have a responsibility to the employees and stockholders to keep the company safe from financial ruin.

Your brand cannot run for office or make policy, but your brand can lose the popular vote. Although I can't verify my theology on this, I don't believe a company can receive eternal salvation in Heaven. However, a company can go to Hell. We've all seen that happen.

It's a complex moral question. Should we sacrifice our business on the altar of our moral cause? That depends.

Consider the Oregon baker who refused to make a cake for a lesbian wedding. The bakery held values based on the personal religious convictions of the owners. The business brushed bankruptcy after losing $135,000 in state-ordered damages. Depending on the editorial bias, the online banter labeled the bakery either heroic or homophobic. Unlike for Trump, the immense national coverage did not help the bakery. It was forced to shut down during the height of the controversy.[20]

The owner, Melissa Klein, along with her husband, was morally free to sacrifice her bakery and livelihood for personal religious beliefs. However, what if a publicly traded bakery franchisee took a similar position? Should an employed cake baker or brand manager have the same moral right to sacrifice a publicly traded brand on the altar of his or her personal convictions?

Or perhaps you think your personal acceptance of various sexual orientations will protect you from a negative outcome? Think again. These unpredictable social movements have strong currents in both directions.

THE RESTROOM WARS

At one point during the 2016 election season, the online firestorm around retail restroom use was the only social-media meme that was trumping Trump himself. By allowing any-gender bathroom use through self-identification, Target faced the largest boycott in its history. All of this protest came because of

Target's desire to live its stated core value of "diversity" by extending compassion toward transgender people. But many who disagreed felt that their own values were being violated by the brand.

As one Instagram post read, "Telling me you're ok with men walking into the bathroom behind my baby girl actually doesn't make me feel like I belong. ... Basically, Target just told us — and millions of concerned parents — that we're no longer accepted, respected and welcome in their stores."[21]

A boycott by more than a million customers cost the company $1.5 billion in stock value in the first week, accelerating to a $6 billion wallop within a month after the announcement. A *Business Insider* article noted that Target's reputation score tumbled by more than 14% among consumers who previously said they would shop at Target. For the first time in years, same-store sales actually began falling at Target.[22]

Many consumers felt their values were violated by the brand, but unexpectedly, it wasn't the transgender issue that surfaced in social media. It was the safety issue that rose to the top of the social charts. Parents posted concerns that their girls would be unsafe from male predators who might use the transgender policy as a loophole to take advantage of women. When Target's other customers told these parents they were "wrong to feel this way," the secondary comments actually positioned Target as intolerant. Sides were cemented. Planned or unplanned, Target became a political brand.

Does diversity sound like a no-win proposition? It kind of is. So, be careful out there. However, there might be a middle way.

Consider the response to this same dilemma by Kroger, which took a different path in restroom politics. In an attempt to find the common ground, the retailer introduced a single-occupancy unisex bathroom policy that allowed privacy for each customer, regardless of their gender orientation. The social media chatter about this solution was very positive in contrast to the online banter about Target's approach.

In a formal release, Kroger stated, "We have a UNISEX bathroom because sometimes gender-specific toilets put others into uncomfortable situations." Not only does this appeal to the LGBTQ customers, Kroger also said the unisex bathroom appeals to mothers with infant sons, fathers with infant daughters and the mentally or physically disabled."[23]

Kroger's customers posted and commented, "Love this ... now really, how hard is that?" "It's all to do with common sense," and "I knew there was a reason why I shop with you."

Kroger avoided a drop in stock value and found a way to avoid a boycott from either side of the argument by taking into consideration all of the gender-orientation sensitivities, safety concerns and religious convictions of the majority of its customers. Of course, they didn't win everybody over, but Kroger managed to navigate these difficult waters. So can you.

The reason Kroger could respond with a more universal appeal is because they had strong brand values in place to use as their gauge. Below are the Kroger values,[24] clarifying the importance of diversity balanced by inclusion, safety and a unified approach that values consumer opinions:

Honesty: Doing the right things, telling the truth.

Integrity: Living our values in all we do, unified approach to how we do business and treat each other.

Respect for Others: Valuing opinions, property and perspectives of others.

Diversity: Reflecting a workplace that includes a variety of people from different backgrounds and cultures, diversity of opinions and thoughts.

Safety: Watching out for others, being secure and safe in your workplace.

Inclusion: Your voice matters, working together works, encouraging everyone's involvement, being the best person you can be.

With Kroger's value statement, "Your voice matters," I am reminded of one of the most important social values consumers expect from brands: "Listen."

It's important to note here that Target entered the fall of 2016 essentially refusing to acknowledge publicly that the continuing boycott of its stores by Americans concerned about its restroom policy had anything to do with its rather sudden swoon in store traffic, sales and profits. Yet after taking time to meet with the leaders of the boycott, CEO Brian Cornell announced that Target would spend $20 million to install single-occupancy unisex bathrooms in its many stores that didn't already have them.[25]

Since Target took the time to listen and respond to the consumer, the tide of boycott and negative social posting has subsided. Brand management is always a work in progress, and even the most angry consumers have been shown to make room for brands who take the time to listen. Brands cannot control the next unpredictable wind that threatens to push them out to sea. However, as Kroger has shown, these winds can be navigated successfully.

WOULD YOUR BRAND SPONSOR THIS?

We might choose to be conscientious objectors and therefore sit out the restroom wars, but there are plenty of other ways to kill your brand out there. One way brands are literally taking life and death in their own hands — both their own figurative lives and the very real lives of individuals — is by sponsoring ridiculous human stunts.

My most memorable days as a child included Evel Knievel preparing for a death-defying motorcycle jump. Long before the X Games or Red Bull's sponsored daredevils, he invented sponsored insanity. The Harley-Davidson and Mack truck brands managed to survive their deals with him even after Evel Knievel's crashes and failures. But, he did live after all. To many of us, he was our hero.

Much more recently, one day as I was browsing my LinkedIn newsfeed, I ran into a video of a guy doing a backflip over a speeding race car, in a stunt apparently sponsored by Qualcomm. With his back to the car, it raced under him at 60 mph.[26] I thought to myself, "Wow, that would be a great way to get 2 million views without paying for the media." Then, my rational side kicked in and the angel on my shoulder told the devil on my other shoulder, "What are you thinking?"

So, I simply posted some food for thought to my marketing friends. "Would your brand sponsor this? Just wondering ..."

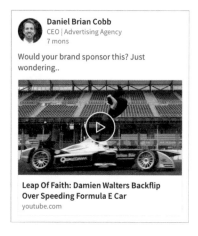

Daniel Brian Cobb
CEO | Advertising Agency
7 mons

Would your brand sponsor this? Just wondering..

Leap Of Faith: Damien Walters Backflip Over Speeding Formula E Car
youtube.com

Of course, we all know the potential outcomes of this risky endeavor. If the guy makes the jump, the brand gets free media and the associated cool brand factor. However, if his timing is off and a race car slices through him at 60 mph, the headlines would read much differently. The viral image of blood on Qualcomm's logo amid the tragedy would never be deleted from the internet — or our minds.

We live in a new world.

The old world was interruptive and disconnected from content. Brands that advertised during the live Evel Knievel broadcast were firewalled from this type of negative exposure. We created ads that found a home among content that was created by someone else. Now, renting space in canned media environments isn't enough. Brands must become the content creators to be relevant, interesting and authentic.

New brands are defining this game. Ever-present in the realm of PR stunts and sports marketing, Red Bull sponsored the Supersonic Jump[27] back in 2014, as a parachutist jumped from a weather balloon in the stratosphere to the earth below — forever claiming its "brand territory" as the producer of extreme sports content. It's a unique (but increasingly mimicked) approach that has Red Bull pumping out content to a highly engaged audience.

Tragically, there have been seven recorded deaths that our research team could find related to Red Bull-sponsored content.[28] Although this is the worst possible outcome for Red Bull, we could find no violations of their brand values in sponsoring these events. Red Bull Media House's marketing page said that the brand is "on a mission to fascinate" applying what it calls Red Bull Values: "Red Bull gives you wings, letting your dreams come true."[29]

I love extreme sports, but even Evel Knievel spent hours of planning and calculating his risk. As a challenger brand in the soda-pop category, this kind of risk might be sustainable for Red Bull. But, what if the sponsor was Coke? Would taking this type of unpredictable risk be right for the brand? These are the values that we must wrestle with before we sponsor or create content we could regret.

LESSON FOUR: FROM A SAFE PLACE, GO FOR IT!

After two days of kiteboarding safety training, we were ready to go. This is the fun part, unless of course you're deathly terrified after the first three lessons.

Perhaps by this point, you are afraid to take any risk at all. Unpredictable winds, waves and a potential wind storm that pulls us out to sea? How is this going to be fun? Perhaps we should just anchor our kites by the harbor.

Don't think you are safe in the harbor either. Remember the boats that washed into the city like bathtub toys?

One Christmas holiday to Busselton, Australia, a man and his two sons were swimming near Geographe Bay Yacht Club when a sudden rip tide sucked them more than 350 feet out to sea, and still moving quickly. The rip tide was caused by an earthquake off the coast of Indonesia, and created tsunamis throughout Asia. The offshore current was so strong, no matter how hard they swam against the current, even these strong young men continued to be pulled out farther.

Luckily, Ian Young, Australia's leading professional kiteboard instructor happened to be out teaching a lesson that day. Not only was Ian able to use the power of his kite to fight the tsunami-induced current to save his own life, Ian was able to save the lives of the man and his two boys that day. As stated on a kiteboarding forum, "He helped them ashore by dragging them back with the kite. Good show, Ian."[30]

Lives were saved that day because of a decision made by Ian Young years before. He was willing leave the harbor and learn something new. All personal growth involves risk, but we never know the difference we can make until we head into the abyss.

There is an opportunity cost to avoiding controversy in marketing, too.

The fear of repercussions from an off-color social post might cause many brands to retreat from the public eye altogether. And, who would blame them? But, this is a mistake equal in gravity to making the stupid post in the first place. That's because the unforgiving and relentless tide of social media will banish these silent and fearful brands from social relevance. Just remember what happened to the mild-mannered Republican candidates in the 2016 presidential campaign, if you can remember any of them.

The real opportunity of the Participation Age will unfold through meaningful social engagement, but not through communication that is void of any critical content that might offend one group or another. We must not hesitate too long and remember to heed Katada's insight to the students that "it's natural to be reluctant." Like he taught the children, the secret to success is understanding the purpose your brand stands for, so leaders will rise up an act without hesitation.

You can't win them all, but you *can* lose them all. In the attempt to avoid controversy, we should not go silent. The opportunity cost is too great. If you don't like expressing your values, you will like irrelevance even less. We might lose half our customers by taking a stand on the wrong social platform, but we will most assuredly lose all of our consumers by taking no stand at all.

Consumers are demanding emotional connection to brands. They want connection to our values, so don't hide them. Refine them to withstand the turbulent waters ahead.

When we know who we are, we won't sway from month to month. Conversely, when our brand shifts with every wind and every wave, we offend one group one month, and we offend our remaining advocates the next. Consistency in brand values is the North Star of brand management in the Participation Age.

Remember the boats that went out to sea before the tsunami? There is no safe harbor in the Participation Revolution. It's time to explore new waters.

Start small. Your brand might not be ready to sponsor the next death-defying leap from space. There are plenty of other engaging ways to excite and connect with the values of your consumers. I'm thankful that my kiteboard instructor led me to the safe waters that were knee-deep for miles. It was much better kiteboarding there. The wind was strong enough to power my kite, but it was manageable.

SAMPLE VALUE DRIVERS

Where should your brand start? Here are a few effective purpose-driven platforms that can power your brand without plunging into potentially disastrous stands on hot-button social issues or losing control of your brand reputation on social media:

Children are always a great cause, especially if they have a physical need. Shoes, housing, education, computer and entertainment brands will do well by associating with children's causes.

Poverty is almost always a cause that people can get behind. Food and shelter brands such as consumer packaged goods and mortgage companies can do well by engaging these social issues.

Safety is an effective value driver in both vehicle and food sales. Car companies have done well by promoting crash test results to families. Non-GMO organic foods are exciting to health-conscious, educated and upper-income consumers.

Animals are loved by many; just look up popular cat videos on YouTube. Pet-supply brands or zoos might consider centering their cause around either highlighting funny and entertaining animals, or calling attention to lost and abused animals.

Victory is a value that is best understood in contrast to the underdog. People identify with the desire to win, but many must overcome difficult circumstances and would appreciate inspiration or encouragement from athletic or apparel brands.

Sustainability is a great cause for most people. Nobody's protesting industrial businesses, oil or chemical companies that want to make an honest effort toward a cleaner world.

> **Joy and togetherness** is an age-old and tested brand purpose. Beverages, food, entertainment and apparel have all used these values to refresh consumers with laughter, family and healing in the midst of life's daily challenges.
>
> **Health and health care** are great ways for health-related brands to gain momentum in their communities. Nobody will ever complain about your efforts to end cancer, unless, of course, you represent a cigarette company.

These are only a few ways to connect with the values of your consumers. In no way is this an exhaustive list. More important, these values aren't squishy. They have a tangible impact on real business. Consider how Nike inspired the value of victory among athletes and won the sports shoe category. When consumers watch you show remark-worthy concern for their community, they will call your brand "remarkable." Inspired consumers will passionately make the sale for you.

LOVE IS THE GREATEST VALUE DRIVER

Discovering your brand values starts with finding opportunities to improve the human condition in a relevant way for your consumer. All brand values can be summarized under one universal value that is common to us all: Love. Every human being agrees with this value. That's why the Coca-Cola brand is so universal. For decades, Coke's advertising has been refreshing audiences with images of joy and togetherness rooted in the value of "love."

While Coke's iconic ad sang about building the world a home and furnishing it with love, it was more about what the brand did than what it said. It presented a diverse world brought together for "a Coke and a smile." Specifically, Coke showed how brands must demonstrate selfless love toward others to become remarkable in the consumer psyche. Although no medical professional will tell you that sugar water offers health benefits, mental health professionals can show how delivering a smile can release endorphins and improve health. In this way, the Coke brand advertising is good for your health, even if the product isn't.

Love has a reciprocal effect. When brands demonstrate love, a psychological bond is formed with their consumers. Coca-Cola actually has a measure for the impact. They call it "brand love," and it's as important to them as market share. In fact, brand love is more important than taste. In the Coke vs. Pepsi challenge, only 38% preferred Coke with the labels off. However, with the labels on, Coke won over 64% of the taste testers.

Once you have determined the core value you provide to your consumer, you will find plenty of ways to contribute to the world in a socially sticky way. But, be creative. Don't get lost in the piles of one-for-one shoe contributions. Look for new ways to express your unique passion and make a difference in the world. Nike, Coke and TOMS Shoes each led their own movement. You can't make the same impact by being a follower.

This is not about donating money to a cause. Building up UNICEF, United Way, Salvation Army or any other well-meaning organization is great, but building up other cause brands will have limited impact differentiating the values of your brand. Every major company has a philanthropy department. Giving money alone doesn't create a movement. Like Coke showed us, values branding is about becoming the cause itself.

SOCIAL CAUSE IS THE NEW PERSONAL SERVICE

As technology replaces personal service, commoditized industries such as banking are seeking a new differentiator. In one study,[31] we explored value drivers that could have the propensity to create preference besides rates and fees. In our study of the general market, cause associated with the bank's social responsibility was equally valued to the service the bank provides. One in four respondents told us they would be willing to switch banks for a more socially responsible brand.

More interesting, when we tested Millennials, the results changed. More than half of all Millennials told us they were most likely to switch to a "socially responsible bank, one that leads with integrity and invests into good causes and makes a difference in my community." As a value driver, personal service and expertise dropped from 41% of the general market to 10% of Millennials. Also, app-based service increased as a value driver from 7% of the general market to 20% of the Millennials tested.

What does this mean? These findings align to the verbatims we discovered in focus groups, indicating the following significant findings among Millennials who are moved by brand value drivers other than price:

1 Millennials are most moved by cause and social values

2 Millennials are more moved by social values than the general market

3 Self-service apps provide the best service, and personal service is no longer a primary value driver in comparison with technology and a strong social cause

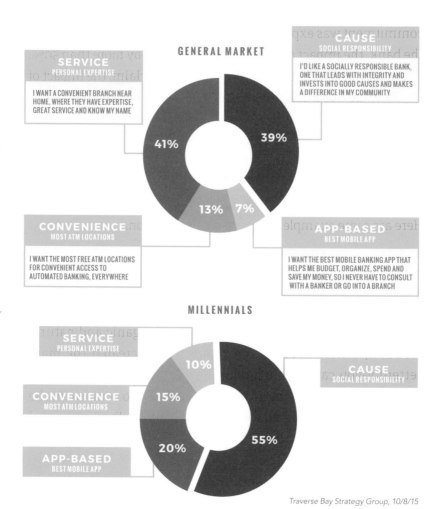

GENERAL MARKET

SERVICE
PERSONAL EXPERTISE

I WANT A CONVENIENT BRANCH NEAR HOME, WHERE THEY HAVE EXPERTISE, GREAT SERVICE AND KNOW MY NAME

CAUSE
SOCIAL RESPONSIBILITY

I'D LIKE A SOCIALLY RESPONSIBLE BANK, ONE THAT LEADS WITH INTEGRITY AND INVESTS INTO GOOD CAUSES AND MAKES A DIFFERENCE IN MY COMMUNITY

41%   39%

13% 7%

CONVENIENCE
MOST ATM LOCATIONS

I WANT THE MOST FREE ATM LOCATIONS FOR CONVENIENT ACCESS TO AUTOMATED BANKING, EVERYWHERE

APP-BASED
BEST MOBILE APP

I WANT THE BEST MOBILE BANKING APP THAT HELPS ME BUDGET, ORGANIZE, SPEND AND SAVE MY MONEY, SO I NEVER HAVE TO CONSULT WITH A BANKER OR GO INTO A BRANCH

MILLENNIALS

SERVICE
PERSONAL EXPERTISE

CONVENIENCE
MOST ATM LOCATIONS

APP-BASED
BEST MOBILE APP

CAUSE
SOCIAL RESPONSIBILITY

10%

15%

20%   55%

Traverse Bay Strategy Group, 10/8/15

ACTION SPEAKS LOUDER THAN WORDS

Be careful that this data doesn't mislead you to manipulate consumers with empty social gestures. This generation possess a strong authenticity barometer, so don't promise values that you don't activate in the real world.

Your values must be demonstrated to be owned. In an extension of our study, we tested assertion against demonstration of values. Values expressed as an assertion such as "committed locally" tested lowest of all possible value propositions. When local commitment was expressed as a specific financial contribution by the bank, the impact of the message increased by more than 50%. When financial accountability was tied to the claim, the impact of the message was increased by 250%.

Specificity is critical. Rather than claiming your brand contributes to the community, present the dollar amount and its impact. Similarly, if your brand is in retail food distribution, don't just claim to use healthy food, ban specific foods that are not healthy. Here are some examples of values demonstration.

WHOLE FOODS: CONSCIOUS CAPITALISM PAYS OFF

Banning 70-plus additives, leading in labeling transparency, and offering their 365 line of private-label organic and natural products, Whole Foods Markets essentially created the mass better-for-you category in a retail-food space that everyone had assumed was already oversaturated. Declining to compete in the "my cost is lower than yours" battleground, Whole Foods conceded this territory to Walmart and created its own playing field.

Today, Whole Foods enjoys its rank as number 30 on the Change the World list[32] for all of the social benefits the brand has delivered to its "granola-eating, Prius-driving, yoga-practicing clientele." Adding locations in underserved communities, including an inner-city neighborhood of Detroit, Whole Foods has stretched its values-based approach beyond the quality of food that it provides. The company focused on the humanitarian causes that the brand serves.

While the entire retail grocery category was struggling to stay in the game, Whole Foods Market became the leader of a category that previously didn't exist. Sales doubled from $8 billion to a record $15.4 billion in just six years, and profits have tripled from $284 million. At $970 in sales per gross square foot, Whole Foods is the industry leader.[33]

However, being the organic food leader is not without its challenges. For one thing, sometimes it's difficult for the brand to reconcile its legendarily high prices — it's not called "Whole Paycheck" for nothing — with the notion that better-for-you food ideally should be available to as many Americans as possible. But the cost of raising and manufacturing organic ingredients and foods is significantly higher than for conventional equivalents, and Whole Foods' business model, which insists on a plentiful staff of relatively well-paid associates who are well educated about their products, is costly.

As a result, Whole Foods has been as lambasted for its business practices in recent years as it has been lauded. A particularly damaging segment on *Last Week Tonight with John Oliver* had the comedian accusing the brand of overcharging its customers.[34]

Another challenge is Whole Foods' Co-CEO and Co-Founder John Mackey, who has been known to voice his political views in ways that have not helped the brand build trust with its progressive consumers. Unfortunately, he publicly has picked sides in controversial political debates, gaining negative coverage and social shares because of articles such as the following excerpt from CBS website *MoneyWatch:*

> 66 Mackey has shot off his mouth on a number of controversial topics, from opposing Obama's health care reform to publicly stating his disbelief in global warming. Despite media uproar, it doesn't seem to have hit the chain's sales volume. That's because, as Mackey proudly points out, he is not Whole Foods.
>
> – *CBS MoneyWatch, Sept. 1, 2010*

Such viral coverage from Mackey's comments have prompted some of Whole Foods' valued liberal customers to boycott the chain from time to time. But thankfully for the brand, Mackey has learned to keep his personal political agenda separate from the company in recent years. In fact, he continuously pushes forward what has been called "conscious capitalism" — the idea that being socially and environmentally responsible and making a profit are not mutually exclusive goals.

So Mackey's various passions have been some of the brand's greatest assets, as well as its greatest liabilities. But it is by associating its brand values with the cause of popularizing organics that Whole Foods has even gotten into a position where Americans care what its co-founder believes.

FAST CASUAL: NOT CASUAL VALUES

If you think you've got problems, maybe you should run a fast-food company for a day or two. McDonald's, Burger King, Taco Bell and other fast-food giants are facing stagnation in their businesses, mainly because they've been outplayed at the branding game by fast-casual competitors whose brands mean more — and deliver more of what modern consumers are looking for. *Values.*

Brands like Chipotle and Panera Bread are proving it's no longer a race to the bottom on speed or price. Millennials are willing to pay more, and even wait longer, if a brand can deliver a healthier product, help create a better environment — or even espouse a superior worldview.

Lured by sublime brands and more healthful menus, Millennial consumers have been flocking to fast-casual outlets and leaving behind traditional fast-feeders — and so have more Baby Boomers. As fast-casual brands continue to expand the value they provide, they are exploring consumer experiences and even humanitarian endeavors that price-obsessed fast-food providers could never compete with.

Known for its bold moves, for example, Panera has somehow continued to approach the edge of outright altruism without falling over it. The brand's experiment with a handful of "pay-as-you-go" cafes serviced more than 1 million urban Americans without any required payment. The St. Louis-based chain also took the risk of sharing some of its values more explicitly by opening a handful of pay-if-you-can stores in some economically hard-hit cities, including its hometown and Detroit.

In the "Panera Cares" locations, about 20 percent of customers left more than the suggested donation; about 60 percent left the suggested donation; and 20 percent left what they could, but often significantly less.

Panera eventually relegated the experiment to urban training locations since they didn't deliver a mass-reach financial model, but the effort was applauded by advocates for the brand. And, creating brand advocates was what the "Live Consciously, Eat Deliciously" campaign was all about. Panera Cares cafés have driven more than 2 billion media impressions to date.[35]

"We really wanted to talk more about why we exist as a company, rather than simply talk about what we do," explained Michael Simon, senior vice president and chief marketing officer at Panera Bread.

HOW BRAND VALUES ENGAGE THE CONSUMER BRAIN

There are brands that consumers trust and there are brands that consumers love. Love is not easy to achieve. It requires a certain tipping point of positive stimulus in the consumer brain. We are mistaken if we believe a brand can be loved by meeting the personal preferences of its consumers. There is no measure

> **❝ Love is an unconscious motivator that moves the human condition past the base motivators of self-interest ...**

of contribution a brand can make to achieve love by satisfying consumer preferences in relation to self-interest.

That's because the human emotion of love is not associated with self-interest. Love is more closely associated with selflessness. The old model built on self-interest was never able to fully explain why people would choose to have children, or why they would sacrifice so much for them. Love is an unconscious motivator that moves the human condition past the base motivators of self-interest toward social awareness, or even preference toward others.

In Nobel Prize-winning economist George Akerlof and Rachel Kranton's hypothesis on Identity Economics, they questioned the original concept of behavioral economics. They found that belonging and values of community are core to human identity. That's why values are often the most powerful force of influence in consumer behavior, or any behavior for that matter. Indeed, they wrote about the rules for behavior saying modern scholars "agree on the importance of anxiety that a person experiences when she violates her internalized rules."[36]

That means the consumer brain feel less anxiety over choices about features and benefits than they do when they make choices that might violate their core purpose or values. These core values are tied directly to the most powerful motivator in the consumer brain: love.

The consumer brain is less interested in meeting its need for preferences toward features and benefits than it is in maintaining its need to get love or provide love to others.

Let's talk tactics. How can we make this practical in the auto-motive industry, for example. The values of the automotive manufacturer are more important to its consumers than the features and benefits. People don't fulfill their need for identity from a car that tested high in crash safety. However, that doesn't mean that crash safety features and benefits are irrelevant either. In fact, these features and benefits may become critical to demonstrate your brand values.

Perhaps you think it's silly for a brand to promise selfless love to its consumers, but consider Subaru. It wasn't flattering to show a car smashed in a commercial about Subaru. In the commercial titled "I'm Sorry," after a teenager gets in a car accident, the mom says, "You're OK? That's all that matters."

When Subaru demonstrated safety as a selfless value owned by the brand, they earned the right to say, "Love, it's what makes a Subaru a Subaru." They were able to tie crash safety features to emotionally charged values of self-sacrifice that Subaru demon-strated by showing its vehicle smashed.[37]

Values such as love are verified by action. That's because the evolved consumer brain is acutely perceptive. It possesses an authenticity barometer that will test your values to be sure they are true. Before the consumer brain assigns love to your brand, your brand will need to demonstrate love first.

In this belief structure, the brain's left hemisphere weighs in on your brand's emotional promise with a desire to see action. That's why you can't fake your values in advertising. What good would it do if Subaru said it loved your kids, if their cars put them in danger? In this commercial, Subaru never had to say they loved your kids. They demonstrated love by their "lifetime commitment to getting them home safely" through crash survival outcomes.

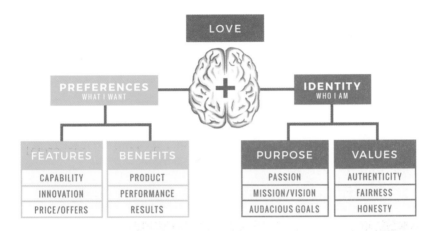

In our updated belief structure, we must appeal beyond the preferences of our consumers to identify with their values. The consumer brain seeks preferences in the "what I want" part of the brain, but it will never violate its identity, or the "who I am" part of the brain. The latter function has been proven to short circuit self-interest. As we meet the preferences of our consumers to come into alignment with their identity, we will find values alignment. That creates a condition where love is found.

BEST PRACTICES FOR EMPLOYING VALUES

Consumers connect emotionally to your brand values. These are not soft, intangible feelings. Leading brands are *flipping the pyramid*. Brands are feeding and clothing consumers who can't afford to pay. Brands are healing people through commerce. Brands are giving purpose to employees and to the consumers who love these companies more than any generation before us ever thought they could.

The longer brands take to get into the movement, the more

they will look like inauthentic followers of this powerful trend. Significant benefits will be rewarded to brands who act now with authenticity, seizing control of early-mover advantages.

These are the key best practices to keep in mind:

1 **Determine North Star Values for your brand:** Establish a moral true north for your brand values that guides everything your company and its employees do. Plan a safe launch for these brand values in today's socially charged marketing landscape.

2 **Love is the greatest value driver:** Most importantly, love is the universal value driver. If in doubt about a complex values question, test it to see if it falls under the definition of selfless love that you can demonstrate as a brand.

3 **Social cause is the new personal service:** In recent studies, a brand value proposition tied to social responsibility has shown more impact than personal service, which is being replaced by mobile apps and self-service.

4 **Action speaks louder than words:** That means demonstration is better than assertion. So, don't be anxious to promote your values in your ads by talking about them, unless you can show accountability.

❝ Even a fool who keeps silent is considered wise; when he closes his lips, he is deemed intelligent.[38]

– *King Solomon, Proverbs 17:28*

DOES ANYBODY CARE THAT CHIPOTLE CARES?

BLOG POST: SEPTEMBER 29, 2016 – Chipotle is a brand that exudes its brand values. The progressive and health-oriented raison d'etre for the Denver-based chain — which, ironically, previously was owned by McDonald's — includes the promise to use only "natural" and healthful ingredients and to support family farmers and sustainability. Chipotle also puts cool, philosophical musings from random authors on its paper cups and bags. All this happens with freshly made food served in a trendy environment. Consumers are willing to pay more for this experience.

Another interesting part of the Chipotle brand persona has been a nasty flipside to its utopian message about "food with integrity": attacking food and brands that it believes lack the same integrity. In fact, a major aspect of Chipotle's branded content over the last several years has been to produce animated videos that use a narrative to explain the evils of Big Food processing of fast-food restaurant fare that relies on antibiotics, artificial flavors, preservatives and other things that Chipotle says don't belong in food.[39]

Delivering 100% GMO-free, antibiotic-free and ethically sourced food creates a quality control and supply problem: There aren't yet enough GMO-free farmers to fulfill the Chipotle promise. When sourcing problems undercut the chain's ability to supply enough antibiotic-free pork in early 2015, Chipotle determined to tell the truth. Instead of quietly supplementing their high quality food with less desirable options for their popular *carnitas* burritos, Chipotle publicly posted signage stating they were unable to meet their requirements for the day, and rotated the shortages regionally. This necessarily went on for several months, but the brand's transparency further sealed the trust of Chipotle's fans.[40]

However, Chipotle's fans proved to be not so forgiving when, in late 2015, poor food-safety practices resulted in several outbreaks of bacterial and viral poisonings of hundreds of customers at a handful of locations. Such are the risks of attempting to create a new food-delivery process while ignoring the safety practices that the fast-food industry has had years to develop. This time, consumer-approved values worked against the brand, but for an unforeseen reason. Chipotle executives quickly acknowledged the need for better food-handling systems and pledged to make a priority of overhauling them.

Yet in the year that it took the chain to unravel the problem and to figure out and institute a variety of solutions, Chipotle's sales took a bath. Millions of Americans stopped frequenting Chipotle's, many presumably out of concern for their health — but no doubt many also because they were turned off by the idea of a brand that promoted the "integrity" of its food, but apparently didn't care enough about the health of its customers to use tried-and-true safety practices.

In the end, Chipotle will write either a case study showcasing the ability of one of the original purpose-driven brands to leverage that advantage to overcome a self-inflicted wound — or showcase a lesson in how hubris can sink a brand built on transcendent values.

4

LIFE AFTER TV ADVERTISING

HOW BRANDED STORYTELLING WILL EVOLVE

> ❝ Those who tell the stories rule the world.
>
> – *Hopi American Indian Proverb*

As workers got out of their cars by a factory on the shore of Kamaishi Bay, one of them paused for a moment to glance out at the ocean and gather his thoughts for the day. Over the three decades they watched construction of the gigantic breakwater nearby, they had grown confident — almost lackadaisical — about their safety.

Recognized as it was in the Guinness Book of World Records for its depth and breadth, few doubted the invulnerability of this $1.5 billion monument to man's ingenuity. The workers were all sure that the engineers had been careful to consider every contingency. This was the 21st Century, after all. And this protective bulwark wasn't called "The Great Wall of Japan" for nothing.[1]

So when the workers saw the shallow pool of water come into the factory during the first wave, they were surprised — but the puddle looked nothing like the result of a tsunami. It came in slowly, like the way a basement will flood after a big rain. But this wave was only the first surge from the ocean caused by the quake more than a half-hour before.

The second wave, higher than the first, flooded the first floor, as well as the workers' concerns. Then one man who was perched on top of a building nearby shouted, "Wow, look at the shape of the breakwater! It's collapsed."[2] And yet because the ocean receded after the highly destructive second wave, some were waiting for the sirens to end, thinking they needed to start the huge task of cleaning up the water.

As the water receded outside the factory, many inside thought to themselves that the tsunami was over. The breakwater was built to contain waves up to 25 feet or more; it had done its job. Nobody had ever heard of waves higher than that. Little did the workers know they were only minutes from a wave that would set new records.

Suddenly looking out to the horizon, the workers who stayed by the shore saw a surge of water approaching more quickly than waves were supposed to move. The massive turbulence took no time to reach up to the third story of the factory. There was nothing the workers could do. This was the tragic end of almost 20,000 people in Japan that day. Some cities, including the northern side of Kamaishi, faced walls of water more than 75 feet tall.

Katsushika Hokusai, The Great Wave, 1829.

Most people don't act. They don't imagine catastrophe could happen to them. In the land of quakes and sirens known as the "Ring of Fire," there were so many false alarms that people rarely took notice. And there was much to get done, so they got on with life as usual.

I think of the times I've stayed sitting in a conference room during a fire alarm, waiting for the drill to end. I've made presentations right through fire drills. So what would I have done during a tsunami drill? What would you have done?

WATER IS LEAKING UNDER THE DOOR

Imagine the village that advertising lives in. Before a disruption strikes, nobody believes it will happen. We depend on our wall that has worked in the past. However, the future will look nothing like it did in the past. The wall presents a foreboding metaphor for the overconfidence we have in TV advertising.

Just before any wave of change, there is always a receding of the waters. This drying up of what once flowed unchallenged is the most ominous of the signs of what is to come. The drying up of the beach with fish flopping in the sand represents the reduced viewership we are beginning to see in our media post reports.

Broadcast television and cable TV networks quietly lost half of their audience over the past decade, and they will soon face another half-life.[3] They paved the way to a golden age of streaming TV, along with "second screens," including smartphones and video-playing tablets.

The jolt of social media and the tremor caused by the use of digital analytics also have rocked an industry that already was on edge. Yet most of us don't understand the implications of the water leaking under the door from those first and second waves of change.

And now the third wave is coming, in the form of Millennials who are cutting their television cable en masse. With 80 million subscribers to Netflix alone,[4] this single streaming-TV media network has eclipsed the entire cable TV industry, which quietly fell to almost half as many subscribers.[5] As the viewing time of Millennials is mapped out, the trend line reveals a unsettling silhouette of the great surge taking place.

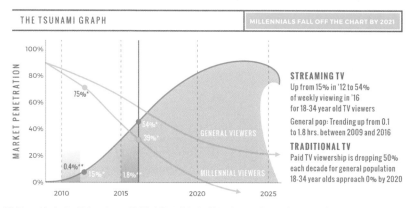

THE TSUNAMI GRAPH — MILLENNIALS FALL OFF THE CHART BY 2021

STREAMING TV
Up from 15% in '12 to 54%
of weekly viewing in '16
for 18-34 year old TV viewers

General pop: Trending up from 0.1
to 1.8 hrs. between 2009 and 2016

TRADITIONAL TV
Paid TV viewership is dropping 50%
each decade for general population
18-34 year olds approach 0% by 2020

*18-34 weekly viewing % time: State of Cable & Digital Media, 2016, Horowitz Research **Hours/day/customer UBS. 2015

Already, 54% of Millennials' viewing time is spent on streaming TV, leaving less than a quarter of their viewing time allocated to live TV. Streaming has surpassed traditional television for the next generation. Now, a quarter of Millennials subscribe to no paid TV at all, and that number is increasing quickly.[6]

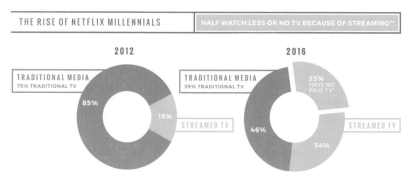

THE RISE OF NETFLIX MILLENNIALS — HALF WATCH LESS OR NO TV BECAUSE OF STREAMING**

2012

TRADITIONAL MEDIA
75% TRADITIONAL TV
85%

15%
STREAMED TV

2016

TRADITIONAL MEDIA
39% TRADITIONAL TV

25%
HAVE NO
PAID TV*

46%

54%
STREAMED TV

*"One-Quarter of US Households Live Without Cable, Satellite TV Reception," GfK, 2016 (Web). **"Millennials Stream
More than Half of their TV; More Likely to Turn to Netflix for TV than Live, Says Horowitz," Horowitz Research, 2016 (Web)

We can't use the old, proven models anymore. Measuring TV Gross Rating Points (GRPs) is no longer a viable media model to reach a mass market. The mass audience isn't there anymore. Furthermore, the cost per impression to TV advertisers to reach this dwindling crowd has more than doubled. It used to take three weeks to effectively reach 90% of the population in the U.S.

via TV, but now it takes more than eight weeks to reach only 60% of the that same audience, at best.

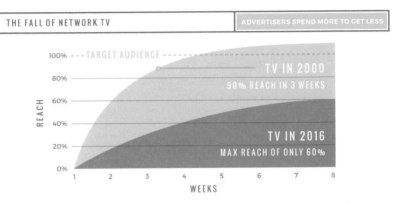

eMarketer "US Connected TV Usage: Digital Content Gives the 'First Screen' New Life," Nov 2015

> 66 I would call this the calm before the storm, on the brink of a whole new set of services that are more compelling than the ones we have now. ...
>
> – Cable Analyst Craig Moffett

It wasn't long ago that my kids mentioned the cable TV system had been down for a week at my house. Funny. Nobody missed it. Although they all sat watching the flat screen for hours, it was all streamed video programming. That's when it hit me. I never see advertising in our family room anymore. My wife suggested we should just cut our cable subscription because nobody uses it. I thought to myself, "Wow. Is this already happening?"

Many Millennials have either ended their cable plan or never subscribed in the first place. After my daughter left our house and got married, she never subscribed to any TV service. My daughter uses Apple TV. Others use Roku or Netflix on their

Xbox. Most of these new services don't allow advertising, so my daughter hasn't seen a TV commercial in a year. She is typical. Only 16.9% of new households subscribe to pay TV.[7]

Will advertising survive this shakeup? Currently, some analysts are running for the hills. Most ad execs are still perched on top of their great advertising factory, watching their great wall. They are busy planning their next million-dollar TV spot.

I recently read a report[8] from Morgan Stanley about the state of broadcast TV. It built the case that TV advertising is a house of cards nearing the end of its viability. Although this paints a bleak picture of the future for marketing professionals, let's look at the same picture from a different perspective. The tsunami is coming, but advertising isn't the village being struck. In this analogy, advertising is the wave.

BE A HIRO

If new advertising media is the wave and the old advertising industry is the village, where does that leave us? We could run from it, or we could harness it to propel an entirely new golden age of advertising. But, is it even possible to ride a tsunami?

Nobody in their right mind would seek out a tsunami to surf, but one man might know the answer to that question. Consider the story of Hiromitsu Shinkawa; Hiro for short.[9]

The morning of the tsunami, Hiro remembers a hint of sulfur in the air as he said to himself, "Rise now, Hiromitsu, man of men, and accept your fate, this day in mid-March." A fourth-generation son of rice farmers, Hiro lived in a concrete home reinforced with metal pylons that his family built among hundreds of wooden houses. After dusting the chicken coop with a grain and barley mix, he was off to work.

While other workers got out of their cars slowly that morning, stopping to stretch and look at the bay, Hiro went straight into the factory to work at his table saw. He distinctly remembers the smell of cedar dust. Later in the day, lost in his work, it was 2:46 p.m. when the earth shook. Time slowed as if to numb his senses as Hiro was violently thrown from one direction to the other. Stacks of wood clattered to the ground. Massive machines rocked back, then lunged forward without respect for what fell in their way. The quake measured a magnitude of 8.9.

Still shaken, Hiro stumbled to his car and raced along the broken road back to his house, swerving to avoid sunken patches of asphalt, downed electrical lines and fallen trees. Hiro found his house in disarray from the jolt. He remembers picking up a bottle, as if he had time to organize the mess. He began to search for items to bring to safety. Then out the window, he suddenly saw another house whooshing by. Hiro realized he had taken too much time gathering his things and had squandered the time he was given, and before he knew it, the only thing Hiro could do to save himself was to scramble onto his roof.

But quickly, the irresistible rush of water, laden with debris, swept him off his roof and flung him into a watery abyss. He asked himself, "Is this up or down?" Lost in the blackness, there was no source of light to follow. Hiro was tempted to gasp what seemed to be dark air in the deep. Finally lunging above water by a miracle, Hiro fought to catch his breath. The frigid and oily water shoved Hiro through tree tops, until he finally found a roof to hold onto. It was his very roof upon which he had been standing just moments ago, being hurtled forward by the rush of dark water.

As Hiro surfed his roof deeper inland, his first thought was, "Where has the whole world gone?" After slowing down, Hiro was tempted to jump off and take his chances to swim toward a crane arm extending from the flood, but he hesitated for just one second. Then having missed his opportunity, Hiro began a rapid and accelerating surf back out, toward the ocean. Quickly and violently, he was pulled miles out to sea.

The stark cold was next in Hiro's gauntlet of terror. Experiencing near-zero temperatures, with a smell of diesel in the air, he listened to the distant sounds of helicopters flying relentlessly through the night. Upon daybreak, rumbling aftershocks shook the sea. His "life preserver," the waterlogged roof, was sinking as Hiro faced dehydration, hypothermia and freezing temperatures well into the second night. His only glimpse of light to break the oily black water was phosphorescent jellyfish and ocean mushrooms glowing with a neon, bluish light.

Nine miles out to sea, Hiro began to regret his overconfidence in what he always considered his well-built home. He reflected on family members he was not able to save. As his roof was now sinking into the black ocean, he wondered why he had stopped to pick up that bottle. As he shivered uncontrollably, he asked himself, "Why didn't I just run up the hill?" By now, it was Hiro's third day.

But hours later, he could see a boat on the horizon, filled with rescue workers dressed in green thermal suits. Hiro heard himself cry through his own broken voice, "Help me!" to which a reassuring voice responded, "We're here."

That is the *true story* of the man who surfed the greatest tsunami in the history of Japan — on the roof of his house.

This is a story of resourcefulness. If we are going to ride the wave that is falling upon us, we will need to use whatever we've got. And, as long as we have ideas, we are not without means.

 FIND YOUR ROOFTOP

There are no rules in tsunami surfing. Our new competition is, literally, *anything*. Now, anything that distracts from your next sale is your competition. Any small piece of content on LinkedIn, Facebook, YouTube, a mobile app or a competitor's website is your competition. It all competes for your consumer's attention.

This change came without warning. It's no longer our given right to purchase effective advertising reach. We can't simply buy our way to mass market awareness. Mass media doesn't reach the masses anymore, and paid media is slipping or "skipping" from our grasp. It's all becoming earned media now.

We also face a higher bar on what we can consider "compelling." An ocean of highly engaging content is aimed at your listeners. The noise of it shouts more loudly than you could ever shout. It all compels your audience to ignore you. If your content isn't more entertaining than the outrageous cat video with 50 million likes, then your content will get missed. Lost. Wasted.

We need to get resourceful like Hiro did. We need to use whatever we've got — to bring lift to our brand. Find your rooftop and shout from it.

Do something to get your consumer's attention. Do anything. Step out of your comfort zone. Innovation can be messy. That's OK. This is new territory. There is no class or booklet on how to lead into the future. Nobody had ever surfed a roof before either.

So, be a Hiro. That means find your platform, and try random things. Be unconventional. Don't be afraid of trying long shots. Look for anything that can float in this turbulent environment. Find entertaining content your brand can climb onto and ride it. Surf that silly cat video. Blow up a pizza with dynamite (Be careful. We did that once, and the police didn't like it very much). But, do something to stand out in this sea of content.

Ride on the heels of mommy bloggers. Some of our clients are even building partnerships for premium Hollywood content from Disney, Fox and Warner. Advertisers are now competing in a world of entertainers. It makes sense, therefore, that if you can't beat them, join them.

For example, we once did a live social video post with Angelina Jolie. It drove 26 million views without paying for a single impression. Our social syndication with *The Hobbit* drove even more, at 350 million free page views. Partner with any entity that will give your brand lift.

In the next Golden Age of advertising, advertisers won't just be the interruption. They will be the featured event — if they want any attention at all. We need to get the permission of our viewers to engage them, because they don't have to listen to our stories anymore. That's why a recent study reported that nearly a quarter of advertisers budgeted half of their advertising dollars toward content marketing in 2015, with a projected 34% increase in "native advertising" in 2017.[10]

We have to earn our way back into the hearts of our consumers. The art of storytelling will evolve as it has always done. It will cleverly find its way into the new media as inventive new storytellers apply the ancient principles that will always define the next evolution of storytelling.

FROM INTERRUPTIVE TO ARRESTING

It's only appropriate that one of the master storytellers of all time, William Shakespeare, actually coined the word "advertising." Stories capture our attention and persuade people to think differently. We are enamored by stories of those who succeed, like Hiro. They give us meaning. We yearn to understand the "why." If we learn from the context of a story, it organizes our thoughts. Somehow, we intrinsically know these stories make us smarter.

Movies. TV shows. Books. News. Religion. They're all storytelling. In fact, the average person spends the majority of their day consuming stories.

Why are stories so important to us? Like waves that come in sets of three, life is full of patterns. We tell and read and hear stories to help us understand these patterns, so we can navigate the challenges of life that are common to us all.

Most of us will never face a tsunami off the coast of Japan, but all of us face change in our lives. All of us face some sort of impossible odds. We all grasp for meaning. We all seek hope so that we will overcome these challenges like Hiro did.

Why would I, as a storyteller, position H-I-R-O as our H-E-R-O? Because I have had life experiences, passions and emotions regarding my subject matter that I cannot easily transfer to you as the reader. And if I can get you to understand the feeling I have about the coming wave of change through a story about Hiro, maybe I can persuade you to understand the importance of preparing for that change.

Maybe my readers will put down the bottle of complacency and try something unconventional. You could "be a Hiro" of your own branded movement.

Emotion educates better than information. That is the power of story.

REDISCOVER THE CRAFT OF STORYTELLING

We must get back to the basics. I'm pretty sure Shakespeare didn't come up with the word "advertising" to describe a 30-second TV commercial to promote his next play.

Advertising was invented long before TV, and its influence was seen long before there was a word for it. Advertising will surely stand the test of time. But it will not continue as we currently define it.

Let's get back to its original intention. Advertising is story-telling for the purpose of persuasion, and stories are used in persuasion because they are the best way to articulate meaning. Consumer psychology has shown that stories wield the most effective power to organize complex information and create emotional connections to brands. Stories laced with arresting visuals and sensory language create emotion and can cement new constructs within the human brain to be subconsciously recalled later.

The brain draws from these constructs to be used as decision-making models to answer a broad range of questions in life: What to do? What to think? What to purchase?

For example, here is a story:

> *"The Mayo Clinic treated a broken Olympic athlete, who finally won the race of life."*

Add some impactful images and sound design for a TV spot, and fleshing out a 15-word storyline such as this can help build a brand. From a small town in Minnesota, the Mayo Clinic has built the world's leading health care brand based on stories like this, and a core value they call a "Culture of Storytelling."

Note the fact that this story about Mayo contained no promise to save your life. It offered no evidence for better mortality scores or national rankings of the hospital. By using a concrete example, this story simply implied, "If Mayo is good enough for Olympians, it's good enough for you."

Stories are often most effective because they provide powerful models of truth without overpromising or creating inflexible expectations that can fail under the complexities of reality. There is no perfect model in storytelling. As statistician George E. P. Box said, "All models are wrong. Some are useful." That's why it's impossible to communicate everything about your brand from a single TV commercial. It takes a series of stories to get the full picture.

This endless need for story development is what keeps the advertising industry well fed. Telling stories for decades, ad agencies have evolved into TV-commercial factories. As the formula has changed from interruptive commercials to permissive content, the role of the advertising agency is changing, as well. Advertising is no longer interrupting entertainment but is being integrated into it. In fact, the two are becoming one and the same.

This is why the Mayo Clinic gets involved in entertainment. I recall a Mayo Clinic marketing director who was most proud of the fact she had engaged the TV series, *The Simpsons*. When Homer Simpson went to the Mayo Clinic to get a colonoscopy, he was surrounded by medical researchers, students and foreign dignitaries, all awaiting to experience the medical expertise of the Mayo physician.

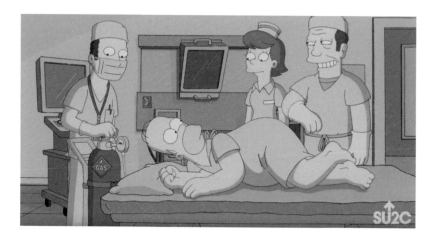

The Mayo Clinic wasn't embarrassed by this public exposure in content. They were actually writing the script.[11]

These opportunities present themselves when we dare to explore the very purpose of advertising and ask ourselves why we exist. We don't merely exist to make TV commercials. Our job is to create stories that sell products and services. New media has redefined the sacred art we produce. No longer commercial factories, relevant agencies are evolving to produce "branded storytelling" like this.

A LEGACY OF STORYTELLING

Let's face it, branded content isn't new. We put a new polish on the idea of storytelling and call it whatever the latest guru names it. Branding, advertising, communications, engagement, memes, conversations, blah, blah, blah. Like we invented any of it? From the beginning of time, and in every culture, tribal leaders have told stories that influenced and changed the world.

Most people wouldn't call the story of David and Goliath a marketing campaign, but it did help establish the brand of God as the force in the universe who believes in the little guy. Most of the tribalism of Western culture — including Judaism, Christianity and Islam — all subscribe to this ancient writing by one storyteller named Samuel.

It's interesting that Samuel was called a "prophet," because it's the storytellers who not only predict the future, but craft the future. Whether the storyteller was Jules Verne, Ray Bradbury, Buddha, Moses or Jesus, our very culture has been crafted from the words that were documented years ago.

Today's prophets are producers. Think about how our culture has been influenced by movies. The movie Rocky inspired the fitness craze in the '80s. We all went to the gym. I even remember attempting to drink a glass of eggs. After the movie Top Gun, Navy aviator recruitment increased 500%. I even remember buying the leather bomber jacket that everybody wore in our silly attempts to look like Tom Cruise. The movie Animal House famously redefined college. What used to be a place of education and self-improvement, became redefined as an escape for toga parties, lewd initiations and beer pong.

Now that more people go to movies than go to church each week, movies are the storytelling venues that have replaced the pulpits that create our worldview. Cynical producers are the prophets who expose our dark side, yet hopeful storytellers build a vision of new possibilities. I personally watch Jimmy Stewart in It's a Wonderful Life every Christmas because it inspires me to become the best version of myself each new year. It's a spiritual experience for me.

Let's not forget, a 30-second TV commercial is storytelling, too. Think about the brands that live in our worldview as a result of these snippets of branded storytelling. Kellogg's Tony the Tiger, the Keebler Elves and the Marlboro Man[12] — these characters emerged from the minds of advertising storytellers in the '50s and '60s. Men like Cary Grant have depicted Don Draper-like mad men to personify these storytellers who branded American retail mythology. These are the men of the Golden Age of Advertising. With the advent of the printing press, the radio and television set came a new generation of prophets who changed the world.

Millennial mad men are more digitally tech savvy than Don Draper and quirkier than Cary Grant. The creative-class executive of today looks more like a hybrid spawn between a movie producer and a social media nerd, with tattoos and ear gauges. Still today, the best story wins.

STORYTELLING AND THE CONSUMER BRAIN

Neuroscientists are beginning to study the impact of storytelling on the consumer brain. In one Princeton University study, neuroscientist Uri Hasson found:

> ❝ The results showed that not only did all of the listeners show similar brain activity during the story, the speaker and the listeners had very similar brain activity despite the fact that one person was producing language and the others were comprehending it.[13]

These findings indicate that storytelling creates a formidable bond between the teller and the listener. When we hear a story, it engages us in the same way it does the person who is telling it. ...

Consider the Wynn Casinos culture of storytelling. In every department, they have a pre-shift meeting where they share a story — a story of something interesting that happened with a customer, or how an employee went above and beyond. These stories create a powerful community bond where the values of the brand are shared, so they can be can be lived and breathed.[14]

Storytelling isn't just about creating advertising stories for our customers. Our most important consumer of our brand is actually the employees who represent the heart of our message.

Let's start telling a story or two inside our culture and watch the heartbeat rise.

As Maya Angelou said, "I've learned that people will forget what you said, people will forget what you did, but people will never forget how you made them feel."[15]

STORYTELLING STRUCTURE

Thirty years from now, will you be more likely to remember the facts, business rules and stats from the many case studies in this book, or will you remember the fish flopping on the sand before the black wave hit that destroyed the coast of Japan? Exactly! Storytelling is much more entertaining than facts.

Our brain is better at remembering those disruptive images that tell an entertaining story. This is why philosophers including C.S. Lewis and J.R.R. Tolkien used allegory to express their philosophical points of view on the adventure of life. This is why prophets taught in parables. We are creatures who live in story. A modern story is best told through the storytelling art we call "entertainment."

Branded entertainment is not really different than any other form of storytelling. A TV commercial is just a tiny movie, after all. All good stories need to feature lead characters, establish conflict, encounter unexpected twists, reach a climax and resolve with closure. For TV commercials, all of this has to happen in 30 seconds. For branded entertainment, there is no such time restriction.

For these reasons, long-form branded content will most likely look more like a movie than a commercial. If that's our future, where should we look for inspiration?

THE PIXIE DUST BEHIND PIXAR

Think about the amazing stories told by Disney's Pixar Studio. How do they get it right so many times? Let's explore the Pixar story-arc model[16]:

> **"** Once upon a time there was _____. Every day, _____. One day, _____. Because of that, _____. Until finally, _____.

This story arc is familiar to us because it represents every Disney or Pixar film we have ever watched. This ground rule is only one of 22 filters used to evaluate all content before it's distributed by Pixar Studios. Here are some other Pixar filters that can be helpful in developing our own branded content.[17]

Cast an unexpected "Hiro": You admire characters more for trying than for their successes.

Don't advertise, entertain: Keep in mind what's interesting to an audience, not what's fun to do as a writer. They can be very different.

> **Instigate conflict:** What is your character good at, comfortable with? Throw the polar opposite at them. Challenge them. How do they deal?
>
> **End first:** Come up with your ending before you figure out the middle. Seriously. Endings are hard; get yours working up front.
>
> **Where's the "gotcha"?** Discount the first thing that comes to mind. And the second, third, fourth, fifth. Get the obvious out of the way. Surprise yourself.

Let's use these Pixar filters to help you find a way to evaluate storytelling for your brand, starting with:

Cast an Unexpected "Hiro": We love a common man or awkward protagonist like Hiro. The word picture of Hiro "dusting the chicken coup" was an important picture of his humble world. Don't pretend that your brand is more heroic than it actually is. All the consumer needs to see is your brand trying harder. Curiosity and failure are actually attractive brand characteristics to your consumers. Remember how Chipotle won customers by telling them the stores were out of GMO-free, responsibly raised pork? Rather than casting your brand as perfect, let others call your brand great. When you control the content, self-deprecating humor and humility will appear less self-serving, and that will build trust.

Han Solo was no more likely to become a hero than was the character of Luke Skywalker in *Star Wars*. Rocky was never supposed to beat the world champion. Cinderella was not considered worthy to dance with the prince.

Remember how we originally met the old, yellow Chevy Camaro

that became Bumble Bee in the first *Transformers*[18] film? This unwanted rust bucket identified with Shia LaBeouf's character. The shabby Chevy brand was on a co-journey with him as the unlikely hero.

In the end, LaBeouf got the girl, but the Camaro saved the day. Its transformation from the old, backfiring rust bucket to the new, mouth-watering design was accompanied by hero music as the Camaro drove by in slow motion. Oooh, I wanted that car. So did my kids. I could hear them all lust for it. Every time we ever saw a yellow Camaro after that, my kids would point out the "Transformer Camaro."

I didn't want to ruin the magic by telling them this, but the film was funded by a $50 million promotional contribution from General Motors.[19] That means GM had to invest to promote the film in their ad campaigns. In exchange, the new Camaro was written into the film, which was also produced in Detroit.

Other car companies have tried their hand at product placement, but nobody has done it like GM. It reminded me of how Pontiac Firebird Trans Am sales increased by 30,000 cars after Burt Reynolds drove his black Firebird beauty in *Smokey and the Bandit*.[20] No automotive TV commercial has ever been so effective.

> 66 Pontiac saw a marked increase in their stock prices. The value of their stock rose a startling 70 percent after the film's release, and to show their appreciation to Reynolds, the president said they would give the actor a new car each and every year.[21]
>
> – CinemaBlend.com

Don't Advertise, Entertain: Stop lecturing about facts. Facts are boring and, therefore, forgettable. Start telling stories. Better yet, start showing stories. Our memory is better at recalling what we see, feel and even smell. Hiro smelled a hint of sulfur in the air in the morning and diesel through the night. Paint word pictures through senses. Don't write into the script what the creative brief says. In fact, if you can avoid words, don't use any at all. The best stories are not verbal. They are visual. Your consumer audience doesn't have to watch your content; in fact, they don't even want to. You have to earn their attention.

Instead of wordsmithing the message that is outlined in the strategic plan, take the time to understand why the plan exists. Tell the story that fulfills the objective. Show consumers something visually entertaining first. They will repay you by not cutting you off when you present your case. By infusing facts into pictures and stories, you keep your listener engaged.

GoPro, for instance, never even attempted to sell its camera's features listed on the creative brief. Instead, they demonstrated them at the point of sale with some of the most interesting extreme sports footage ever seen. The GoPro video kiosk must have really frustrated the copywriter on the account. Even if words could have helped, retailers kept the videos silent.

At first glance, the GoPro story seemed to be missing a plot line. If you analyze these videos on the surface, they seem to merely be a montage of unrelated, cool shots of extreme sports and stunts. But, make no mistake. The story is still there.

The GoPro itself was always cast as the hero of the story in our minds. We saw the euphoric expression on the face of a snowboarder as he flipped off a cliff, and we asked our minds to figure out how that video angle was even possible. This created conflict. Our minds answered with a story:

> ❝ Once upon a time there was <u>an amazing snowboarder.</u> Every day, <u>that snowboarder did unbelievable tricks that nobody could experience but him.</u> One day, <u>he stuck a GoPro on his head.</u> Because of that, <u>he could share his experience with the world.</u> Until finally, <u>everybody wanted a GoPro.</u>

This story has been told a million times on YouTube, and although there are no words, the story gets more interesting every time. My kids and I own two GoPros, and I'm considering another one. My son-in-law interviewed for a job at GoPro's headquarters in San Francisco because the brand so captivated him. And GoPro never used a single word to persuade him.

Instigate Conflict: Conflict is captivating in the story of Hiro. Had he not faced a tsunami, the world would not know his name. It's hard to build drama like this in branded entertainment because brand managers don't like to sponsor anything negative. Although conflict can make ad executives squirm, it's more than OK to have an antagonist in your branded content. If you haven't seen it, watch the movie *Megamind.* Bad guys are the reason good guys exist.

I remember pitching TV shows to Henry Ford Hospital in 1998. After they agreed to produce a show, I actually got seller's remorse. Reality shows weren't popular yet, so I thought to myself, "How are we going to make a reality TV show about a hospital interesting?" Where would the conflict come from? Then I met a 17-year-old girl who needed a heart transplant. I met her worried mother. Time was not on their side. The possibility she might not make it was very real.

As part of the production team on *The Minds of Medicine*,[22] I remember directing a camera on the physician assistant when the call came in. We witnessed the distress on his face as he said, "I'm sorry to hear that." I never felt so awkward as when we followed him into the patient's room with cameras as he told the mom and her daughter, "The heart is no good." Conflict introduced the show. This represented the daily challenge at the hospital because they don't have enough organ donors. When we shamelessly promoted organ donation at Henry Ford Hospital, no viewer felt used or sold. Viewers felt compassion.

Of course, by the end of the show, a good heart came in and the girl was saved. But, I'm sure viewers wondered for a moment. I sure did. That is the conflict that drove the show's ratings to a No. 1 ranking for a primetime show on the local ABC affiliate. That's also how an infomercial for a hospital won Emmy Awards and drove patient volumes up by 1,800 online appointments that year. The program paid for itself after the first referral came in from the TV show.

Let's get comfortable with conflict. In fact, our tendency to be uncomfortable with conflict is often cited as the primary reason team members water down great creative in advertising. Our job as the reviewers and leaders is not to resolve the conflict in advertising stories before we approve them. Conflict creates cognitive dissonance in the brain. This makes us all uncomfortable, so our brain seeks out a path to remove this conflict. Resist the desire to remove conflict from your advertising scripts. It's there to engage the mind of your consumer. That means we should resist our desire to remove risky, strange, confusing or unexplained things.

It was risky to show potential failure at Henry Ford Hospital. It was tempting to let consumers know they shouldn't worry, but life doesn't telegraph the end of the story. Authentic reality holds tension, and allowing this truth to be exposed builds trust in the Participation Age. Thankfully, we had a client who understood this.

Here is a good test for successful creative content. If you are not nervous to launch an ad, it's probably too soft. Do something uncomfortable if you want to avoid becoming forgettable.

End First: Hiro lived. That would have been a terrible title for his story, but a great ending. The ending is the most important part of the story, so give it top priority. The end should clear up all confusion, present a gotcha or resolve a conflict. All other content is simply support for the conclusion at the end of the story.

So leave enough time at the end to let it sink in. The ending completes the whole point of your story, so don't rush it. In a video lasting only 30 seconds, you'll need 10 seconds for the end, so make time for it. Don't ruin your emotional climax by rushing it or smothering it with proof points. Let it breathe instead.

Our brains have a psychological requirement called "closure." It's the need we all have to secure the resolution of conflict in our minds.[23] It's why we are so filled with suspense during the movie, *The Sixth Sense*.[24] We want to see the end, because we need to know why Haley Joel Osment sees dead people. The end is always the point.

Never give away the end, because that will end the conflict, and you will lose your viewer. That's why every news break ends with a broadcaster who teases us with an impossible image or a statement about how the world might implode. They'll use a small clip from a video of a ridiculous dog trick — anything that our minds need closure to understand. We watch every commercial, just so we don't miss the rest of the story. If you create conflict and put enough thought around an amazing ending that resolves it, people will watch just about any tedious content you put in front of them about your brand.

There is one way to know if you created a great ending. You should feel an emotion. Laugh. Cry. Feel pride or joy. The particular emotion doesn't really matter. The test of emotional engagement might sound simplistic, but it's been proven true in every study on advertising creative. Never let your proof points get in the way of this end goal.

Where's the "gotcha"?: Ask yourself, "What's different about this story?" Avoid the temptation to ever use a montage of lifestyle shots in advertising. If it can be found in a stock photo library, don't shoot it again. The world has no use for one more photo of generic humans.

Nobody notices nice advertising. People notice when you punch them in the gut. Make your advertising do that. Grab the attention of the viewer in the first shot. Shock them with an arresting jolt of visual smack. Use word pictures. Start the content with something irreverent, amazing or disruptive. Surprise the audience with an unexpected ending.

Surf a tsunami on the roof of a house. Make your reader say, "That's crazy!"

Remember how the consumer brain works. If there is no emotion, there is no advertising. Don't get lost in the sea of formulaic ads. If you've seen it before, or if your idea feels safe, start over. Safe is the enemy of great. Good advertising should make you nervous. The most effective advertising usually gets the most consumer complaints. That's because it gets noticed.

Brainstorm with somebody who thinks strange, random thoughts. Partner with class clowns, nerds and people who blurt out awkward things without social filters. Look at odd photos in stock libraries off the beaten path. Listen for that moment that makes you react with an emotion. Any emotion will do. We've found these secrets are most likely to inspire something worthy of remark in advertising.

Always remember that the consumer brain is visual. Test your ads with the sound turned off. Assess your ad without reading the words. Studies show that even if you do all of this right, only one in five consumers will read your body copy. So, if your message depends on your amazing copywriting skills, you have already lost. Follow the eighth rule listed in David Ogilvy's *Confessions of an Advertising Man*, who said, "Avoid blind headlines — the kind which mean nothing unless you read the body copy underneath them; most people don't."[25] This is where we bury all of those proof points that the consumer doesn't seem to care about anyway.

> ❝ More is not better. Different is better.

More is not better. Different is better. Great advertising is about the simplification of a singular outrageous idea. Most often, the gotcha comes from the story you show, not the story you tell. Old Spice figured this out. It was known as the old man's aftershave brand. If I'd been there, I would have asked, "Could Millennials ever really be attracted to a brand like that?" Yet, Old Spice set the tone for unexpected advertising with a surreal setting and a quirky former football player spokesman who said from his bathroom, "I'm on a horse. ..." as he appeared suddenly riding bareback on a white horse in the Caribbean. Gotcha![26]

It was odd. It was unexplained. We all needed closure, but Old Spice wouldn't give us the satisfaction of an explanation. They kept our attention. They kept us wondering. That expanded the story for the next time we could grab a glimpse of more obscure antics from their unexpected shirtless spokesman, online or offline.

Response to the TV campaign drove the Old Spice guy into social media, where he appeared to reach out to Millennials to engage them personally. He would respond to requests within minutes. Even a marriage proposal. This increased social interaction by 800%.[27]

Today, Old Spice is a case study for turning a brand around. There was no path for them to follow. Instead when they saw the fish flopping in their brand relevance scores, they left behind the old model and rode the new wave. Fans drove digital activity as a result of traditional TV commercials. The brand never even talked about the product features to anybody. Instead, they sold unexpected moments that took consumers off guard, and we all wanted more. Especially Millennials. Not long ago, I saw a stick of Old Spice deodorant in my son's bathroom, and I asked him about it. He said, "Old Spice is cool."

HOW STORIES DISRUPT THE CONSUMER BRAIN

Our job as storytellers is not only to entertain, but to change thought patterns in the human brain. We employ various tools to create cognitive dissonance, forcing disinterested consumers to pay attention and engage. Moving the consumer brain from disinterest toward loving our brand requires more than a rational argument woven into a story structure. Effective branding requires emotional disruption.

Although we know disruptive storytelling like the Old Spice series can build emotional connections with consumers, we don't know exactly how it works. We've found that certain kinds of stories consistently create emotional responses that correlate to increased brand preference and sales. Beyond that knowledge, our models become hazy at best. This is because the consumer brain relegates some of its most sophisticated thinking to unconscious processing. This is where the mystery of emotion resides. Somehow the consumer brain trusts its emotion to be more intelligent than its own conscious cognition.

Because the unconscious brain can be a bit of a black box, various imperfect theories and models are used to help us understand these "dark" processing patterns. One popular theory among psychologists is the "Triune Brain" model. This model suggests that the unconscious functions of the brain are made up of three components: the basal ganglia, the limbic system and the neo-cortex. This belief system asserts that the most successful storytelling engages all three of these components, therefore, it's important to understand their individual functions.

The basal ganglia, also known as the "reptilian complex," is the primal fight or flight mechanism of the brain that responds to disruptive sensory input such as loud sounds, falling, threatening movement or any exciting visual stimulus that could pose a threat or promise the brain a reward of pleasure. This is the critical function of the brain that Hollywood film producers use to engage people and bring them into a story. Emotional disruption is a cheap but effective trick. For action films, directors use fast and erratic movements or surreal special effects. In romance films, directors use beauty and seduction. In comedy, the actors fall to the floor to coax laughter, etc.

The second component of the brain, the limbic system, is most commonly associated with the human need to engage social relationships. As we've discovered in our studies discussed earlier, social identity can be the most powerful driver of decisions. If consumers can't find a social relationship to the story, they disengage emotionally. However, even building a strong social purpose isn't enough to create this connection, especially if nobody knows about your cause or embraces it. That's why using bold creativity to deliver the brand story can be as important as the message itself.

This brings us to the third part of the brain, the neo-cortex. Unique to humans, this is the most complex and advanced component of brain processing. It's the part of the brain that stores complex concepts in the form of metaphors. By converting the brand promise into a concrete visual, we cement a "theory of brand" in the consumer brain. This visual metaphor becomes stored in the consumer psyche, providing an actionable belief system that will become available for efficient recall at the time of need.

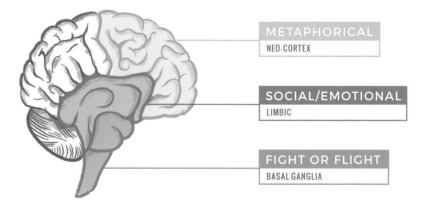

According to the Triune Brain theory,[28] when we employ all three components, a highly engaged and emotional response will become triggered. This is how brands achieve the proverbial "wow factor." However, engaging all three components at once is the most difficult job in communication. Below is a summary of what is required for high-impact storytelling on all three components of the consumer brain:

First, be disruptive: Without conflict, shock, comedy or an experience of pleasure, the human brain remains disengaged from the story. Disrupt the emotional status quo of your consumers. If your advertising story doesn't make people feel something, it's not finished being developed. You might even need to start over.

Second, be purposeful: Importantly, don't get so caught up in creating emotion that you forget your purpose for telling the story. A worthy advertising purpose should create emotion, not get in the way of it. So, don't bury your message in the tag. Make it the point of your story. Before you go forward with any creative concept, always ask the question, "Why do I care?"

Third, be metaphorical: Finally, without a clear and concrete visual device or metaphor, the price, features and benefits of your brand become lost in a list of unemotional proof points. So, wrap it all up in an arresting picture that says it all. Be specific and concrete. For example, use a tsunami. Build a picture of a man named Hiro, visualize a wall or boats going out to sea. Like muscle memory, these pictures build an actionable reflex in the mind.

Many creative experts say, "Keep it simple, stupid." Of course, K.I.S.S. is a great rule of thumb, but cramming a disruptive, purposeful and metaphorical concept to fit into a 15-second advertisement is really hard. From the strategy department to legal, compliance and political powers that plague the industry, great creative concepts must survive the gauntlet of a thousand points of death. Don't allow the process of critical review to complicate your message or remove any one of these three pillars.

Storytelling is difficult work. The difference with great storytellers is that they don't allow themselves to get discouraged. So, keep the faith to the end.

METAPHOR VERIFIES MEANING

Although the Triune Brain theory remains imperfect, it models the importance of disruptive visual stimulus in the unconscious brain. This need for visual metaphor in communication has been verified by neuroscientists during the study of split brain patients.

While the left brain has been commonly found to process words and information, the unconscious right brain has shown more aptitude for processing pictures and concepts. Compelling communication engages both sides.[29] For example, trust can be difficult to build on a phone call between two people. Why do you think conversation is more effective in person? Because the human face communicates volumes through the 43 muscles that sometimes tell a different story than the mere words being used.[30]

Likewise, when both sides of the brain are engaged in the visual demonstration of any brand, the consumer brain's unconscious calculation toward trust is confirmed. In other words, the consumer brain evaluates both what it hears and what it sees as a way to verify a rational conclusion. This means we should not fall into the trap of selling products without first establishing an visual brand metaphor that portrays the central message and social purpose of your brand. This is also why the use of stock photos of generic humans never build a proper metaphor for brand differentiation. Many brands use similar photos, and your visual metaphor tells consumers you offer nothing different.

Let's explore the best practices in the use of visual stimulus. Nobody has used metaphor better than Apple. It all started with the fearless, feminine champion of the people in 1984. More than an advertising campaign, Apple's metaphor created a movement. Disrupting the status quo with an ominous picture of an army of dull, head-shaved minions, Apple entered the scene through a woman, dressed in full color, carrying a sledgehammer to shatter the image of "Big Brother." In a single Super Bowl spot, Apple branded itself as the selfless leader of change in the world.[31]

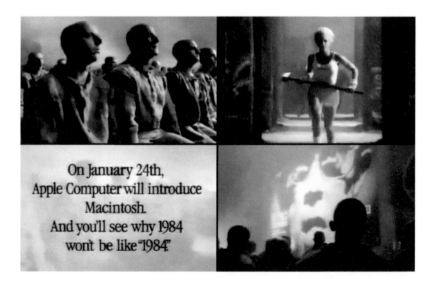

Just like he did in 1984, Steve Jobs came back in 1997 with a new plan to use metaphor and even avoid featuring any computer at all. The turning point for Apple was signified by the famous Apple brand campaign featuring Martin Luther King Jr., Einstein, Gandhi and Sir Richard Branson. Using great leaders and innovators as the metaphor, Apple was able to *flip Maslow's Pyramid* and appeal to self-actualized consumers. Driving a message of selfless, bold leadership, many joined the movement.

The powerful call to duty read by Richard Dreyfuss inspired people to "Think Different." By the time the iMac was available in stores, people weren't shopping for reasons to believe. Inspired followers were seeking features that would give them permission to believe.

With these teaser campaigns, Apple ushered in the age of branding. Apple demonstrated purpose-driven brand values by never showing the product, and not asking for the sale. The disruptive conflict was unmistakable. Consumers could not figure out why Apple would advertise without even making an attempt to sell. It felt as if the cause was more important to the brand than the product itself. This act of selflessness was refreshing. It represented a disruptive form of authenticity.

Years later, the impact of this campaign still casts its shadow on advertising. Just think of how many times your creative team has attempted to hide or remove your product from your ads? You can blame Apple for starting this trend toward pure branding. However, even Apple's board would have most assuredly refused to fund the 1997 campaign, if Apple actually had an interesting product to sell at the time. However, there was none. Whether it was intentional or unintentional, this computerless social metaphor effectively paved the way for the product that would finally verify Apple's stated purpose.

The people who are crazy enough to think they can change the world are the ones who do.

Apple's 1997 commercial concluded with the profound statement that would define the brand for the next two decades: "...because the people who are crazy enough to think they can change the world are the ones who do." Many employees and consumers were effectively convinced: If those people in the Apple ads changed the world, then they could, too. And they did.

But, keep in mind, very little actually happened immediately after this campaign ran. Remember, there wasn't even a unique product to sell until almost a year later. As we've heard a thousand times, branding takes time. So do unique products and services. More important than time, branding campaigns need verification with actual products that demonstrate the brand through practical features and benefits. Gasp! The creative department will not want to hear this, but branding messages alone cannot carry a brand.

Never forget, the product itself eventually needs to fulfill the promise of the branding, and you eventually have a second campaign you will need to produce. Yes, we must fulfill the brand promise by launching a specific product-line or service-line promotion. For Apple, the promotional campaign launched with a new, disruptive visual metaphor: a kalei-doscope of computers delivered in color. Beyond disruptive to an industry of beige, metal boxes, the iMac was visually stunning. And, the claim of each new iProduct was equally disruptive for its day. For the iPod, the headline read, "One thousand songs in your pocket."

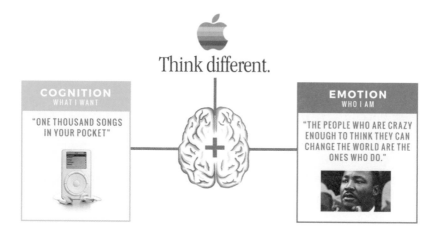

The arresting imagery of the iMac, the dancing silhouettes of iPod users and the swiping motions of the iPhone itself became metaphors for the brand. Each metaphor more disruptive than the other. Each metaphor fulfilling the greater purpose and changing the world. These products represented evidence to support the purpose and values that Apple had been promoting during their "Think Different" campaign. This is how cognition verifies emotion, and ultimately, metaphor verifies meaning.

I've heard the complaint from many brand managers, "But we aren't Apple. We don't have the budget for branding. We need sales!" Some forget that at the time of launch, Blackberry owned 50% of the smartphone market.[32] But under the power of Apple's branded movement, Blackberry's brandless phone was crushed in sales by the iPhone. There was no promotional campaign or discount

Blackberry could employ to challenge the force of the Black Wave that powered Apple.

When a brand builds an expectation aligned to the purpose and values of the consumer, then proceeds not only to meet but exceed these expectations, a visual demonstration of brand purpose verifies the consumer brain's theory of the brand. This creates the perfect storm for brand sales growth.

The problem with weak branding campaigns is that we often don't think big enough. Market-driven leaders like Jobs understand branding is more than advertising. It's the product itself. William C. Taylor describes the importance of this effort to disrupt the status quo through product innovation in his book, *Simply Brilliant*. He said, "Stop trying to be the best. Strive to be the *only*."[33] That is the essence of thinking differently when making your brand story.

BECOMING REMARK-WORTHY

Market disruption can make your brand "remark-worthy." If we "wow" our consumers with disruptive innovation, they'll consider our brand worthy of remark. That's when we can most effectively leverage the power of Participation Media. Consumers don't go online to chat about parity products, but they will passionately share their commitment to brands that exceed their expectations, such as Apple.

This assertion obviously assumes that Apple can continue to create the disruptive innovation that was consistently achieved under the leadership of Steve Jobs. Unfortunately, the early returns following Jobs' passing aren't encouraging. New, visionary brands such as Samsung have arisen with purpose-driven passion to fill this void in smartphone leadership.

Innovation theorist Peter Thiel explained it this way:

> ❝ Many have tried to learn from Apple's success: Paid advertising, branded stores, luxurious materials, playful keynote speeches, high prices and even minimalist design are all susceptible to imitation. But these techniques for polishing the surface don't work without a strong underlying substance.

Don't think you can copy Apple. Many have tried and failed. Many have attempted to copy the pure branding model, but lack the disruptive core purpose necessary to build a movement. Many have tried to present product simplicity, but without featuring any product disruption.

Even Apple can't copy Apple if it wants to win. That's because a copy never disrupts. You'll have to find a creative solution to disrupt in your own way. Colored computers, white earbuds and a dynamic leader wearing a mock turtleneck won't be the secret to your success. If you wear New Balance shoes to your next business presentation, you won't look like Steve Jobs. You will look like a nerd.

Remember to follow principles not pathways. The pathways previously used have already been disrupted. Clichés never work because they are built from previous disruption. The success of your brand cannot be built on a cliché either, because other brands who journeyed before you have already established that position. That's why it's a cliché.

There is nothing disruptive about a rerun. Your brand was born an original. Don't let it die trying to become a copy. You can't make a TV spot like Apple did. That age is over. This isn't the age of TV advertising anyways. Learn from the principles the previous age taught us, but let's explore new territory online with the skills we have acquired offline.

For a company to achieve remark-worthy conversations online, the product or service itself must be revolutionary in comparison with the competition. Often, successful companies are not willing to do the extra work to invent something that brings more value. Possibly because they don't want to take the risk. Perhaps they don't understand the benefits. Whatever the reason for it, we must overcome our tendency to copy what others are doing. Industry leadership is hard work, but it's worth the effort.

If your brand story doesn't continue to include something completely new to show or talk about, your brand reviewers will award you with the most unwanted prize in social media: the title of "also ran." That is, if they bother to mention your brand at all.

The importance of maintaining a marketing mindset from the top of the company is best expressed by Richard Branson, who said, "I don't go into ventures to make a fortune. I do it because I'm not satisfied with the way others are doing business." His Virgin America airline went public with great fanfare, with its in-flight experience being compared with using an Apple product for the first time. Not only does that attest to the success of Virgin's products, but to Apple's, as well.[34]

In Hollywood, a storytelling maxim says, "The best way to tell a story is to use no words at all." The movie critics and Hollywood insiders at my office have actually watched the original film in the Indiana Jones' saga *Raiders of the Lost Ark* as a silent movie, as an homage to the wordless art of Steven Spielberg.

In branding, the highest form of storytelling is no different.

The best stories are not told, they are made, often using no words at all.

In the words of St. Francis of Assisi,

> ❝ Preach the Gospel always. If necessary, use words.

STORYMAKING EXPERIENCES

As people move from advertising observers to brand participants, they transform from consumers of our message to co-creators of our message. This means advertisers must shift their focus from storytelling to storymaking.

Storymaking is about creating tangible value. Leading-edge CEOs are granting marketing departments real authority to design more than advertising: They engineer the customer experience as well as the product, from a marketing perspective.

For example, Chick-fil-A has found a way to be generous to its "guests" and distinguish itself from other fast-feeders by focusing on families.[191] Chick-fil-A has always been a leader in bringing families together, but the brand determined to become even more intentional about it.

Calling customers "guests," Chick-fil-A employees have been known for responding to their customer's appreciation with the famous phrase, "It's my pleasure." Other examples of being intentionally generous to their guests include an operator walking from table to table with an enormous pepper grinder to add pepper on request, and the toilet paper in the bathrooms is even folded as it's done at exclusive hotels. These examples of serving families were a natural extension of this experience.

Storymaking starts with understanding the needs of consumers. For example, most Millennial parents say if they had an extra 15 minutes in a day, they would spend that time with family.[192] So, Chick-fil-A introduced "Bypass the Line" with the Chick-fil-A One mobile app. That's why it became one of the top downloads from the App Store in 2016. However, convenience and amenities are not the only ways this brand found to serve families a better chicken experience.

Chick-fil-A focused on ideas to encourage family time, such as "Daddy-Daughter Date Nights" and "Family Dinner & A Mystery" nights. The consumer posts in social media, with their candle lit tables and fast food adventures, outpaced every other quick service restaurant online. "Our focus is on providing a remarkable experience that brings families together," said David Salyers, marketing innovator of the brand and co-author of the book, *Remarkable*.[35]

At Chick-fil-A, the kid's meals are not packed with toy incentives but with creative resources that teach object lessons. Take, for example, "Surprise it Forward" gift cards. They were designed to teach respect for elders. An online video about a child giving a Chick-fil-A-branded thank you card to an elderly neighbor drove 4.3 million views on Facebook, with some of the most likes of any branded video for the QSR industry in 2015.[36]

Interestingly, Chick-fil-A never mentioned the chicken in the online promotion of these kid's meals, but the customers didn't forget to bring it up. One online post read, "Love it. Thank you for your compassion. And chicken, don't forget the chicken."

Socially friendly storymaking strategies like these have positioned Chick-fil-A as a leader in appealing to kids and families. Recently Sandelman & Associates named Chick-fil-A No. 1 in kid's meal appeal, becoming the first brand to pass McDonald's in this category in 20 years.[37]

Today, the Chick-fil-A brand enjoys the fastest-growing position and highest same-store sales volumes among the top ten QSR chains. As Chick-fil-A became the leader at $3.4 million per store, McDonald's moved to the No. 2 spot, not only in kid's-meal appeal, but in sales, as well. When a brand provides remarkable value to their consumers, consumers pay them back.[38]

It all goes back to the product itself. From Chick-fil-A to Apple iPhone to Virgin Airlines, competitors can no longer succeed by simply making incremental improvements on last year's model. More than ever before, your product itself is the most important marketing tool you have. Social media has augmented this power. Without a truly standout product or service, marketers are left with very little to work with. Your product or service is core to your brand story.

This is why it's strange that marketing still has no seat at the table on the boards of most companies. In the Participation Age, the CEO is the chief marketing officer, too. Rather than forcing the marketing department to sell what we want to sell, we should first consider what the customer wants to buy. The current organizational structures are all wrong for this. Product development and customer experience innovation should report to marketing. Not the other way around.

In advertising, the objective of storytelling is to cement a mental picture of your brand in the consumer brain. We use words like "awareness," "relevance" and "preference" to describe the degree of cognitive impact we've made on our consumers. This is how we measure the effectiveness of our stories, however, there are some storytelling tricks that can short circuit the consumer brain and acquire more mental real estate than any other form of storytelling.

The physical presence and visibility of your brand in the real world is the most relevant form of your story to your consumer. More storymaking than storytelling, it's a battle for real estate in the community where our consumers live.

If you work in franchising, you've heard it before: "location, location, location." The three rules of real estate are also the three rules of retail chain marketing. Despite the movement toward online engagement and e-commerce, much of the game continues to be played in the field. A physical field, that is.

Let's not get carried away with digital and allow ourselves to forget to execute the basics of our industry. Year after year, our studies show that brands get more than half of their total store traffic from people who "drove by and saw a sign." This holds true today. And these numbers are not much different among various franchise locations, including QSR, banking and health system chains.

In fact, with all of the ATM and online banking access we have available today, we see that the No. 1 influence on the total quantity of regional bank deposit accounts is still squarely aligned with the physical bank branch footprint. It's almost a direct correlation. Even focus groups of customers who never walk into a bank tell us they are looking for branches in their neighborhood above all else. As a bank marketing director and I joked behind the glass wall of one consumer focus group, "A bank branch is just a $2 million billboard." But it's the most important billboard a bank can own.

From these studies, we can view "Share of Branches" as the primary market share factor for a bank's success. This phenomenon is not confined to banking. By simply improving the design of a retail sign, we have created an average increase in sales between 20% and 30% per location.[39] Let's take a pizza chain for example. Although pizza chains are moving toward mostly online ordering for delivery with very few physical visits, a physical signage update has been shown to significantly increase the number of online orders. How does that happen?

Think about your own behavior. When you drive through a new neighborhood, you probably notice all of the pizza-franchise locations in town. Your brain stores those physical images to be recalled later. When somebody says, "Let's get pizza," your brain reverts to that image of a pizza store just down the street. You may never need to visit that store if you call or click in your order. Functioning as a visual metaphor in your brain, the storefront and signage simply act as a billboard for your online experience.

Here are three ways that the old-fashioned concept of real estate, maybe in some new-fashioned ways, can play a crucial role in being a metaphor for your brand:

Share of Square Footage: Even storefront footage makes a difference. When quick-print shops, including American Speedy Printing, were confronted by the explosive growth of the Kinko's and FedEx chain, we did a study on consumer behavior. It was not the brand, but the amount of street-facing real estate that positioned Kinko's/FedEx to get first trial by consumers. And, they dominated.

By simply improving its sign and street visibility, any quick-print shop would increase sales by an average of 26%.[40] This explains the success of the big-box retail store. The power of square footage is actually quite simple: Bigger stores are bigger billboards that drive more traffic and more sales.

Share of Shelf Space: We saw the same phenomenon in retail Consumer Packaged Goods. Gerber baby food was the leader in shelf-space acquisition. When this icon of the category wanted more shelf space, it would add another vegetable, soup or cereal SKU to the line. The wider the Gerber shelf got, the more of that brand's baby food sold.

Consider the launch of the Gerber Graduates line. By adding this line of food products targeted at an older baby, Gerber not only retained customers longer, but added shelf space for the Gerber brand. The product line delivered $2 billion in incremental revenue with limited mass consumer advertising. Most of the "advertising" was tied to in-store shelf talkers and end caps or targeted collateral dedicated to the B2B initiative to gain shelf space.[41] This is why some brands, like Gerber, have limited needs for consumer mass media. Through shelf space acquisition, the most effective advertising is the product itself.

Share of Social: Social media is a "real estate" game, too. There are many "storefronts" to browse online, from Facebook to Instagram. And the "signage" changes by the second, as new posts push old posts into unsearchable depths. If you posted only once this week, your consumer probably never saw it.

To maintain visibility, we must compete in the mounds of content. This is a hard sell within most marketing departments because we have already spent the marketing dollars on TV commercials and outbound media buys. CMOs will say, "There was barely enough budget to be on TV last year." So how can we cut budget from our outbound media that has been proven to work, so we can fund experimental inbound social campaigns in the future? It's a matter of priority and balance.

Of course, we won't be able to produce $25 million film productions for every social video post. The need for quantity must be the driving force to balance our desire for quality, but we need to make sure it's exciting enough to leverage consumer sharing. We can't simply throw quantities of weak content at the consumer just to see what sticks. Not only will your content never get shared, your brand could become permanently unfriended. This is a precise balancing act.

THE ART OF RECOVERY

As online participation provides increased levels of consumer feedback, angry consumers are participating in your story as well. That's why we are entering a new era of corporate listening. We have all purchased our license to social listening tools such as Radian6 or Sysomos™, but what do we do with all that power?

Don't be like some of those who have purchased Salesforce.com subscriptions without integrating it into your systems and operational structure. Otherwise, these tools can become just an expensive Excel spreadsheet. They can be incredibly important, but they only perform well if you have properly outlined the goals and principles of use. Ultimately, it's about what real humans do with the data that these tools provide. One of the most important functions of these tools is building customer satisfaction.

According to a study by American Express, fewer and fewer people talk about their good customer experiences. Nearly half of your consumers admit that they tell negative stories about brands in social media. Don't miss the opportunity to turn these negative comments into a positive story. Up to 63% of your consumers are willing to give your brand two or more chances to recover.[42] A simple online response to a negative tweet, or a recovery effort to refund the customer can gain a customer's loyalty for life.

When a brand masters the art of recovery, consumers actually lend a higher level of loyalty than they had given your brand before the mistake occurred.

It turns out my mother was right: Manners matter. Consumers are always happy to receive a credit or refund, but surprisingly, customer satisfaction is not finally earned without an apology. Monetary value alone won't cut it. Studies show that refunds or other compensation might only earn you 37% satisfaction after a service failure. Consumers want to know that you care. You can double your satisfaction score to 74% or higher by offering an online apology. In many cases, loyalty is even stronger after the apology than before your brand made the mistake.[43]

When customers get answers to their concerns in real time, this is a remarkable — and remark-worthy — moment. And, all of the friends of these customers get to experience this recovery moment together. So, never let a service failure opportunity go to waste. It's a great chance to write a completely new story.

If you have your graphic services department posting ads in social media, that's nice, but it can further frustrate angry consumers. The last thing they want to see in a response to their complaint is a branded meme about your stellar service.

Adding a service-recovery team to your social media strategy can be expensive, but consider the cost of staying in the harbor and not winning over a loyal customer for life.

This is one more way to make your story known — by having others tell it for you. As these new models of storytelling are redefining our approach, this reveals the second of three principles for surviving a black wave ...

KEY PRINCIPLE NO. 2:

LEAD WITH AN INNOVATIVE ATTITUDE

This means being proactive and optimizing each situation by making the best of it. Katada taught the children of Kamaishi East how to think outside of the box by insisting there would be no rules that could save them when the tsunami came. During the chaos of a tsunami, the children would need to be resourceful and creative to find a way out.

The chaos of disruptive change in business is no different. Our second principle of black wave surfing is captured by the story of Hiro:

 FIND YOUR ROOFTOP

As the old platforms of media fail us, we must find new platforms to use. Find a rooftop and shout from it, if necessary. Grab onto anything that will bring lift to your brand.

There are no rules in tsunami surfing, so try unconventional ideas and find a new storytelling platform. As storytellers, we must face the fact that we are all competing in the entertainment business. We are the service experience department.

We are in the real estate, product development and product placement division. We are on the service recovery team, so don't forget to use all of the tools available in our toolbox:

Rediscover the craft of storytelling proven by Pixar and the entertainment industry:

1   Cast an unexpected "Hiro"

2   Don't advertise, entertain

3   Instigate conflict

4   End first

5   Where's the "gotcha"?

Disrupt the consumer brain, appealing to all three pillars of effective storytelling:

1   Be disruptive

2   Be purposeful

3   Be metaphorical

Build storymaking experiences that empower consumer word of mouth.

Invest in share of mental real estate to gain visibility in the marketplace and online.

Master the art of recovery by using social listening tools to resolve conflict.

I still remember the photographers who told me digital cameras would never replace the rich quality of film. Almost every photographer I knew made fun of me for believing digital cameras eventually would get better-quality images than the professional film-processing industry. It must have seemed like a threat to their skills. Perhaps the simplicity of click-and-view cameras threatened to diminish the value of their mysterious art and processing alchemy.

For whatever reason, most professionals denied the future. But today, almost anybody can shoot like a pro on a digital camera, and processing filters are automatic.

Photography is yet alive, but it has evolved. Life will go on after TV, too, but a new kind of expertise will need to emerge. The art of branded storytelling will survive this change as it always has, so avoid hesitation, grab a surfboard — or a roof — and keep your storytelling skills sharp as our new future unfolds.

CALL ME CRAZY

BLOG POST | JANUARY 12, 2017: This new year will bring us millions of new channels and unlimited options to consume content. As marketers, our greatest risk will be the wasting of our resources on creating content that is lost in the clutter. The search for safe advertising is the hunt for an elusive creature. Advertising must take risks to get noticed.

The first reaction I get to the idea of branded entertainment is, "Oh, that's not for our brand. We aren't that cool." My response is always, "Why?"

Why can't your brand participate in this new arena of media? What was so cool about soap and cereal? Some would argue not much, but those companies premiered sponsored radio and TV dramas of the '40s and '50s. Who's cool now?

Henry Ford Health System engaged Hollywood production, producing a prime time TV series that won Emmy Awards. They are not alone. Following this lead, Johns Hopkins, Cleveland Clinic, Penn Medicine, Uhealth, Advocate, and many others, have all produced TV shows about their hospitals. What is so cool about hospitals?

Why do we look to others first?

I discussed this at length in an earlier blog post of mine:

> 66 When we start out in advertising or marketing, everyone wants to work for the provocative companies. The brands that get mentions in the industry rags. The brands that get to cut loose. "Red Bull is so daring," they say. "Look at what Nike just did!" they chant. "Did you see the production Coke just pulled off? We could never do that," they lament.
>
> My question is, "Why can't you?" Isn't that our job? If we can't make hospitals, banks or deodorant exciting, we should find another career. Limiting yourself or your advertising efforts because of a preconceived notion about your industry can be harmful.
>
> Imagine, for example, you lived in the 1960s, and your retail client asked you to create ads for a boring product such as a shoe. Nobody then would have imagined that Nike would later do what it did for the shoe industry.
>
> Instead, look up and out.

Let's take, for example, an insurance company. Look past what your competition is doing. This works for any "uncool" industry. Instead, study the best companies doing the best work. Look at the Coca-Colas and the Nikes.

Or, take a look at what North Face has produced. Their efforts can inspire yours, even if your industry is vastly different.

Recently, North Face took a few pages from the extreme-sports playbook. Partnering with other relevant sponsors — including Red Bull, one of the leading extreme-sports brands — the outfitter has found its place in the homes of cable-cutters through its wildly successful branded ski documentary, *Into the Mind*. North Face ventured into uncharted mountain ranges for the film, but it was the media buying strategy that broke new ground. The brand didn't pay to be on Apple TV. In fact, targeted consumers actually paid to see the brand's advertising on their digital set-top boxes. The reviews for the film were off the chart.

"Last night was the first time I've ever heard anyone get shushed at a ski movie. ... 'Shut up,' the viewers seemed to be saying, 'I'm concentrating here,'" stated Heather Hansman of *Powder Magazine*. "It's an unquestionably beautiful film." In fact, viewers not only paid to watch this commercial, they were "concentrating" on this commercial for one hour and 25 minutes. How many times does that happen for your brand? What would you pay for that much emotional engagement with your consumer?

Branded extreme sports media began with a vision of a marketing V.P. at Red Bull. The mission of Werner Brell, the managing director of Red Bull Media House, was to build a media business that would be more profitable than the drink itself. Brill said, "What we do always has to come with some form of paycheck, whether advertising, licensing or a co-production deal."

Their plan is much like kid's movies that break even at the box office, while the revenue is made on the products that sell in retail outlets after the film is no longer in the theater. This allows Hollywood to create bigger-budget films than ticket sales can justify.

Advertising of the future will be no different. Leading advertisers such as Red Bull are building a model where the ad campaign has a bigger budget than the drink sales can justify, but the Netflix sales are making up the difference. And today these online films and TV events have placed Red Bull to become ranked No. 74 on the *Forbes* list of top brands in the world.

Valued at $7.9 billion, the Red Bull logo is worth more than the annual gross sales of the company itself.[44] This is in no small way a fulfillment of their mission to have a media company that would outperform the product. They have effectively flipped the marketing model. With revenues quickly approaching $100 million, Red Bull Media House makes more money than most advertising departments spend.

History has proven that people will call us crazy if we challenge the status quo. It's time to get on board with this movement. It's time to start planning your entertainment strategy for your brand. That might sound crazy, but I'd rather be crazy than irrelevant. How about you?

INBOUND MARKETING: WANTS VS. NEEDS

BLOG POST | APRIL 11, 2016: Finally. I finally get it. I figured out why most marketers don't get around to giving priority to inbound marketing. It feels like a *want* fighting for resources in a world of *needs*.

I followed my own blogging patterns recently, and I'm embarrassed to even act like an expert in this area. When my schedule becomes filled with immediate opportunity, my blog gets put off for another day. That becomes another week, and next thing I know, goodbye consistency. I remember when I was ranked No. 1 among 4,000 peers in LinkedIn for my constant engagement with the community. Today, I'm ranked No. 279.

What happened? Where did I go wrong? Well, I remember at the time, we lost a very big account, and I needed some activity around our agency story. Now that we've nearly doubled our business, I've been too busy doing the work to take the time to plan for getting more business.

There you have it. I feel like I'm in a blogger support group airing all my dirty laundry, but perhaps this will inspire me to get back in the habit.

In this case, I'm just talking about one form of inbound marketing — blogging. Anything from public speaking engagements to app development can be inbound marketing. Bringing customers to your brand, rather than inundating them with your traditional advertising (outbound), is what makes inbound special. It creates trust and authenticity in an overly inauthentic world.

Here are some reasons to consider a new focus on inbound marketing:

The best service is self-service. Consumers are doing their own research and don't want to engage a pushy salesperson. A potential consumer can move through 57% of the buying process before even talking to a sales representative.[45] That means digital content can replace the need of a sales pitch for thousands of engagements.

Court search engines to get some love. If you have a consistent and valuable presence on your site and your social media channels, you have a better chance of a higher ranking on search engine results pages (SERPs). In fact, 93% of online experiences start with a search engine.[46]

You get higher ROI over the long term. Blogging is one effective facet of inbound marketing. If you are producing great content, you're not only making search engines happy. You're also giving your social media manager consistent, valuable social fodder.

I don't think inbound is just a *want* anymore. It's becoming more of a *need*. I'm ready to start treating it as such. How about you?

5

DON'T JUST BUY THE MEDIA BE THE MEDIA

TECTONIC SHIFTS IN THE WAY
BRANDS ENGAGE CONSUMERS

> **❝ The best way to get media coverage is to own the media.**
>
> – *Author is unknown (but all-powerful)*

Suddenly, your peaceful moment is disrupted by a seismic shockwave. You feel the boom of an earthquake offshore. The thud reverberates to your core, as if God Himself just pointed His finger into your chest. As captain of the cruise ship, you are responsible for a passenger list of almost 2,000 souls, and it seems all of their faces of desperation flash before you. As a plume of dust rises over the horizon, you have a choice to make: Will you motor into shore or go out to sea?

It was 2:46 p.m. local time when the North American and Pacific tectonic plates off the coast of Japan slid together and created the 2011 Tohoku earthquake. It sent a 500-mph shockwave rippling across the ocean. That's the speed of a commercial airliner. The shockwave was so powerful, if it could have been harnessed, it would have produced enough power to run the city of Los Angeles for a year.

The tsunami that struck Japan in 2011 was a result of the largest tectonic plate shift in recorded history. It caused the earth to slide 164 feet into itself. Traveling a mile every 7 seconds, the waves generated were approaching the speed of sound. Imagine these waves as they targeted the ships anchored along the shoreline.[1]

Once these high-speed waves reach shallow depths, they hit the seafloor, compress and rebound upward, gathering to form an unnaturally fast wall of water. This would not be like the beautiful white and blue waves you see rolling gracefully toward the shore of a surfer's cove. The jet-speed impact of the seismic blast of water on the seafloor would dislodge sediment, junk and debris and roil it into a shock wave three stories tall. The impact of the wave was so jarring, it shifted Japan's main island of Honshu eastward 8 feet. How would you get out of the way of that?

In contrast, we who manage large brands are accustomed to slow-moving waves of change. We stand by and watch as our competitors create a new technology. We wait and see as newcomers employ innovative media platforms, and we have always had time to react with a quick adjustment to the media plan just in time for the following quarter.

The problem with this reactive model of media planning is that it assumes we will always have time to see every media tactic coming. It also assumes brands will always outsource their customer relationships to third-party media like Facebook, YouTube and Google.

One day, we will wake up and realize that Facebook, YouTube and Google know more about our customers than we do. And, that they are holding our data hostage.

When we finally realize we've outsourced our analytics, that's when owned media networks will emerge. Well, no — they will shift into the market with seismic impact. Innovative marketers are realizing that they don't have to *buy* the media when they can *be* the media. Most advertising and PR professionals understand "paid media" and "earned media." These are time-tested models. "Owned media" presents a certain mystery because it's less formulaic.

In some ways, owned media isn't a new concept at all. The phenomenon has existed for years. Cereal and soap companies were the pioneers of TV advertising, first innovating branded content with owned media in the '50s and '60s. This branded content led to the term "soap opera" when referring to daytime dramas. Long-form content actually existed before the 30-second commercial format.

Owned channels are everywhere. And we all have a website, don't we? That's owned media. We own storefronts, signage and packaging that we can design however we want. All of that is a form of owned media.

Owned media is not new. Yet what we're seeing unfold here is truly revolutionary, not just in a matter of degree or magnitude — but it's a shifting of our business on its axis, like the Earth shifting after the 2011 quake.

The next wave of change will look nothing like what we are used to. The imperceptible speeding wave of media disruption is stealthy, but almost upon us. Behind the scenes, the rapid adoption of new technology is being developed by startup companies, unknown challenger brands and your most aggressive competition. The wave of change may take time to fall upon your brand, but it's coming at a speed that will not afford you enough time to react.

Don't be caught, like Hiro, wondering, "Why did I stop to pick up the bottle?" That's exactly what happened to Blockbuster. By the time they built their own streaming video platform, consumers were content with their Netflix subscriptions.

The platforms of media have shifted like the great tectonic plates under the sea. Change is coming to your industry. You may have already felt the jolt from a competitive platform. As the children of Kamaishi were taught, now is not the time to hesitate. Now is the time to become proactive and lead your brand. You could lead your industry.

CONSUMER-DEFINED ADVERTISING

Before we explore market-proven solutions, let's take a look into the future. Even as marketers gain almost unlimited power to measure the impact of media, they will become stripped of their power to control it in any way. We must, rather, ride the wave of consumer-defined advertising, and go where it takes us.

No longer will advertisers dictate the consumption patterns of consumers. Consumers will set their own user preferences to either allow or block advertising content, and they will decide how it will be permitted to engage their world.

Because the parameters of this advertising will be defined by the consumer, advertisers will have to earn the right to engage consumers, resorting to incentives for content consumption. This will inevitably motivate the creation of consumer rewards and loyalty systems unlike anything we have seen before.

Of course, Netflix and Apple TV are commercial-free for now, but that will change — just as commercial-free cable TV did in the '80s and '90s. The margins of media distribution are too small and advertising dollars are too big to ignore these forces forever. New technologies will enable marketing solutions to arise for nearly every consumer desire, expressed or unexpressed.

Her story begins in a neighborhood like yours, in a home like yours. Now, picture the bedroom. It's like yours, too. It's early morning and the birds are chirping their routine sound as the darkness dissipates. But now everything that's familiar is gone.

When the alarm goes off in the master bedroom that morning, it actually greets CB by name. Of course, the voice is synthesized, but it sounds real. She selected the voice of her favorite Australian action hero. But as much as she likes the amiable persona of Hugh Jackman nudging her into action each morning, there's still something not quite right about it. She can't put a finger on the feeling she has. But something about connected technology rouses thoughts in her often — of government conspiracy, or perhaps something even more sinister. Some days it seems to CB that everyone has become a part of a revolution she doesn't understand.

Anyway, CB turns over and pulls her sheets close to her face. The radio persona speaks as a friend who is cautious to disturb her familiar awakening routine. "Would you prefer the Starbucks channel this morning?" he asks CB.

She groans, "Yes, that might help. I'd like my coffee at the door though. I don't think I can make it to the car without it." He responds — with an accent that she used to love — "Of course, mate." The coffeehouse-inspired music begins softly, and finally CB opens her eyes.

There are no commercial breaks on the Starbucks channel. In CB's world, advertising doesn't interrupt her life — or at least she doesn't think it does. Her media preferences are set to block advertising on all channels. She even turned off her Facebook camera because she read a blog post about the new Facebook artificial intelligence engine. Cameras connected to deep learning freak her out.

Her kids make fun of her aversion to technology. As she sends off the kids, they each put their hands to their face gesturing as if they are holding a camera to take her picture. She laughs it off. At least, for now.

You see, CB is like most other consumers — but not quite a full-fledged member of the future. She's a careerist, a wife, a mother and totally modern in the brands she buys and allows to serve her and her family. But CB is still figuring out whether she really likes how brands access her life — it's just so different than in her mother's day. While advertising doesn't interrupt programming, it's a constant presence in her life: From the Starbucks channel to the Nike Plus fitness center, she understands that she ultimately controls their invasion, but somehow it seems less volitional, maybe even intrusive. There's something almost Big Brother-ish about it.

But that doesn't mean CB has no relationship with brands. To the contrary, her relationships with brands have become symbiotic. And those brands she carefully selects have become exclusive relationships. Only the companies she trusts to bring value to her life have become part of her community. These brands have earned a place in CB's life as long as she believes their values align with hers. And as long as these values are authentic. But then that's where her tacit arrangement with brands can run into problems.

REALITY OR FANTASY?

CB's world may seem imaginary and far away, but all of the technology exists to create it today. For that reason, many experts believe that immersive and automatic, but customized media and advertising experiences will become a reality in our lifetime. Possibly sooner than we think.

So, this is an exciting time to live. It's a sobering responsibility, too. We who work in the marketing and advertising industries will define the future. The leaders of this change will become the leaders of their respective industries and the culture itself. They will build their own media platforms and create their own communities, replacing mass media as we know it.

Consider the pizza industry. By the time the pizza chains realized Domino's online ordering app was a game-changer, consumers were already loyal users of this new form of media. Developed undercover for almost a year from a small digital shop in Detroit, nobody saw this media innovation coming. The Pizza Hut media team will obviously never have the option to buy in or place media on the Domino's app. So Pizza Hut had to scramble to develop their own customer relationship network.

By the time Pizza Hut started playing catch up to the simple media application, Domino's was doing them one better by adding gamification experiences and pizza tracker capabilities. And since then, the pizza brands, including Hungry Howie's and Papa John's, have each continued to try to out-hustle one another by adding new digital ordering platforms at a furious pace, via everything from Twitter to Snapchat to Ford's Sync infotainment system to emojis.

Given that an average pizza buyer spends almost 30% more when they use an app,[2] Domino's has been happy to lead this new race in the pizza industry. More than half of all orders already come online for the leaders. It's been such a successful media innovation that Domino's eventually ran a TV campaign telling their customers to not call.

Pizza isn't the only industry to be disrupted by an online ordering app. I have to admit, after I downloaded the Starbucks app, I stopped going to other coffeehouses. I liked the fact that I never needed to explain my Grande coconut milk, caramel cappuccino with five pumps of caramel. I simply click reorder from my car and pick it up the minute I walk in the door of my local Starbucks. No lines. No re-swipes of malfunctioning credit cards. No misunderstood orders. I'm hooked.

HOW CB EXPERIENCES OWNED MEDIA

Capitalizing on the power of owned media, Domino's, Papa John's and Hungry Howie's have inadvertently joined forces to change the media paradigm for an entire industry. Soon, these pizza shops won't need third-party media to communicate with their customers. For customers on their network, they have become the media. Likewise, Starbucks doesn't need to reserve, lease or negotiate with media representatives. The brand can push-notify their advertising on consumer mobile phones for free. There is no cost for that kind of media impact. With a 98% open rate,[3] push notification is the most effective media on the planet, but it's not for sale anywhere. It's a small leap for Starbucks to add value to their members by distributing music, news or other branded content, such as a voice-synthesized alarm clock that has become normal in CB's world.

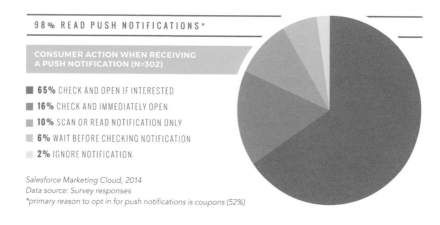

98% READ PUSH NOTIFICATIONS*

CONSUMER ACTION WHEN RECEIVING
A PUSH NOTIFICATION (N=302)

- **65%** CHECK AND OPEN IF INTERESTED
- **16%** CHECK AND IMMEDIATELY OPEN
- **10%** SCAN OR READ NOTIFICATION ONLY
- **6%** WAIT BEFORE CHECKING NOTIFICATION
- **2%** IGNORE NOTIFICATION

Salesforce Marketing Cloud, 2014
Data source: Survey responses
*primary reason to opt in for push notifications is coupons (52%)

CB still isn't sure she's OK with all of that. She blocked ABC, NBC and CBS — and their advertisers — from her screens years ago. Sure, she lets Starbucks, Hungry Howie's and many other brands push promotions and reminders to her, unblocking a pre-approved list of them to respond to her ongoing needs. So, advertising has found a way to integrate into her life to help CB with countless conveniences. Yet, sometimes she wonders if her approved brand roster is running her day instead of the other way around.

Her block list, on the other hand, is meticulously managed. When she turned off her Facebook camera feature, that was her latest attempt to block what she calls "Big Brother." Her kids are obviously not old enough to understand the meaning of this reference to 1984. CB only remembers her parents using the term "Big Brother" when Amazon first became aware. A lot has happened since then.

CB mulls over these misgivings as she takes her morning commute in her self-driving Google sedan. A message interrupts the continuous stream of coffeehouse music: "Today at Mobil, CB, there's one free gallon of gas waiting for you."

It's not really gas, of course, but the hydrolyphic fuel breakthrough that never found a name they could force consumers to understand, so people just call it "Google Gas."

Soon, other brands compete for her attention via personalized billboards on the sides of the roads that appear to overlay green-screen panels. In some places, whole buildings seem to be wrapped by advertising messages. CB never blocks these messages because she would feel wasteful to turn off the billboards, as she would lose the free offers on gas. Anyway, she justifies to herself, these ads don't interrupt her view in an obnoxious manner. These sprawling billboards aren't like the noisy signage in, say, Times Square. Unexpectedly, it's as if the landscape takes on a beautiful array of artistic expression. Fields come alive as if the advertising messages all dance together in a great choreography of subtle light and sound.

Each message is personally tailored to CB's preference settings — and through a virtual-reality application in her Google Glass 5.0, visible only to her. Her preferences are set regarding pricing, diet, lifestyle and shopping wish lists. And because they don't need to be concerned about distracting a "driver" who no longer is actually operating her automobile, CB's favorite brands load up these billboards with much more specific and even immediately actionable information than in the old days of static, analog billboards that were criticized as visual pollution.

Today, CB notices a new repeating billboard for the Chipotle breakfast burrito. Of course, this offer meets the requirements of her personal nutritional profile as maintained by the Mayo Clinic. After passing by the third virtual billboard for the steaming breakfast burrito, CB cuts short her quandary by blurting out with resignation the simple voice command: "OK, I'm in." Immediately the virtual roadside banners for Chipotle dissolve from her view, some of them moving on to promote Alka-Seltzer because CB's Mayo Clinic profile also includes the fact that she lives with intermittent IBS.

And already, the Chipotle a mile away is preparing her breakfast burrito for drive-thru pickup.

Social media and mobile tech have enabled lots of conveniences for CB, but most of all, food in her world has become a radical convenience that simply happens on demand. Later, at work, for instance, CB's wristband alert will sound off, "It's noon, and you've earned loyalty rewards for a Jimmy John's No. 8! It's free if you accept it in the next 10 seconds." Of course, delivery of this one-click order would be "freaky fast."

However, CB decides to apply her food points to other restaurants participating in this particular loyalty network. She starts by viewing the favorites list produced by her Yelp community. Within seconds, Yelp finds her the perfect salad delivery from Sam's Food Truck.

CB often takes advantage of food convenience at work. But she religiously maintains old-school eating traditions at home, including something she preaches about to her bemused neighbors called the "family dinner." She strongly feels that her kids also deserve the love of a mother who actually walks the aisles of a grocery store as her mother did — albeit assisted at every end cap by beacons that feed her smartphone promotional deals to entice her. Price is another reason why she refuses to get all of her family's meals dropped at the door by Walmart's delivery drones.

After work, CB drives by a billboard that blares, "Kyle just gulped down the last quart of milk!" The image of her teenage son caught in the act by the new fridge cam makes her laugh uncomfortably as she pulls up her Waze navigation app. It asks CB, "Would you prefer the lowest milk price or the fastest route to a grocery store?"

Sheepishly, CB steers her Google to reroute to the store where, she knows, a rare Pokémon GO character was sighted earlier today. Closing the app, she looks around in traffic as if she doesn't want to be caught in her outdated and obsessive Pokémon addiction. It's another way in which, perhaps, CB just can't let go of a past that was simpler when her life seemed less programmed.

THE MAGIC OF OWNED MEDIA

> **ff** Those who have access to and control of the platforms have the largest, most powerful source of information about human behavior that anyone has ever had in human history.
>
> – *PBS.org, Frontline*

The future won't be defined by paid media or earned media. The future will be designed to accommodate new forms of owned media. Owned media had its influence long before digital connectivity started blurring the lines between entertainment and advertising.

Among all of the owned-media examples we could explore, the power of owned-media programming never has been more effective than in the half-century relationship between ABC and Walt Disney. Hailed as the captain of family entertainment, Walt was never afraid to go out to sea. He always seemed to understand the importance of disruptive change in the way things were traditionally done. He grew up in a less-connected generation, where parents treated children as those who should be "seen and not heard," and he decided to change that.

For Walt Disney, it all started with an idea. "We believed in our idea — a family park where parents and children could have fun together," he said. And once Disney understood his purpose, the rest was a natural progression toward the family culture we know today. Only, Disney still needed a way to both pay for and promote his dream.

At the time, Disney was a successful family filmmaker, but as such, he detested the lackluster venue of broadcast TV. So, when ABC first approached Disney to have his own TV show, he rejected the idea. It was only upon ABC's offer to invest in the park that Disney decided he had to take the TV deal.

Planned or unplanned, *The Wonderful World of Disney* television series was the catalyst for Disneyland. The hours of coverage and promotions featuring the likes of Ronald Reagan and Art Linkletter on ABC created fanfare that Disney never had to pay for. The millions of TV viewers became millions of park visitors. There were only three TV channels to choose from at the time, so seemingly the entire nation witnessed Disneyland's opening day.[4]

Disney didn't need an advertising budget. The Disney TV programming itself was the advertising. And Disney kept using its own programming on its own cable TV channels to promote its parks and movie properties instead of relying in any way on interruptive TV advertising. In fact, the tail eventually wagged the dog when Disney purchased ABC in 1995.[5]

"CUSTOMER RELATIONSHIP NETWORKS"

Unlike Disney, companies of the future won't have to buy broadcast networks or install towers or massive satellite dishes. With affordable digital platforms, anybody can own a broadcast network online. Innovative companies will no longer need to buy or beg for media in a world where they can *be* the media.

The unique benefit of digital media is its ability to provide Customer Relationship Marketing. CRM has always been sold as the evolution from broadcast advertising to narrowcast advertising using data-informed direct marketing at a highly targeted audience.

But let's face it, CRM has seldom offered more than a managed direct mail or email list. The new term arising for marketing automation is "Customer Relationship Networks," or CRN. In contrast to CRM, Customer Relationship Networks utilize real-time data to enable two-way digital conversations with individual consumers and brands.

Rather than employing stagnant database management systems, CRN uses fluid Big Data (short for "Big Brother Data") on a mass-media scale. By adding automated decision-making, these platforms will help brands understand and engage millions of customers individually, and in real time. Ultimately, CRN replaces generic mass marketing with individualized, variable messaging to the masses.

All of these marketing-automation platforms are built to incentivize customers to stay within the network. Remember when the titans of the Industrial Age created monopolies? The titans of the Participation Age have grand ambitions, as well. They are all after the power of media influence.

DOES CB OWN HER MEDIA – OR VICE VERSA?

Finally back at home after shopping, CB unpacks her grocery bags and syncs her food choices with her new Samsung smart fridge. Then she glances at her husband, Gabe, who is putting down his work and reaching for the TV remote.

Before immersive TV programming, CB and Gabe didn't even know their neighbors' names. But now their family has a relationship with the neighbors that is difficult to describe and, to CB's way of thinking, maybe even a bit unsettling. In particular, Gabe and their neighbor next door, Jim, have this thing they do when they both get online with their TVs. They'll look through their windows at each other and point downward, each grinning like mischievous children when they're about to jump off a cliff together.

This odd male ritual — along with other strange behaviors, exhibited by the kids — all started with a game show called *The Neighborhood*. Literally, the whole neighborhood logs into their smart TVs to play against one another. CB clearly doesn't get it. But then again, she never understood that fad of role-playing sitcoms, either.

CB remembers when TV was a passive form of media that she strategically used to disengage the world. Perhaps that's another reason why she took so long to subscribe to the Amazon Prime Home Rewards network. "Why must we insist on voting, competing or role-playing in every TV show? Why can't we simply go to our separate rooms and watch TV?" she quietly asks herself.

But then her train of thought shifts slightly and more optimistically. "Somehow," she admits under her breath, "the kids love it" — and by "kids" she includes her husband, who was previously an addicted video gamer. To CB, *The Neighborhood* is just another video game. But she realizes that, better than video games, this new fad actually inspired her family to engage with real human beings, and people who live close to them at that. "Without that TV app, we probably wouldn't know our neighbors," she says to herself.

After dinner, as the kids gather around Gabe and the TV, a series of rapid menu selections appear: "Virtual Challenges," "Physical Challenges," "Brain Challenges," "Sit-Coms," "Soap Operas," "Shopathon," "War."

Kyle selects "Kellogg's Physical Challenge," which promises free cereal to winners. Suddenly, the family all leap up from the couch and start running toward the door, shouting things like, "OMG, Kellogg's just released a level-1300 Pokémon in our front yard!" As they scramble around the yard looking at the world through their cell phones, CB enjoys a moment in the house to herself.

Noting this spontaneous moment of rapturous joy for her family was "sponsored" by Kellogg's, the moment gives her pause. As she peeks out the window at her children jumping on their dad in the front yard, she asks herself, "But, what's so wrong about that?" She realizes that there was never anything she could do to get them to go out and play before *The Neighborhood* was released as a TV app. CB concludes: "That app doesn't make the moment any less real, does it?"

CUT ANCHOR OR DROWN

Now, back to the ship. As captain, have you decided whether you'll go out to sea, or do you plan to keep your cruise ship in the harbor? It's your call, captain.

Do all of these ideas about media innovation and disruptive change worry you? Perhaps you are like CB, and you like the way things used to be. Perhaps, as the captain of your ship, you would rather not go out to sea. There are terrifying possibilities and risks when we innovate ways to invade our consumer lives. What if we go too far? What if it fails to work? What if ...

By now, if you have hesitated to move, or if you have chosen to motor your cruise ship to shore, you just lost 2,000 souls to the tsunami of Japan. The statistics show that most ships would be better off sailing out to sea. The faster, the better. The deeper, the better. Typically, navigating water that is 150 feet deep is sufficient depth to survive a tsunami. Veterans of the sea know this rule.[6]

Some seasoned captains have even experienced the almost-supersonic passing of a shockwave at sea. After an earthquake, sailors have attested that the thrust of a shockwave sounds like rocks hitting the ship, but it doesn't do any damage when at sea.

The most dangerous place for a ship to be during turbulent water is anchored near shore. This is why many ships go out to sea during great storms. This principle holds true for companies during times of great disruption. Now is not the time for your brand to stay anchored at bay. It's time to go out and explore the deepest opportunities for innovation.

The future of CRN and Big Data platforms might seem ominous, but there is no reason your brand can't navigate these waters. You are probably already building your platform, and didn't know it. The pioneers are quietly forging these new networks under a seemingly mundane initiative, currently called "loyalty programs."

Every brand is currently focused on building customer loyalty networks. It's all based on the classic business idiom: "Your best new business is your current customer." It's true. Gartner Group research can show that 80% of an average company's future revenue comes from just 20% of its existing customers.[7]

Motivated by new technology platforms and findings like this, the corporate rush to gain loyalty has become almost comical. Marketing automation consultants are being hired and Salesforce.com is being licensed in marketing departments but without regard for a cohesive digital plan for integrating accounting, sales and the call center. Brands are aggregating consumer data without even knowing how to use it. After in-house attempts have failed, some brands are signing license agreements with white-labeled loyalty packages, only to find that canned software is restrictive and not differentiating at all.

If this innovation chaos sounds familiar, you are not alone. Market disruption is a learning process for everyone.

That's why strategy is more important than technology per se. What will we do with all this data and unlimited consumer access? We must never forget that consumer attention still has to be earned. Consumers can easily block email, delete apps or turn off notifications if we constantly annoy them with pushy advertising messages.

The data we gain on our consumers could be very personal, lending Big Data the potential to become Big Brother. This

is at least a subconscious source of CB's unease with her relationships with brands in the future. Brands' knowledge of exercise habits, eating patterns and current location can be used to build consumer relationships ... or destroy them.
Your relationship with your consumer will be like a marriage. We might have the power to tell a consumer they are eating too much and haven't been to the gym in a month, but should we?

Brands are just like people; there are people we like to be with and people we don't. We must practice restraint. If we focus purely on product advancement and extracting the sale, people will be left with the feeling they are being used, rather than appreciated. We're all familiar with that feeling.

Author and marketing expert David Salyers once said, "Big Data gives us all of the power to be generally right, but get everything specifically wrong." Initially, Big Data was viewed as a scientific way to get more customers. But what if we changed our thinking? Let's dare to consider how we can give something more meaningful than points or free products after 10 purchases. What if loyalty made your customer's lives better? What if we could make rewards more fun?

Imagine this: A consumer downloads an app from his favorite restaurant while on a road trip with his family.

All of a sudden, an alert comes through on his phone:

"You've driven a long way! Why don't you take a load off at exit 35 and have an appetizer on us?"

What about this one: "You've come to see us quite a few times in the last couple of weeks. Let us buy you a coffee."

Once, when I went to a resort, my wife and I were greeted when we got out of our car by a valet saying, "Welcome, Mr. and Mrs. Cobb. Happy Anniversary."

I'm still trying to figure out how they did that.

This is what Big Data can do for us.

But not if it stays locked up in a database managed by the I.T. department. We must activate Big Data to serve our customers. The Customer Relationship Networks are becoming core service experience and marketing tools that need to be driven by the leadership of every organization.

CB DECIDES

As her family settles down to watch the movie, CB recalls fondly the days when she watched an alphabet soup of TV networks: ABC, NBC, CBS. Sometimes she even misses those old annoying TV commercials. She's wondering whether they were actually better because they made her feel more in control ... when suddenly a beautiful dress worn by her favorite actress flashes across the screen during the movie.

Abruptly abandoning her previous train of thought, CB grabs the TV remote so she can make a double-click order from Amazon — though her family barely notices as CB completes her order from her mobile phone. The Amazon virtual mall has replaced hours upon hours of shopping, mostly because CB can't get over her addiction to watching Amazon Soap Operas.

Using the Virtual Dressing Room app from her mobile phone, CB views herself in the dress. As her husband glances over at her mobile screen, he exclaims, "Wow, you look great in that!" CB smirks as she thinks to herself, "He's just trying to earn real-world points for later."

Just as the movie starts getting interesting, family movie night breaks for a Kids vs. Kids game sponsored by Hasbro. But this commercial break isn't like the interruptive promotions that CB grew up watching on TV; these breaks are actually fun, and they bring the family together. Sometimes, it's a race or a face-off; other times, it's a "Where's Waldo?"-type of quiz segment that rewards the person who finds the special "Easter egg" clues while watching the movie.

Usually, Kyle wins because he captures every detail of every movie, but this time the competition is over quickly when little Elle uses her "unlock" code that she found earlier in the Purina puppy-food bag. Nobody could top the "humanitarian points" that Elle had acquired by feeding the neighbor's puppy. With that many points, only Elle remained in play. There was nothing anyone could do to beat her. But CB says, "Great job, Elle!"

With a nonchalant groan, the remainder of the family slouches back into the couch and returns to the movie. They know that as the winner, Elle now controls it. Elle excitedly heads off to cash in her snack points by printing her free Mars bar at the 3-D candy printer in the pantry. "Only one rule!" CB shouts after her: "No candy printing unless you share with the whole family! Print one for your brothers, too," she says. "And don't be long. You are in charge of the storyline for the rest of the movie now. If you're not here to make story choices, the default plot line could take us all on the director's cut."

"Yeah, get back here quick!" the boys shout.

CB savors this moment of true family togetherness, Brought To You By Your Favorite Brands. She looks around at the children on dad's lap and sitting close together. It's one of those rare moments that comes along, meant to be savored. No fighting. No whining. Not one of those three words echoing in her head, "Stop touching me!" She only hears laughter. As Elle jumps back, squishing into her spot on the couch, nobody complains. It's that moment. The perfect moment she remembers with her mom and dad, brothers and sisters, sitting together and having fun.

Reaching to snap a photo that she will keep forever, she stops — she realizes that in her earlier paranoia, she had blocked the camera feature on her Facebook phone. "I'm silly," she says with regret. Then it hits her. Putting her hands over her face, CB works to hold back her tears. Struggling to see through a fog of emotion, she looks around at her family laughing and hugging each other.

This moment crystallizes her world. It's not ever going to be like it was with her mom and dad, the way it used to be. It's going to be better. This is her family, and this is her world, and it's not so bad.

And as the movie ends and the kids all get ready for bed, CB's thoughts finally go back to what she was thinking about when the day started: the old days when brands were not part of her family. The days before advertising ended.

As she reaches for her mobile preferences and clicks on her Facebook camera module, she pauses a moment looking at her blocklist as she had often before. She says to herself, "What could it hurt?" as she welcomes brands' embrace with a single sliding button labeled, "Unblock all."

GO OUT TO SEA

Unfortunately for most brands, stories like CB's still sound like science fiction. That's a sign that many ships are still anchored at bay. Leading brands have felt the rumble of change in their industry, and they've gone out to sea. They are exploring new technology and steering toward the wave. These are fearless captains of industry, and they have been headed out toward the deep unknown for years. They are navigating for a world united and powered by interconnected networks.

As described by Joshua Ramo in his study of the coming Age of Networks, "The last great shift of the Enlightenment was a violent and wonderful transformation. It produced winners and losers, triggered tragedy and lit fresh triumphs. What lies ahead of us is the same."[238]

Now, let's move beyond the theory and beyond illustrative scenarios like CB's story from the future. What do Customer Relationship Networks and Big Data platforms look like in the real world today? Here are three case studies:

APPLE: THE KING OF CONTENT MARKETING

Question: Is Apple still a hardware company? Or, has it become something else?

My photo library is stored in iCloud. My music library is stuck in iTunes. Now, my home video library is held hostage by Apple TV, and I don't seem to mind at all. I would suggest that Apple is no longer a hardware company but a Customer Relationship Network. I pay a premium for their hardware — but only to stay connected to my content. And even as challengers to Apple arise to steal market share among Millennials, invested dogs like me will probably never switch.

Since the loss of Steve Jobs, the future of Apple has been clouded. However, regardless of whatever Apple is today, its success during the Jobs years is undeniable. It has been the most-capitalized company in the world for a while. And with 94% year-over-year profit increases, Apple distributed $11.47 billion to shareholders in a single year, making it the largest dividend-paying company in the world ... ever.[8]

The secret to the success of Apple during its heyday was Jobs' unwillingness to stay in his lane. While traditional business-school theology would have preached, "Stay within your core competency and focus on great technology," Jobs took Apple into the entertainment business.

Jobs once had to course correct his own marketing team about just what is the core value of Apple. He said, "What we're about isn't making boxes for people to get their jobs done. But, Apple's core value ... is that we believe that people with passion can change the world for the better. That's what we believe."

Jobs learned early on that his technology wouldn't make a difference in the world without partnerships with great content — other people's content. Driven by his passionate principles, he looked for content that would change the world. Whole industries were born of Apple's content partnerships, including Microsoft's Office platform, Adobe's Creative Suite and countless audio-visual development tools on which the media industry depends.

When Apple needed a solution to market its MP3 player, Jobs looked to content again. This time Apple struck gold with a curated-content strategy that changed the music industry: iTunes. Early on, Apple secured 63% of all digital music downloads,[9] putting Apple on track to sell more than a billion iPhones since its launch in 2007.[10]

So, is Apple a hardware company or an entertainment company? By building a Customer Relationship Network that engages its customers with the content they want, Apple pioneered and remains a major player in both industries.

Apple's participation model originally broke ground with custom playlist selection, replacing CDs and network-dictated "playlists." Participation is now encouraged by user reviews, sharing, gifting and recommendations from the "Genius Playlist." While other music apps including Spotify, Pandora and the emerging threat from Vertigo are improving participation, Apple is staying in front by moving on to the next innovation curve: TV apps.

After replacing the CD, Apple TV also replaced the DVD. Now, it's on its way to replace cable TV. By its second year, Apple already owned half of the market share of paid digital movies. I've lost count of how many Apple TVs I own. I don't buy these devices just for the technology. I buy Apple because the content selection is better and new movies are there long before they come available on a Roku box or Cable On Demand. Apple felt the seismic shift and responded before the waves reached the harbor.

God only knows if Apple eventually will become its own "Big Brother" from the vision in its iconic Super Bowl ad that channeled 1984. But content is king. And, Apple is the king of content marketing.

AMAZON: ARTIFICIAL INTELLIGENCE FOR SHOPPING

Amazon is a great name for the soon-to-be world's largest retailer. What started out as a cute idea for an online book store has ventured far outside of its lane into every category of retail distribution and has made its visionary founder, Jeff Bezos, one of the world's richest people. From books to electronics to media and every other aspect of our lives, this mother of all e-commerce destinations keeps going after new categories that it can dominate.

Recently breaking into the apparel business, Amazon already owns 43% of all online clothing sales and is surpassing Macy's as the biggest apparel retailer in the U.S., with a forecast of $52 billion by 2020 in apparel alone. Amazon has even introduced seven of its own designer clothing labels, including Franklin & Freeman men's shoes and Society New York women's dresses.[11]

Why is one retailer able to dominate so many categories? Amazon is delivering an online experience that traditional retailers are struggling to match. The Amazon platform has aggregated members and purchasing patterns to build the world's most powerful recommendation engine. Letting consumers know which styles and sizes sell best by region, Amazon can help any individual find the right fit at the right price.

"Years ago, when you walked into a department store, there was a salesperson who knew you and knew what to show you," said the CEO of Camuto Group, Alex Del Cielo, who sells shoes and apparel. "That's what Amazon has done with technology."

According to a recent study by the Pew Research Center, user reviews have become the most powerful asset in e-commerce. Consumers trust online reviews from other customers on Amazon.com five times more than the messages crafted by the brands that created the products. People would even rather buy Nike products on Amazon than purchase them at the Nike website.

By providing user participation in product accountability, the consumer has gained the power to find the best possible product. All this has happened on Amazon's behalf without hiring a single sales representative. The consumer is the sales staff. That's efficiency! In fact, when I purchase a new lens for my Canon 5d camera, I can read reviews from dozens of expert 5d users. No pro camera shop can give me that much expertise. That's how Amazon became my single source for lenses.

Now Amazon is repurposing user data to make shopping recommendations. My purchase patterns are combined with user ratings and the purchase patterns of others. All of this data adds up to enable real-time marketing that directs me to purchases that I don't even know I want to make.

Amazon actually has integrated artificial-intelligence software to learn about me over time. Now, when I go to the Amazon home page, it's full of Canon lenses that I would love to own. Big Brother? The politically correct term is "Big Data." Big Data combined with real-time recommendation engines are the future, and the next obvious step for marketing automation.

Amazon is testing physical distribution centers with same-day delivery. Meanwhile, Walmart keeps struggling with the performance of its bricks-and-mortar stores, slowing down the pace of construction of new ones, and deciding to pour significantly more resources into e-commerce in an effort to catch Amazon online. And so now there's a real race for which company will be the world's top retailer — and it will be won and lost online.[12]

NIKE: JUST DO IT

Driven by its stated purpose of "bringing innovation and inspiration to every athlete in the world,"[13] Nike set itself apart as more than a shoe manufacturer long ago. Nike was years ahead of the wave and even helped usher in the Participation Age as the first brand to start a conversation with their community.

It started in the '80s. Remember then? While other shoe brands followed the classic advertising model of differentiation based on price and product features, Nike began speaking with the athlete in a dialog that motivated runners to "Just do it." No reference to nylon fibers, no diagrams of reinforced cushion pads and no hard sell. The buyer felt respected, even honored, to be part of the club.

Steve Jobs said it best, giving Nike credit for the strategy that relaunched Apple as a leading brand in the world. He said, "The best example of all and one of the greatest jobs of marketing the universe has ever seen is Nike. Remember, Nike sells a commodity. They sell shoes. And yet, when you think of Nike, you feel something different than a shoe company. In their ads, as you know, they don't ever talk about their products. They don't ever tell you about their air soles or why they are better than Reebok's air soles." Jobs asked his marketing team, "What does Nike do in their advertising?" He said, "They honor great athletes and they honor great athletics. That's who they are. That's what they are about."

Today, Nike continues its purpose beyond the sale of its shoes with the Nike Customer Relationship Network. They simply call it "Nike Plus" (Nike+). When you put on a Nike-compatible wrist band and register your personal data into their corporate CRN, you are provided access to monitor and track your "Just do it" progress. Download the mobile app, track your miles and your speed. You and your friends can even join a worldwide race all within the world's most popular runner's club. That's why Nike has been named innovator of the year by both FastCompany and BizBash.[14]

Nike expanded on its history of connection to famous athletes like Michael Jordan by connecting consumers to Nike+ Run Club coaches. Comedian Kevin Hart sponsored 5K runs around the world. His Nike+ Run Club, named "Run with Hart," connected the brand to 15,000 runners.[15] Today, with more than 28 million users, Nike+ has actually engaged more people than the famous commercials that once promoted the brand on TV.[16]

Why would the Participation Generation buy any other shoe brand? Nike provides the motivation to get started. Nike provides tools to help track and maintain your commitments. Besides, it's not very fashionable to wear Adidas while using the Nike app. When Nike felt the shift, they began to make the changes long before the waves of disruption reached the high ground where they previously stood.

It all started more than a decade ago, when Nike's CEO, Mark Parker bet the shoe store on emerging technologies. Cutting traditional media by 40% back in 2006, he redirected the funds toward a mobile app. Since then, Nike revenues and profits were both up almost 70%, and its market cap doubled, increasing its share of the U.S. shoe market from 48% to 61%.

When Nike was founded, there was little hope for an American branded shoe made in Japan to beat the Germans at their craft. But, since these innovations, Advertising Age has declared Nike the victor over Adidas by asserting "Adidas remains stuck on the sole of the shoe, whereas Nike has engineered a system for the soul of the athlete."[17]

BE A SUBMARINE

One strategy for taking on a tsunami is to be on a submarine. It's the international symbol for stealth power. They have a special advantage when they go out to sea. They are different from other boats.

One U.S. submariner posted the following account: "No matter the surface conditions, it's typically very calm while submerged. The only time we were ever affected by weather was when we had ported in Guam. A hurricane (or a typhoon in the Pacific, I guess) was headed toward the island, so we actually headed out to sea and submerged. With the storm raging 400 feet above us, all we noticed was a gentle side-to-side rocking of the boat."[18]

These great ships are out there patrolling the entire ocean, but no one is the wiser. Under the surface, new technology is operating in business, too, and it gives companies first-mover advantage in the midst of the black wave.

Harvard Business Review studied[19] the differences between companies that lead their industries and companies that lag behind. In this study, the leading-edge companies reported a much higher usage of real-time decision-making, customer-experience metrics and rewards systems. We are finding that laggards in digital customer experience miss out on more than just the "trendy tech spotlight." The sales of these lagging companies suffer, as well.

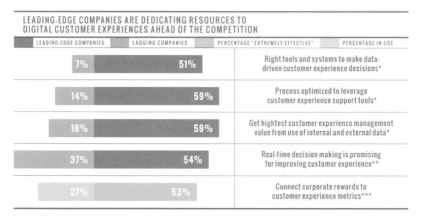

LEADING-EDGE COMPANIES ARE DEDICATING RESOURCES TO DIGITAL CUSTOMER EXPERIENCES AHEAD OF THE COMPETITION

LEADING-EDGE COMPANIES	LAGGING COMPANIES	PERCENTAGE "EXTREMELY EFFECTIVE"	PERCENTAGE IN USE
7%	51%		Right tools and systems to make data-driven customer experience decisions*
14%	59%		Process optimized to leverage customer experience support tools*
18%	59%		Get hightest customer experience management value from use of internal and external data*
37%	54%		Real-time decision making is promising for improving customer experience**
27%	53%		Connect corporate rewards to customer experience metrics***

"Lessons from the Leading Edge of Customer Experience Management." White Paper. Harvard Business Review, 2014 (Web)
Please indicate your level of agreement with the following statements. (Percent "Somewhat" or "Strongly Agree")
**In your opinion, how promising are the following emerging technologies for improving your organization's ability to manage the customer experience? (Top Five Emerging Technologies)*
***Please rate the effectiveness of the practices your organization currently employs to manage the customer experience on a scale from 1 to 10, with 1 meaning not at all effective and 10 meaning extremely effective. (All saying "extremely effective." Top box scores of 8-10; among those who routinely employ the relevant customer experience practices)*

In final analysis of their study, the *Harvard Business Review* concluded, "Leading-edge companies are dedicating resources to digital customer experiences ahead of the competition."

Like the stealth power of a submarine, it's amazing how new technology can help us face even the most disruptive forces of nature. But, what immersive innovation will defy the coming media maelstrom? Let's look at the leaders. While others are trying to figure out the future, four industries have seen the white crest of the black wave and are already silently leading the charge under the radar: health care, retailing, banking and entertainment. They are using owned media platforms to submarine the media industry with innovative media of their own.

Health care: Nike, Fitbit and, now, hospitals and health systems are developing wellness apps and discharge apps. Lives are being improved and even saved as the lines become blurred between marketing and medicine.

Retail: In addition to what Amazon is doing to define a new category, restaurants and franchise food chains have become online brands via mobile ordering apps. From retail food and QSR to consumer packaged goods and franchising, Customer Relationship Networks are becoming powerful to proactively meet every unexpressed consumer desire in real time.

Banking: Mobile banking technology is making every transaction easier with real-time access to services previously provided by a branch manager. No more lines, no more ATMs. No more cash. It's just a matter of time before we won't even need the credit cards in our pockets.

Entertainment: Apple TV, Netflix, Hulu and Amazon Prime are leading the industry toward a new kind of home-entertainment experience. This is the sneak attack of our generation. After the computer found its way to the family-room TV set, this audience watches what they want, when they want it, and without interruption from advertising. When this war is over, broadcast TV won't even know what hit the industry.

REBUNDLING HEALTH CARE

Technology is changing a $3-trillion industry. Actually, health care is facing a disruption of its own making. Before health care reform, the more people who went to see a doctor, the more money that doctor made. This has all changed because of new reimbursement legislation playing out under the banner of "Population Health Management." Now health systems and Accountable Care Organizations will get paid for performance. For the first time in American history, health care providers are governmentally incentivized to keep their local populations healthy. Hospitals will even face readmissions penalties if their patients don't follow the doctor's orders.[20]

Now, doctors are automating the care of patients through technology and connected home care services. It's called, "Self Health." By creating a more informed population, placing more of the responsibility on the patient and their family to manage their own care, the cost of national health care falls while quality goes up.[21]

How will health systems engage this new patient experience? Many are looking to that omnipresent device: the smartphone.

Mobile devices have changed our lives. Next, they will save our lives. Too good to be true? Tell that to the millions of Kaiser Permanente Healthy Lifestyle app users at who reported that they are losing weight (56% of them) and quitting smoking (58% of them). The health system reports that 70% of their nine million patients are active users of their patient relationship network. Initially, most of their patients were driven to access the network for a more convenient way to engage their physician, but now they are engaging in more advanced wellness and health management services.[22]

The Mayo Clinic has joined the telehealth revolution as well, reporting a 40% reduction[23] in cardiac-patient readmissions through its discharge app. In one significant breakthrough, Trinity Health System made headlines when they became the first to use heart rate data from a patient's Fitbit to properly diagnose and save a patient's life.

As the physician gets paid more for simply keeping people well, they will start pushing these apps, wearables and other new "internet of things" that will help individuals avoid ever having to go into a doctor's office in the first place. And, who wouldn't be OK with that?

Now that physicians are being measured against their ability to communicate with consumers, the practice of medicine has moved to the communications department. Don't make the mistake of installing brochureware about your health system on a mobile app. This new advertising is less about communication and more about improved customer experience and utility.

Don't look to the I.T. department to develop these strategies. The physicians are too busy with patients to make this a priority. The decision to build Patient Relationship Networks must come from leadership or marketing. This reminds me of a recent assertion by *Advertising Age*:

"Marketing can't just communicate your ethos anymore; it has to deliver access to your brand through mechanisms that let people experience the value in everyday life. That means the brand job only starts at aspiration and has to incorporate a range of technologies for realization."[24]

ARTIFICIAL PHYSICIANS?

Treating the well instead of merely treating the sick is a noble cause that is arising in the health care industry, so each battle is celebrated by all parties, regardless of the team that makes the win. One company featured in *Fortune*'s "Change the World List," IBM, will probably be at the forefront of the innovation that could unite the health care industry.[25]

IBM is working on a $100 million project focused on mobile health applications. The initiative is an extension of Watson, the artificially intelligent computer developed by IBM that competed in the show *Jeopardy!* Billed as the world's most powerful medical library, Watson was able to answer more questions than a room of medical physicians. Now, Watson is being reconfigured to respond directly to customer inquiries as a 24/7 health and wellness repository.[26]

Imagine if the world's leading medical supercomputer was unleashed on hundreds of millions of medical records. Once common strains of health conditions can be compared with lifestyle habits and minute-by-minute vital signs, we might find the cure for a myriad of diseases, previously misunderstood.

The race to big data in medical care is on. In a currently unrelated study by a compendium of leading medical groups including Henry Ford Health System and the University of Massachusetts, researchers are setting the stage for an individualized form of medicine called "Precision Medicine." The database from studies like these will provide insights from thousands of monitored volunteers to create a quantum leap in medicine toward predictive care that will treat patients before they ever get sick.

This new study of patient data and genetic markers for preventive health treatments could become the genesis of a new age of enlightenment that could extend life as we know it.

CASHLESS COMMUNITIES

Health care isn't the only high-security industry moving confidential consumer data online. Banks have moved nearly all functions of financial services so that soon we will never need to enter a branch at all, unless we want to.

Although PC-based banking gets high scores, studies show that consumers are not satisfied with the current level of service from mobile banking apps. Mobile represents 60% of all online consumer activity in every category of business, except banking.[27]

Why don't people use mobile in banking? It's not that they don't want to. The fact is that most banks don't provide the level of capability in mobile banking that they provide online at the trusted old PC. Perhaps the security issues and regulations born of the banking crisis of 2008 stalled app innovation. Whatever the reason, back to the desktop we go every time we make an online banking transaction.[28]

Self-service is the best service: Our studies[29] show the market is ready for a better mobile app experience. Among Millennials, twice as many say they would switch banks for a better mobile app than would switch banks for better personal service.

You would think the banking industry would have the motivation to innovate. When it comes to marketing, banks are a lot like beers. They all basically offer the same products, but with different labels. Regulation restrictions and commonly licensed products have created an environment that makes differentiation difficult.

For this reason, the best most banks can do is create a layer of technology to appear as if the "white labeled app" is a custom experience. Mostly, this layer is like a beer label. However, some banks are developing additional capability into the app that gives the customer real value beyond the standard industry experience. The next generation of bank apps will emerge to offer real-time consumer engagement to help customers build savings plans, budget their money and gain financial advice online that today they can only receive from a personal financial advisor.

RETAILERS BECOME ENTERTAINMENT STUDIOS

Instead of sponsoring Hollywood content, retailers are now producing and distributing their own movies. Amazon, Xbox and Walmart, just to name a few, have been opening their own production studios on their own smart TV applications.

What market force is driving this behavior? Let's start by understanding the perspective of major retailers toward Hollywood content. Walmart was historically the largest seller of Hollywood home videos in the world. In fact, walk-in traffic to buy DVDs has introduced opportunities to sell other Walmart products. Once Walmart discovered this phenomenon, the retailer began leveraging studio content by selling it below wholesale prices — just to draw customers in the door to sell other products.[30]

Following the Walmart playbook, Amazon discovered the same phenomenon on its online retail portal. By selling DVDs and streaming video below market cost on Amazon Prime, consumers became regulars. Regular consumers purchase other products, too. Premium content keeps them coming back, purchasing other products along the way, so more content is better.

When Amazon announced the launch of Amazon Studios and Fire TV, the retailer officially opened a store in the living rooms of its customers. This completes the ecosystem for the next movie studio of the future. Amazon Studios' original shows, including "Alpha House," "Goliath" and "One Mississippi," are available on any family room TV set that has online access. This positions Amazon to give Netflix a run for its money.

We often hear that Netflix is the dominant digital TV channel, responsible for 30% of all internet traffic at peak hours. Yet Netflix's $6.78 billion in sales actually pales in comparison to Amazon's $107.1 billion in total retail sales in the same year.[31] Amazon could give away its entire movie inventory as a loss leader, simply to leverage for sales of its other retail products. How could Netflix ever compete with that?

In fact, while Netflix is reporting $4.4 billion in gross sales, Amazon is reporting plans to invest $3 billion in music and studio content development, just to benefit and retain their loyal customers. This studio platform is a calculated move by this retailer. Amazon Prime members regularly spend almost double the amount on Amazon as non-members.[32] Consumers will find their way to where the overall value is best, and the future will be a battle for content supremacy.

If Amazon is becoming a TV studio, then Netflix may be forced to become a retailer, just to contend with Amazon's financial model. Think about this: As retailers move into the entertainment business, they will likely continue to subsidize the cost of their content as a loss-leader product. This will make sustainability difficult for any stand-alone entertainment network.

The trends look even more dire for the old guard in broadcast TV. Cable cutters are not moving to ABC.com, NBC.com or CBS.com. Most are switching to Netflix, Amazon Prime and Apple TV. Two of these top three networks sell entertainment as loss-leader products to build their primary retail business.

What will happen to ABC, NBC and CBS when their fiercest competitors don't need advertising revenue in their business model?

TV APPS ARE HERE

Traditional TV still works, very well. But, as advertisers, we must watch this trend and evaluate the return on our investments. What year will be the last year it makes sense to buy traditional broadcast TV media? Some experts predict the demise of this advertising space over the next decade.[33]

The online evolution of all media is inevitable as consumer patterns and advertising dollars find their way to replace all forms of broadcast TV with streamed programming. Perhaps brands will find a new way to reach out to consumers on web-connected TV sets.

Many brands will even create their own channels. For example, Red Bull was the first branded TV channel on Apple TV.[34] Many more are coming now that Apple has opened its TV platform. Remember the mad rush of iPhone apps when Apple opened its mobile platform? A *Harvard Business Review* study showed that people now spend more time in branded apps than they do watching TV commercials. The trend toward TV apps could be the new advertising.

What do TV apps have to do with advertising? People want free TV, and there is only one way to fund that — advertising. However, I don't see advertising's iconic 30-second spot retaining its hold in the digital space. Think about it. The whole point of digital TV is watching what you want when you want it. And, if you don't want commercials, there will eventually be a service somewhere that will gladly remove them for you. "Banner blindness" is a phenomenon that will only increase as consumers click the "skip" button for pre-roll ads.

No, advertising will not emerge the same way on Netflix as it currently presents itself on broadcast TV. Cable-cutters enjoy interruption-free TV. And, why in the world would they give that up if they don't have to?

Whatever it looks like, the future will be an exciting time of television innovation. And, advertisers will be the dreamers and inventors of a whole new viewing experience.

KEY TACTICS TO FIND YOUR PLATFORM

Finding a rooftop to shout from can be overwhelming. Advertising isn't so simple anymore. The digital landscape vastly expanded into a science-fiction novel. The line is blurred between advertising and apps, between medicine and marketing, between retailer and movie studio. The line is also blurred between advertising and entertainment.

The big wave hasn't hit yet, but water is leaking under the door of places that were once considered high ground. As previously separate disciplines wash together, we should take note of the signs. More change is coming.

There is no going back. Traditional media isn't gone yet, but the age of network TV dominance is almost over. Those currently in broadcast media just don't know it yet. Health systems, banks and retail brands are the future influencers of every aspect of culture. Branded content and branded channels will be their tools of influence.

The tectonic shift in media will be the convergence of retail marketing with entertainment. New platforms will define this new space. So we must:

1 **Build Customer Relationship Networks:**
Marketing innovators won't outsource their customer relationships. They won't buy the media, they will be the media. Leaders are already creating new customer experiences by leveraging digital platforms and loyalty programs in health care, retail, banking and entertainment.

2 **Go Out to Sea:** Investing in innovation is sometimes the most terrifying thing to do during a recession in any industry, but that is the most important time to look to the future. The drying up of the media industry is only a sign of a new wave of change that will create new industry leaders.

3 **Be a Submarine:** Being the leader often means being first to market. The submarine is a symbol of the sneak attack in competitive environments. As industries become commoditized, we need to change the game and provide new technology for new customer experiences.

Now is not the time to anchor our ships in the bay of last year's business plan. Leading brands are not doubling down on last year's model, they are taking their ships out to sea. While they are there, they are building new ships.

In a fascinating study[35] of the commoditization, deterioration and death of previously great brands, business consultant Clayton Christensen prescribes a steady dose of "disruptive innovation." He writes, "Core competence, as it is used by many managers, is a dangerously inward-looking notion." In his best-selling book, *The Innovator's Solution*, he says, "Competitiveness is far more about doing what customers value than doing what you think you're good at. And staying competitive as the basis of competition shifts necessarily requires a willingness and ability to learn new things rather than clinging hopefully to the sources of past glory. The challenge for the incumbent companies is to rebuild their ships while at sea, rather than dismantling themselves plank by plank."

What does this mean? How do we rebuild our ship while at sea? It's about continuing what works while building new platforms for the future. It's important to build your new platform for business to engage this new digitally connected consumer now, while you still can.

BLOG POST: JUNE 29, 2016 – Describing the future of gamification is like describing the color blue to a blind man. Consider these (relatively) surprising statistics:

- More than half (58%) of those ages 30 to 49 play video games.[36]

- Experts predict that the video game industry will reach $118.6B in revenue by 2019.[37]

- 59% of Americans play games, and the average household in the U.S. has at least two gamers.[38]

Tapping into this group isn't just appealing. It's necessary. How do we reach them and make a difference in their lives through gamification?

Could you imagine your mom saying, "Get off the couch, go outside and play some video games"?

No? I can't, either. But this is not your father's Atari.

Earlier this year, Pokémon partnered with Niantic — developer of the location-based game *Ingress* — to create the augmented-reality game *Pokémon GO*, set to release to mass market in July. You can literally capture Pokémon "in the wild" just like it was done on the show.

Some of the beta gameplay has also leaked online, giving a clearer picture of what to expect. Imagine you are at the beach, enjoying the sun with your family. You open the *Pokémon GO* app on your phone and scan the area with the device.

Your phone is showing you the water (the actual water you are seeing in the real world) through your device's camera when a Poliwag appears on the screen. Since they are water-dwelling, you'll only find them by water. The same goes for the rest of the game, with Pokémon only showing up in their natural habitats. Inside the app, you throw poke balls at the creature inside the app to capture it. You can access those captured Pokémon at a later time to have them do battle with other players' Pokémon in the game.

Even though I've never played Pokémon, I'm awestruck. For those of you who have an inkling of how this game is played, I'm sure you are, too.

And now we can begin to realize augmented reality's potential inside the realm of gamification. I'm spit-balling, but just imagine where we can go with this. While virtual reality creates a new world, augmented reality (or, in this case, gamified reality) engages us during our day-to-day activities. Finally, we can get kids off of the couch to go play games.

The brands that can find ways to leverage this new technological horizon will create the game in which we will all compete.

Imagine that you're at your local retailer, and you are able to collect coupons like you might collect Pokémon, and your team wins when a certain number of coupons are redeemed.

And guess what?

You just created a gamified loyalty app and scored gold for your client.

Game on.

[Only three weeks later, I posted the following to my blog. I wish I could take credit for being a prophet, but nobody saw this result coming. ...]

THIS IS NOT YOUR FATHER'S ATARI, PART 2

BLOG POST: JULY 20, 2016 – About three weeks ago, I originally posted on the upcoming *Pokémon GO* game (link to blog post), and it's been almost two weeks since the game launched. Two weeks ago, there were no users. Two weeks later, the participation wave hit with historic proportions. ...

- Nintendo's market cap has doubled to $42 billion since launching less than two weeks ago.[39]

- Pokémon GO has more daily users than Twitter and more engagement than Facebook.[40]

- Pokémon GO has 15 million users already (and it's about to launch in Japan).[41]

- A new marketplace has emerged selling impressive profiles and Pokémon trainers (humans) available for hourly rates.

- Restaurants and bars capitalizing on this wave are seeing sales surge; one pizza shop reported a 75% increase in sales.[42]

The engagement with this app is off the charts. This wave of participation is driving — or in this case, walking — Pokémon users right into restaurants, bars and retail shops that can capture these users and convert them into paying customers. Gotcha!

Right downtown where our office is located, I've seen dozens of "Pokémon zombies" wandering around with their phones up, ready to snag the next Squirtle that unveils itself. Some of the local restaurants and juice shops have signs out front saying things like, "Pokémon friendly. Come try our daily special."

Even as I was coming back to the office from a lunch appointment the other day, I saw a contingent of our creative department moving around the nearby bank parking lot with their phones — capturing Pokémon. This is now becoming the norm, and I still firmly believe what I posted three weeks ago:

"The brands that can find ways to leverage this new technological horizon will create the game in which we will all compete."

As this platform develops, we see the launch of sponsored stops. Imagine a bank which plays to this and hands users free water for stopping in. Then, instead of promoting a new checking account bonus of $100, they promote Pokémon gear, such as a bracelet, and a $50 iTunes gift card, so their customers can better compete in the game — showing that the bank knows what matters to different individuals.

Can you see the pizza place around the corner that establishes the new, sponsored PokeStop or gym and offers tailored discounts and giveaways to the team who controls the gym? Even today as I checked into a coffee shop on Yelp, they asked me "Is there a PokeStop nearby?"

The Pokémon revolution is just another sign of the Participation Age, another inkling of what is ahead. If last week you thought everything that will be invented already has been invented, just pay attention to what happened since then.

What will your brand do tomorrow? Will you compete on the Pokémon network or will you build your own?

6

BIG DATA SURFING

RIDING A TSUNAMI OF MEDIA INNOVATION

> ❝ It has not all been discovered ... Tomorrow can be as challenging and adventurous as any time man has ever lived.
>
> – Gene Roddenberry

Condition Black is the official status for everyone to stay away from the ocean — but that's when big wave surfers grab their boards and run toward it. The history of big wave surfing is full of chilling tales.

In the 1970s, no one believed big waves could be surfed in California. Jeff Clark changed that. At the age of 17, Clark paddled out to a spot where he saw huge waves breaking. When he first headed out to the mountains of water, his friend refused to join him and instead offered up that he would call the Coast Guard and tell them where he last saw Clark.

Jeff was the first to surf a towering behemoth at Northern California's Mavericks and then live to tell about it. At 25 feet high, this legendary recurring wave was nearly the height of the tsunami that crushed the city of Kamaishi, Japan, in 2011. Clark would be the only one to surf there for 15 years — long before big wave surfing was "invented."

Still surfing big waves today, Jeff described the feeling of riding the huge wave. "I kept my head down and paddled as fast as I could, thinking, if this wave lands on me, it could be really bad. My breath-holding will be tested as far as it can go."[1]

Surfers will tell you that if you can see a wave breaking close to you, it's either going to crush you or pass you. It's already a missed opportunity, and now it's time to look ahead. I am no big-wave surfer, but I've learned that the hardest part of surfing a big wave is getting up to the speed necessary to catch it before it breaks.

Big Data and real-time media engagement comprise the next big wave we all need to recognize. Actually, it is the wave you should have been ahead of, paddling furiously to catch a ride on it. It is the future of brand leadership.

The challenge with Big Data is that no one quite knows what to do with it. Real-time media are even more elusive to most marketers. Sure, we understand the concept — to an extent. We know what it is (again, to an extent). But we aren't sure how to harness its power.

Originally, surfing was a sport made possible by sheer force of human will, with surfers paddling their hearts out to ride waves. The bigger the wave, the harder one would have to paddle, but nobody could break the 30-foot barrier. Surfing "giants" the size of the tsunami that struck Japan seemed impossible.

That is, until Laird Hamilton, co-inventor of tow-in surfing.[2] Tow-in surfing provided surfers the power they needed to "paddle" at superhuman speeds by latching onto a Jet Ski or a helicopter. Hamilton and a new breed of surfers revolutionized the sport, surfing previously impossible walls of water, and finally breaking the 30-foot wave barrier.

In January 2013, only two years after the tsunami wrecked Japan, Garrett McNamara (professional big-wave surfer) used Laird's tow-in technique to *surf* the biggest wave ever recorded. At almost 100 feet, the wave McNamara conquered was three times the height of the tsunami that struck the town of Kamaishi.[3]

For perspective: Garrett's view from the top of the wave was like standing on top of a 10-story building. Most people would not believe surfing a behemoth like that was possible, except that it was caught on video.

Look up the video. I'll wait.

Insane, right?! Innovation found a way to surf a tsunami. The key was the innovative use of technology to get the surfer up to speed and ahead of the fast-moving waves.

Like McNamara's incomprehensible tower of water, Big Data provides unmanageable mounds of information. The enormity of data that we collect from consumers can seem untamable, but we can no longer ignore it. This wave is about to break, and we need to get up to speed. We can try to run from this new wave of disruption, or we can take real steps to actually surf it.

Emerging innovators have already found new ways to harness the power of Big Data. The Big Data surfers of the advertising industry are the programmatic media buyers. Like the tow-in surfers, they use machines to do what previously couldn't be done by humans alone.

Using an early form of artificial intelligence, digital-media buyers can analyze Big Data with enough speed to make it useful. With powerful data management platforms (DMPs), brands can engage millions of consumers individually, in real time, with immediately relevant branded content. These systems actually learn human behaviors and respond to consumer needs in real time. This creates a non-linear, non-interruptive experience that is beginning to look less and less like what we call "advertising."

Combined with new immersive viewing experiences and artificial intelligence, real-time marketing allows marketers the ability to engage millions of consumers on a personal level. As video games become more like movies, streamed movies will become more like video games. The end of linear TV content represents the beginning of a new generation of interactive and immersive advertising, the likes of which are nothing short of a scene from a sci-fi movie.

THE PARLOR WALL IN MY BASEMENT

Today, it's hard to imagine the novel *Twenty Thousand Leagues Under the Sea* was written in the 1800s. I used to think that story was just a Disney movie from the late 1960s. It's astonishing how the Nautilus technology dreamed up by Jules Verne was eventually brought to life in nuclear submarines more than 150 years after his fantastic vision.[4]

Once an idea is unleashed into the imagination of mankind, that idea will eventually find its way to reality. Consider the replicator from the TV series *Star Trek*. Like a small microwave oven, it materialized objects and food from what appeared to be nothing. Gene Roddenberry, creator of *Star Trek*, should have found a way to patent this unbelievable invention. Today, astronauts "beam" digital code from Earth to the International Space Station, where a microwave-shaped 3D printer prints a wrench, custom-designed for space station repair. Yes, that happened in 2015.[5]

If the replicator can jump from science *fiction* to science *fact*, what next? Remember the holodeck from the TV series *Star Trek: The Next Generation*? Will TV evolve to immersive and intelligent experiences that feel like real life? Inventors are already working on it. With all of the technology available today, we are only one imagination away from a revolution in the way we consume media content that affects our lives.

Where will all of this innovation start? Like all innovation, it starts with science fiction — before it becomes science fact.

As we take the next imaginary step into the future, consider this. The media innovations of the Participation Age will at first seem no less spectacular than the Nautilus or the *Star Trek* replicator. What initially seems impossible, will eventually change the world.

Take for example, social TV. When I first heard the term "social TV," I had to ask myself, "How would that work?" I know it seems like the next obvious step in the evolution of Participation Media, however, I couldn't establish context for why we would want it. I thought to myself, "Who wants to be interrupted by pop-up posts by friends during their favorite TV series?"

Then I said out loud, "I'm looking at it all wrong." Social TV will not look anything like Facebook or Twitter. And, even though YouTube and Vimeo offer participation video, that's not social TV either. Those channels offer nothing that we want to see on our big screen TV.

As I continued to ponder the future of social TV, a random thought reminded me of the "parlor wall" as described in the classic science-fiction work, *Fahrenheit 451*, by Ray Bradbury. In the 1953 novel, Bradbury first described audio earphones similar to the earbuds that wouldn't be invented until the 1990s. He described them as "shells" in people's ears. The story also depicts a fully immersive parlor-room television experience. Even more advanced than a modern video projector or big-screen TV, the first interactive video wall would not be developed until 50 years later.

In Bradbury's novel, it was the ambition of common folk like Mildred and Montag to own a four-wall immersive TV that cost almost one-third of their annual salary. On these screens, Mildred would spend her days interacting with soap operas as a participating character in the drama.

The interactive television series of the future was called *The Family*, and viewers spent more time with these fictitious characters than they did with their own families. The primary social behavior of the day would be to discuss *The Family* with friends and neighbors. Although this was a foreboding depiction of the Participation Age, it seems to be unfolding before our own eyes. If this isn't a vision for social TV, I don't know what is.

Of course, the world of *Fahrenheit 451* was a dark place that had no need for books or relationships, so our first inclination might be to fear this future. It was a dystopian vision of a possible outcome under an oppressive government that used media for control. The parlor wall influenced culture much like the holographic TV media in the world depicted by *The Hunger Games*.

Let's not go there.

The Participation Age is not about government-controlled media. It's not even about Hollywood-controlled media or propaganda from the media elite. This revolution is about "We the people" media. This is not a future to fear, but a future to fearlessly create for the sake of the consumers and brands we serve.

Let's take a realistic look at the future. The Sony Walkman and iPod earbuds were introduced decades ago, but these "shells" haven't yet turned us all into reclusive zombies. In fact, many of us use them for music to motivate ourselves while exercising or to focus while working. I use them to listen to books on business leadership.

Even the parlor wall exists today. I have one in my basement. It's a 90-inch theater screen with surround sound. That's where my family enjoys family movie night. It's also where my sons play Xbox. My young son who lives at home interacts with his big brother who is away at college. They each play characters in virtual roles and chat together virtually in a "parlor room" complete with surround sound.

The parlor wall actually brings my two sons together from a long distance while one is away for college. It's how they connect. They talk to each other on headsets and compete in games with other people around the world, making friends and building community in a whole new way.

So much for the media zombie apocalypse.

Bradbury's dark foreshadowing wasn't a warning about technology. It was depicting a hopeless future that could unfold if we neglect to use our imagination. It was an admonition about the importance of maintaining family relationships and free access to the knowledge provided in books and history. It was a caution to emerging couch potatoes of the 1950s, so they would not drone on under the spell of mindless media control.

Social TV might eventually take its cues from Bradbury's sci-fi vision, but it will probably empower more freedom for viewers to engage their creativity and imagination. More video game than broadcast programming, social TV will redefine entertainment. Like all potentially addictive behaviors, it will be up to the viewers to control their own obsessions with it.

Let's explore the possibilities of Social TV by imagining new experiences that will add value to our lives. We might even find a solution for how technology might bring families together. As Ray Bradbury said, *"Jump, and you will find out how to unfold your wings as you fall."*

As immersive technology evolves, so will our use of Big Data to engage a more personal experience. New agencies are already creating ads based on the specific lifestyle interests and behavioral habits of individuals.

Don't look to the web team for the solution this time: This movement is not starting with tech-heads or app developers. Of all places, the revolution is arising from the media department of ad agencies, and the unlikely hero is the data analyst.

Media buyers are using real-time media bidding systems including Google's DoubleClick Bid Manager, Trade Desk or Sizmek, and they are partnering with exchange networks including Rocketfuel or TubeMogul. This represents the first step toward an integrated data-management platform. The most advanced systems are being married to social-media listening tools and CRM-database platforms for ecosystems that will redefine the concept of "integrated marketing."

This all started as a practical solution to a simple problem. It used to be the job of media buyers to meet and interview the sales staff with each of the top five TV networks. They would negotiate in conference rooms. This process would take weeks and consume a significant number of man-hours on both sides of the table.

Today, we have millions of channels to choose from online. How can we treat media buying the same way? We can't possibly have millions of negotiations in sit-down meetings.

Enter real-time bidding.

To save time and money, real-time bidding systems were invented. They offer advertising inventory at the lowest cost as it comes available by the minute. Like an E*TRADE for advertising space, this process of bidding on millions of channels is best done by a computer. The humans simply focus on moderating and optimizing the parameters of the bidding system. And, the system automatically negotiates with every channel plugged into the network.

Think about it this way: Why commit a large percentage of your budget to any one channel in the digital space? With millions of channels, perhaps it's best to commit less than 1% of your budget to each major channel. Maybe Facebook is best today, but Twitter is more effective tomorrow. Have you heard of Vertigo? It's the hottest thing coming.

So stop trying to keep up with the madness by the minute. Program the computer to make better decisions, based on better data. The idea of sitting around a table to make these decisions from gut instinct and personal relationships has become silly.

We have data to help make these decisions: Big Data.

Of course, this data is only available in digital media buying, so we can't apply the programmatic model to traditional media ... yet. Don't think digital is only for banner ads. TV and radio have been quietly evolving into digital distribution for years. Keep in mind: Hulu, YouTube, Pandora, iHeart, Tunein Radio and Spotify are digital media sources. These channels represent a digital revolution that will eventually replace broadcast media as we know it.

When we advertise on these digital channels have data on who is listening to our commercials. We know their individual ages, gender, occupations, purchasing patterns and even their GPS coordinates at this very moment!

With the connectivity of digital radio, barriers to purchase have been eliminated. For example, there is no need to put a phone number in the script for your Pandora radio commercial.

Consumers will never need to read a credit card number over a phone either. With click-to-call features, digital radio listeners will simply activate a purchase through a credit-card-connected phone. This is not the future. At Daniel Brian Advertising, the digital media team ran several successful click-to-call campaigns in 2015. No phone number was ever mentioned on digital radio, but thousands of consumers called in.[6]

In these digital channels, we can directly link a single order to a specific ad. Now we can immediately know which ads on which channels deliver the best results at the lowest cost. Advertisers no longer choose specific publisher networks; we choose audiences and channels, such as video, display or audio. The bidding system automatically selects the best publishers at the most efficient price.

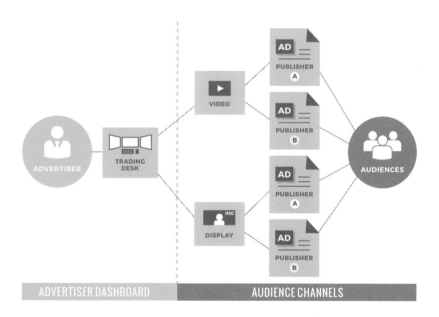

A good platform operator can set up the programmatic system to track cost-per-acquisition (CPA) for each advertisement that runs in the system. If channel A delivers a CPA of $1 and channel B delivers a CPA of $30, the system can be dialed up to focus more media weight on channel A, without the media team even having a meeting to discuss the optimization opportunity.

These systems are changing the conversations we are having in marketing departments. Optimization is a weekly topic. Here is an example of how a typical conversation between the client and agency goes down:

Client: "How is digital media doing?"

Agency: "The cost per acquisition on Pandora is $1, and the cost per acquisition on Spotify is $30, so we are currently shifting budget to Pandora. Spotify might come back when they offer click-to-call features to match Pandora's, so we'll keep them in the system at a monitoring level."

Client: "How is the other half of our radio budget doing in traditional radio?"

Agency: "We don't know. Does your call center track each ad to each sale?"

Client: "No, we've tried to track that for years, but the call center already has too many jobs to do."

Agency: "Then, we can only report impressions. About two million people heard the spot."

Client: "At $1 per customer, we can't afford to miss a sale in digital. Let's maximize our top-performing digital channels, then use the remainder in traditional media."

It doesn't take a genius to see that digital will eventually eclipse traditional media as more and more digital channels can offer bulletproof results.

Our clients never go so far as to quote the Bible verse from

Ecclesiastes 6:9, "A bird in the hand is better than two in a bush," but this dynamic of measurability is exactly why the shift to digital media is so dramatic. Digital media offers answers to the questions clients have been asking for years — "Does my advertising work?"

After a century as the dominant advertising media, we all watched in denial as print was replaced by digital display over less than a decade. Digital radio is currently replacing traditional radio much faster, and emerging digital-TV media will replace traditional broadcast-TV advertising with even more efficiency.

This trend toward digital doesn't mean traditional media is dead. For now, most of our studies show that traditional TV and radio still outperform digital alternatives for mass branding and gross sales volumes. In addition, our research shows that traditional media still provides the needed "air support" for our digital tactics. In most cases, we experience more than double the digital response rates when a proper traditional branding campaign is in place. So, don't walk away from the basics just yet.

No, let's not ignore the power of traditional broadcast and cable TV. As of the publication date of this book, broadcast TV has not been replaced with any meaningful mass audience in the digital space. Broadcast TV is still king of all media. It seems that people still respond best to advertising on a big-screen TV. However, if digital radio is a foreshadowing of digital TV, the next decade should represent a change in the guard.

Follow the data trail, and the future becomes clear. The rise of Apple TV, Netflix, Hulu, and HBO is gaining traction among the coveted Millennial generation. And, while the growth of "cord-cutting" has been both overstated and understated, there is still the reality that, little by little, Millennials are opting out of traditional TV services in favor of the digital options. More than 145.3 million people in the U.S. are watching television online. That's almost half of the population.[7]

Magna Global reports that soon, programmatic TV will account for $10 billion of TV budgets, or about 17% of all TV spending.[8] When we as advertisers can get real-time analytics on our digital-TV buys as we can on our digital buys, it will be very difficult to sell traditional TV to upper management, or even to ourselves. Perhaps this is why Hulu sold out of advertising inventory in 2016 and 2017.[9]

HOW DOES FACEBOOK KNOW I'M HUNGRY

Soon, Facebook will know more about you than you know about yourself.

Imagine seeing an advertisement for $2 tacos ... before your stomach had even growled yet. Through the AI that Facebook is building to help understand everything that you post, this is going to be commonplace.

So, is Facebook becoming Skynet? (A little shout out to all you *Terminator* fans.)

No, of course not. Although the phrase "Artificial Intelligence" usually inspires some factions of the population to warn against the terrors of a worldwide artificial-intelligence network, that representation of AI is fundamentally flawed. Sentient robots with nefarious intentions are fortunately not what Facebook has in mind.

Instead, Facebook is trying to really understand what its users are saying. Using neural networks and deep learning, the technology will use the millions of messages posted each day to learn how to mimic human brain activity. This will help Facebook to understand the meaning behind messages posted instead of just organizing them by keywords.[10]

What no one is talking about is how this applies to advertising.

An even bigger discussion is how we can couple AI with Big Data to deliver the best possible experience for users. Big Data is dark to us, and AI is the switch that turns on the light.

No human analyst can process quickly enough the amount of data that we have access to. AI is fueling the future of Big Data. The new challenge will be to generate the amount of creative output needed to talk to our new structured audiences.

Imagine driving in your car past a diner and you hear a familiar voice coming from your phone. Like an old friend, Siri will remind you of the time you ordered that great omelet with your friend Steve there, and that it has been awhile since you've been back.

If Facebook's AI works — and I'm sure they'll figure it out — the specificity with which advertisers will be able to target consumers will be enough to make any digital media buyer drool. By truly understanding the unfiltered messages that users post daily, coupled with already advanced targeting options, you will be near certain that the eyeballs you are grabbing are the right ones. Only Facebook would know: Tuesdays are taco days for me.

RETOOLING FOR AN AGE OF ADVERTISING INNOVATION

We will need a new breed of innovative advertising and marketing professionals to navigate this new media landscape. It will no longer be possible to separate creative from media as these two disciplines become co-dependent. Those who most understand the tools of this new media will produce the breakthrough creative ideas of this generation.

It's time for the media department to become creative. And the creative department needs to understand these new tools of media. The modern marketing artist will soon have a whole new palette of media options to blend and play with. As each new technology finds its way to reality, we need to experiment with them, so we can begin to understand their new roles in building brands.

New patents and new media technologies are being developed every day. Let's focus on just a few promising new innovations. Speaking with developers, trademark attorneys and industry insiders, we've aggregated the following list of inventions recently acquiring patents. The leading technologies to follow include hot links, embedded advertising, immersive experiences and artificial intelligence platforms.

Hot links: Soon, your TV remote will do so much more than select programming and control the volume. You will have the power to a highlight a car model in a film, inspect its features, tour the interior and even purchase the vehicle without missing any of the streamed program. Ladies will be able to pick out a dress from the closet of their favorite movie star, during the film.

Hot links are much more powerful than previous advertising models. With TV hot links, the purchase process will become dangerously easy. Consumers will no longer have to try and write down an 800 telephone number during a TV commercial. Instead they will click the remote to order products or services in real time. No need to hassle with payment either. The bill will simply be paid by your credit card on file with the digital platform. This will redefine the Home Shopping Network. Market insights will explode as advertisers will begin to measure the consumer interest in real time, rather than weeks after the advertising ran.

Embedded advertising: Often when I see a fictitious brand represented as a prop in a movie or TV show, it kills the authenticity of the story for me. Who drinks a beverage named "Cola" or eats cereal named "Snaps?" I'm sure I'm not the only one who feels this way. Branding exists in the real world, so why wouldn't real brands also exist in our fiction and virtual worlds?

This is not a new idea. Auto companies are paying up to $1 million just to feature their car brand in a video game. In-game advertising is already a $2.8 billion industry. Since 2008, Microsoft's Xbox and Sony's PlayStation have been placing dynamic in-game advertising (DIGA) into car-racing games such as Burnout Paradise, Gran Turismo and Forza Motorsport. These games are actually designed with blank roadside billboards and skeleton car models. Much of this can be skinned in real time from content that comes from an advertising deal long after the game was loaded into the home gaming systems. This comes with real-time analytics and CPM (cost per thousand impressions) reporting for the advertiser.[11]

Soon, similar technology will become available for brands to integrate into television programming. More and more movies and TV shows are being shot with "green screen" techniques that will allow brands to add content later. For example, a beverage container such as a can or a bottle can be painted green for the shooting phase, and Coke or Pepsi can bid against each other for product placement mere weeks or even days before air time. The technology creates a seamless experience that would convince any viewer that the branded beverage was on the set in the first place. Soon, hot links to this content will also be available, creating a new pallet of creative solutions for innovative advertisers.

Immersive experiences: With the invention of visualization technologies including the 360-degree camera and virtual reality (VR) head-mounted devices (HMDs), advertisers will be able to create new interactive engagements with customers. When flat video becomes dimensional, viewers become users and spectators will become players. We can't simply repurpose our flat content for this space.

VR promises immersive experiences: The World Chess Championship was the first sports competition featured. But, what next? Field seats at a football game. A trial getaway to Fiji without the 15 hours on an airplane. A test drive for your next vehicle purchase. And, of course we shouldn't neglect to mention, a one-on-one with one of the world's most iconic villains, Darth Vader.

These virtual worlds are hyper-experiential. VR creates an illusion where you feel like you're there, interacting and listening to a world that doesn't exist in the physical sense, but feels real nonetheless. Explore evidence at a crime scene. Listen in on conversations of characters. In the CSI of the future, you will be the detective.

Deep learning: Advertising will become more and more precise and effective as it becomes more intelligent. Major platforms are focused on making their content smarter. These systems are all beginning to become "aware" of your likes and needs, and they can even recognize your face. As news becomes aggregated by your moods and behaviors, so does advertising.

Search is becoming smarter too. Google's search engine now learns beyond keywords to the intent of your question. As Google learns what advertising might best answer your question, it can provide branded content that you actually want to engage. These systems will eventually remember a series of your search questions to build a composite profile of who you are and what you might need next.

I wonder if Google knows what I should buy my wife for her birthday …

As we explore new technologies like these, two voices will arise. The first voice will cry out, "Big Brother!" People have legitimate reasons to be concerned over corporate and government overreach into our lives. As Edward Snowden revealed in his analysis of these platforms, our data is dramatically surveilled and as a result, privacy and the 4th Amendment are all but dead.

The second voice will come from the creative class of society, and it will use these tools to engineer and experiment with ways for brands to provide more value to their consumers. Some of these experiments will become market-disruptive solutions, creating remarkable brands that will lead the world.

BREAKING THE 30-SECOND BOX

All of these new tools will provide a new palette for creative thinkers. Brand leadership will focus less on producing the best TV commercials. As broadcast media shifts toward digital, consumers won't have to settle for unwanted interruptions in programming anymore. New advertisers will disrupt the market with welcomed integrations that will no longer be confined to a 30-second commercial break.

We must remember: The consumer is in charge now. They don't have to watch advertising. Let's be honest: They never really wanted to watch advertising. They put up with it for years, viewing ads as the toll they had to pay in exchange for television programming. Every once in awhile, a great TV commercial has rewarded the audience with something meaningful or entertaining. But, for the most part, advertising has been an extraction of time that interrupted their lives.

To maintain its place as the primary funding agent of entertainment content, advertising will need to adapt to "advertising-free" environments, such as Netflix and AppleTV. These forces will place a demand on advertising to find its way to become desirable, entertaining and more culturally relevant than before. We can no longer force an annoying sales message into this new pipeline.

Don't worry: High-quality production video will not go away. It will simply evolve to a permission-based experience that will provide more entertainment or informational value to the consumer. Consider the current digital advertising for streamed TV content on YouTube. These digital video ads look a lot like TV commercials. In fact, these "commercials" have proven more effective. That's because they don't allow you to turn channels or skip them.

One study by Cadbury showed that an online TV commercial had more than four times the impact of a traditional TV spot. After all, current digital video advertising delivers a captive audience. Have you ever tried to skip or avoid a video advertisement?

However, most consumer studies show that viewers don't like the interruption at all. Designers of new platforms describe a future where advertising will be integrated into the digital content rather than interruptive. These advertising models will mature as more and more users move to digital TV.

For example, soon Facebook will be distributing more TV commercials to consumers than TV does. The silent, clickable video in their news feed is a welcomed model to many Millennials. Less interruptive, these TV commercials can be swiped away or played on demand. On Facebook, they can even save consumers' videos to their profiles, for watching and laughing again later or for sharing with others. TV can't compete with that.

THE FAMILY ROOM TV SET

The old TV spots won't work in this new space. The first five seconds are critical in this medium, because that might be the only part most consumers see. Sound is irrelevant during those five seconds because viewers won't be able to hear it anyway. That begs the question, "What will our TV spots look like with subtitles?" And, maybe it's time to consider using vertical aspect ratio on these videos, which shows up mostly on mobile devices. Disruptive, permission-based advertising like this will become more and more relevant as the industry makes this transition.

Nielsen released a report that projects the initial growth for streamed TV advertising will shift to networks such as YouTube and Hulu. Netflix, Amazon Prime, Apple TV, and Xbox could eventually be forced to offer advertising to remain relevant and get their slice of the advertising pie.[12]

Unfortunately, even the best consumer studies don't predict what this advertising will look like in the future. The fact remains that advertising as we define it today does not exist on an Amazon, Apple TV or Netflix.

The shift from traditional broadcast advertising to this type of streamed TV advertising can be mapped by projected ad dollars. According to MyersBizNet and Nielsen, digital video advertising represented $6 billion in 2013, and traditional TV represented $69 billion. At that time, no coordination or integration could be found between the two. By 2016, digital video more than doubled to $16 billion. On top of recent media, much of the existing traditional media also became available online. Less than half of that was delivered as traditional interruptive TV commercial advertising during programming, such as what can be viewed on Hulu.[13]

At the current rate of transition, digital video is expected to eclipse and almost fully converge with traditional media by 2020, growing to reach $116 billion.

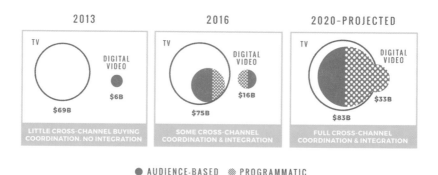

MyersBizNet Media and Marketing Investment Data and Forecasts, January 30, 2013.

The biggest shift will happen on the family room TV set. Some of us are old enough to remember when cable TV began to offer ABC, NBC and CBS. Many of our parents paid the cable subscription and never bent another rabbit ear again. This is what it will feel like to switch from traditional cable TV to digital streamed TV. Today, some content exists in both online and offline channels, but in the near future, digital channels will contain all the same content, plus content that will never be available on broadcast channels.

All we are waiting for is the online distribution of live events, such as sports or politics. It's coming. CBS recently signed a digital partnership with the NFL to deliver streaming of the network's live games to their viewers. CBS won't stream these games for free, however. Access requires a fee-based sub-scription to CBS All Access. This is just the beginning of the retooling taking place on the family room TV set, as four million viewers streamed the Super Bowl live online in 2016.[14] Even more viewers digitally streamed the first presidential debate between Hillary Clinton and Donald Trump later that year.

Netflix already has most of the regular programming offered on ABC, NBC and CBS, but it also adds exclusive programming that's arguably better than what broadcast TV has to offer, including the highly acclaimed series *House of Cards, Orange is the New Black* and *Stranger Things*. Many people subscribe to Netflix for access to these programs alone.[15]

This form of branded entertainment will most likely remain platform-exclusive (i.e., these programs are produced by Netflix exclusively for the benefit of Netflix subscribers). This is what makes the Netflix platform so sticky. CBS responded with the launch of their ALL Access platform and, in 2017, released a new original show, Star Trek: Discovery, as an exclusive show only available to their All Access subscribers. Of course, the first episode was free on the network during primetime, driving more viewers to subscribe to the exclusive platform.

Other winners in this shift will include emerging platforms that offer the latest advertising technology. For example, I love watching the snowboarding documentaries produced by Red Bull and North Face, and I always want to have the best snowboarding gear. Watching these branded entertainment programs on Apple TV, there is no commercial advertising, so currently, I am a missed opportunity for a sale. In the next five years, I'm sure brands won't let opportunities such as this go to waste. With the emergence of interactive advertising on networks that will compete with Apple TV, I will be able to simply click on the gear that my favorite pro is wearing and buy it while watching the documentary. Sweet!

Unlike the pushy and irrelevant advertising platforms of the past, this new wave of integrated advertising will act as a service of convenience, creating connections among the experience, the product and the consumer. This represents an opportunity for first-mover advantage. When the full force of digital integration hits broadcast TV, there will be little time to react. The winners and losers will be defined quickly.

None of us knows what the future will be. But like the school children who survived the tsunami in Japan, your brand will need to have a plan to move to the high ground. When the Third Wave hits with interactive advertising, it will be too late to start exploring branded entertainment models for your brand. Now is the time to find out what is going on. Now is the time to meet the speed of this great wave and drive new innovation that can set your brand apart.

THE GAMIFICATION OF EVERYTHING

I remember when Atari came out in the '70s. After all the changes since *Pong* and *Combat*, interactive technology is just beginning to mature. It's not just for kids anymore. Perhaps that's why average gamers are in their mid-30s. As I played the new *Star Wars* video game with my kids recently, I felt as if I were playing in the movie that I grew up watching as a child.

Of course, what appears to be amazing technology to me is considered normal by my kids. This generation didn't grow up limited by one-way entertainment experiences. They have an expectation to experience whole new worlds that they can live in or even create on their own terms.

This new trend in gaming appears to have overtones of world domination. If we consider ourselves the offspring of a creative God, is it possible that our very DNA cries out to emulate our maker? As creative people designed to want, do and be more, why would we want to do anything less than create worlds of our own?

This is the power of modern gamification technology. From

Farmville to *Zoo Tycoon* and *Farm Simulator*, world building is a growing theme in gaming. *No Man's Sky*, *Battle Plans* and *Destiny* either focus on exploring the universe or taking over the world. Games like *Fallout 4* sold 12 million copies, worth some $750 million, in the first 24 hours. That's more viewers than the Emmy Awards had in the same year, and three times the revenue of *Star Wars: The Force Awakens'* entire opening weekend.[16]

Have you even heard of *Fallout 4*? Or, were you busy watching the Emmy's during its lowest viewership in recent history?

Now, these games are so well produced, I've had my kids' friends come over just to watch other kids playing a video game. These games are more like movies than games. Players don't just want to compete with their opponent in the game — they want the backstory, so they know exactly why they are competing. These games are basically interactive feature films.

As TV becomes more interactive, how will there be any difference between the two? It's time to start paying attention to this Black Wave. In our lifetime, we may very well experience the transition toward the gamification of everything.

Just consider the astounding statistics: At 80% penetration, more people own a gaming device than have a subscription to cable TV. An astounding 42% of Americans play for at least three hours per week. Most gamers are men, but women now account for 44% of all gamers, mostly due to mobile app games. For the first time since Atari, video gaming meets the definition of mass media.[17]

It's a law of human nature: Mass media attract big brands. Tiger Woods, Tony Hawk and others have had their own game titles. I'm surprised there's not already a Nike Sports series. Perhaps Tony the Tiger needs a magical world to explore. What if the Keebler Elves were a game?

Don't laugh. Consider Pokémon. The brand exploded after venturing into its own app-based game, growing its revenue to $46.2 billion that same year.[18] And, if Pokémon wanted to launch a snack food or cereal of its own, it could give both Tony the Tiger and the Keebler Elves a run for their money.

This wave isn't too big for your brand. Somebody at Pokémon had to imagine a future beyond the trading cards and kids toys. Somebody had to start with the faith of a child before they could engage a generation of children. You can, too.

INVENTORS HAVE THE FAITH OF A CHILD

Consider the innovative children who survived the tsunami that struck Kamaishi, Japan in 2011. Why were the survival rates of children so much higher than the survival rates of adults in their town? Some theorists believe they were saved by the very fact that they were children. Adults make plans. They lean on their experience to repeat patterns of the past. Children have no such patterns to cloud innovative thinking. Innovation is a way of life for a child. They have no routine. No patterns. No proven models to use again and again. So, children are free to come up with brand-new ways of solving brand-new problems.

The school children of Kamaishi were taught by Katada to use invention rather than experience to map their way out of the disaster area. That is why the children were more effective against the tsunami than were the adults in Japan that fateful day. There was no historic record of a tsunami like the one that struck Japan, so experience worked against the adults. The children were taught to believe in a wave much bigger than any adult could imagine, so they survived a wave much greater than anyone else could have expected. You can survive the pending tumult too, but you will need to start by gaining the faith of a child.

Before we begin to reinvent the advertising and media strategy for your brand, it's critical that your team builds its foundation on a strong philosophy toward invention. Invention grows from the fertile ground of humility. Pride makes leaders blind to foresee their need for change. It's important to note that successful inventors are often described as being humble with curious and child-like passions. They seem almost disinterested in protecting their pride.

Consider the stereotype of the absent-minded inventor. Such stereotypes are born of reality. Often, forgetful minds are driven to solve problems in new ways simply because they lack the skill to remember. These inventors are not inhibited by pride in their experience, simply because they couldn't recall the past if they wanted to. Often, these inventors have been made fun of their entire life for having this characteristic. Many did terrible in school because they could not recall specific facts for a simple test. This has been the record of school drop-outs such as Edison and my grandfather. However, this forgetful trait makes their minds humble and therefore powerful to imagine new possibilities like children can.

A child-like mind is powerful if managed by the discipline of an adult. Children have no fear. When it comes to invention, fear of failure is a self-fulfilling prophecy. People never succeed when they are afraid to try. That's why invention never takes place in a culture of fear. As leaders, we must control our temptation to protect our pride. Like children, we must charge through our fear of failure. We must encourage a culture that rewards the attempt and seeks the learning, rather than punishing negative outcomes. To succeed, we must learn to hope, trust and believe like a child believes.

Inventors, like leaders in any good endeavor, will passionately affirm the importance of a "no lose" mindset. That means they have a keen understanding of the science of trial and error. The great ones will tell you it's impossible to lose, because success brings satisfaction, but failure brings wisdom. As Nelson Mandela said, "I never lose. I either win or learn."

My grandfather was an inventor. I learned a lot about innovation philosophy from him. He had a hand in many mechanical wonders we take for granted today, from the axles on our cars to the hydraulic garbage truck compactor. I used to love his stories about how he built a shop in Detroit to invent things that were used to win World War II. He would also tell me how invention is not about brains or education. He described invention as an attitude of faith and hard work. It's about believing you can do anything you are willing to work for.

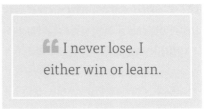

❝ I never lose. I either win or learn.

He once told me a story about how he invented the solution for a problem with the development of a critical component on the first U.S. satellite in space. NASA needed to make a perfect metal sphere. All of the educated engineers couldn't figure it out. Over and over, they would grind down a solid block of metal into a perfectly round shape. But once it cooled down, it always deformed into a useless egg shape.

While the engineers worked hours with their calculations, he went out into the shop and brought back a perfect sphere. My grandfather was only a hired hand with an eighth-grade education at the time. When the humbled engineers asked, "How did you do it?" He simply answered that if it's wrong when you make it right, perhaps the answer is to make it wrong. He overcompensated the diameter of the grinding to address the shrinkage. Once it cooled off, the perfect sphere was formed by the laws of nature. These are laws that he never fully understood; however, he learned to take command over them by the power of raw belief.

To inventors like my grandfather, "impossible" is just a word lazy people use as an excuse to give up. It seems that invention requires a well-developed tolerance for failure and starting over. My grandfather was often called "lucky," to which he would paraphrase Thomas Jefferson with the response, "That's true, I am lucky, but it seems that the harder I work, the luckier I get."

There is no rest for inventors, because innovation isn't a one-time event; it's the constant lifeblood that flows within any successful leader or growing company. Great companies are defined by creating the game that their competitors will eventually be forced to play in. But even successful companies that invented the industry they lead must always innovate to keep up with the competition. This is how Apple held its own against IBM in the '80s and '90s. This is how Samsung already is challenging Apple for the next decade.

That doesn't mean your brand always must be first to market, but it's important to be first to integrate other people's inventions to solve an unmet demand. Keep in mind: Henry Ford didn't invent the car. He didn't even invent the steering wheel or the assembly line. Long before Ford Motor Company, Packard invented the steering wheel and Oldsmobile invented the assembly line. What Henry Ford actually did invent was a platform to ride the unmet wave of demand for the world's first affordable car.

Similarly, Steve Jobs didn't invent the first MP3 player; he was just the first to integrate a music library within an MP3 platform. He simply made it easy to use.

Don't start by inventing things you want to sell. Start by finding problems that need to be solved. As Thomas Edison said, "My main purpose in life is to make enough money to create even more inventions ... I want to save and advance human life." Ultimately, he was relentless in his thousand attempts to make a lightbulb work, not just for more money, but because he was driven to make people's lives better.

Thomas Edison is not alone. Many great leaders have found that when we make things better, money won't be a problem.

Let's take, for example, Walt Disney. Often cited for being an innovator, Disney did a lot to improve entertainment. Nobody would argue Disney was a great storyteller, but it's unfortunate how history has overlooked his role as a great inventor. Disney used so much new technology in his storytelling that it could be argued he built his entire success on a platform of media invention.

Disney...

... *was first to use sync sound:* When sync sound was invented, Disney was first to experiment with the technology. He first tried it on a mouse animation called "Steamship Willie," and Mickey Mouse was born. Without the disruptive innovation of sync sound, Mickey would probably be just another silent cartoon character, forgotten in history.

... *created the first color cartoon:* Shortly after Technicolor was invented, Disney signed an exclusive two-year agreement with the technology, and led the industry in color animation by owning rights until Disney's competitors became irrelevant.

... *produced the first animated feature film: Snow White* wasn't just the best animated feature of its time; it was the only animated feature of its time. Before Disney, nobody ever thought it could be done. There was no competition. Again, Disney invented the space.

... *built the first theme park:* When Disney decided to launch a park, he was not satisfied with the state of the common amusement park. He actually redefined the industry using Hollywood set design, animatronics and storytelling, so that Disney could invent the concept we call the "theme park."

I've often heard young talent tell me they want to be the next Disney, and their end goal is always to make theme parks and animated movies. However, I think they have a wrong view of Disney. Looking at the pattern of his life, it doesn't seem that Walt Disney would be working on his next park or animated movie.

Of course, he was a storyteller. But not just in parks and movies. His legacy depicted a man who was not driven by his fame or even by his art. Disney said, "I am interested in entertaining people, in bringing pleasure, particularly laughter, to others, rather than being concerned with 'expressing' myself with obscure creative impressions." This passionate purpose drove Disney to many firsts. He only lived long enough to make his impact in film, theme parks and animatronics.

Disney's commitment to invention begs the question, "If he were still alive, what would interest Walt today?" I believe he would not only take great interest in digital media, but also he would be the leader in engaging parents and children to bring them smiles through the use of new technology. He might be telling new stories through the use of big data and digital media. The possibilities would have piqued his interest, just enough to coax him in and drive him to dabble in it.

The inventors of *Pokémon GO* weren't afraid to be the "next Disney." Perhaps your brand could be the "next Disney," too.

 ## THROTTLE YOUR SUNFLOWER

There is more than one way to surf a tsunami. On Oshima, a once-beautiful tourist island off the coast of Japan, everyone was running to the hills when the big one hit in March 2011 — but one man ran to his boat.[19] Susumu Sugawara, a 64-year-old sea captain, powered up his pride and joy, the *Sunflower*, quickly passing his fleet of boats as he said goodbye to them all. Some of his other boats were larger. Some had more amenities. He chose the *Sunflower* because it was powerful and could get out of the bay quickly. It was small enough to be agile but large enough to sustain big waves and hold 20 people at a time.

When the earthquake struck, Sugawara knew that if he could not get his boat out to sea fast enough, the island would be cut off without hope of rescue. In an interview, he told CNN, "I knew if I didn't save my boat, my island would be isolated and in trouble."

Other ships tried to get out with the same intent, but the wave came much quicker and was much larger than they had expected. All but the *Sunflower* were lost at sea. Sugawara was not out to sea yet when the big wave came. He said, "I pushed full throttle," ramming into a wave he estimated at more than 50 feet high. He climbed what he described as a mountain. "When I thought I had got to the top, the wave got even bigger." When the captain could see the horizon again, he knew he had made it. Following this, there were four or five more waves that he could remember.

Going back to the island in complete darkness, Sugawara was able to navigate the *Sunflower* nimbly around the wreckage of houses, debris and the remaining fleet boats that were destroyed off the coast of Oshima Island. One ship was so big after being plunked on land, the whole city seemed to be buried under its hull. Under the expert guiding hand of Sugawara, the *Sunflower* spent the next 20 days making hourly trips as the only remaining connection to the mainland for transportation, supplies and help.

One supermarket owner who had given all his food away became Sugawara's assistant. He spoke of Sugawara as the island hero, saying, "Everyone used to look out for themselves on this island, but after this, the whole community is now helping each other."

Although going out to sea is sometimes the best option, not all ships made it out of the harbor. Some were too big; some were too slow. Others did not have the 42 years of seagoing experience as did the captain who navigated the *Sunflower* that day.

Pictured Above: The boat, "Himawari," translated Sunflower.

GO BIG BY GOING SMALL

After the tectonic changes have already taken place in Customer Relationship Marketing, we need to assess the best way to build our teams to address this change. As with Sugawara and the *Sunflower*, bigger isn't better. The huge ships offering seeming safety actually don't have the agility necessary to power over the wave of change that is coming to the marketing and advertising industry.

For example, Thomas Edison's "Muckers" of Menlo Park, the core team at the famous "Invention Factory," was a small group of fewer than 20 innovators, possessing every skill needed to work very fast.[20]

Like Edison, Walt Disney was known to crash together various disciplines into what his team would call "Imagineers." Disney explained Imagineering as "the blending of creative imagination and technical know-how." Biographer, Sam Gennawey described Disney's role on the team as "project cheerleader."[21]

One thing Walt Disney knew more than most was the importance of building a roundtable of experts. He understood that innovation doesn't happen in silos of expertise. From the development of trains to props and animatronic robots, Disney was a master of bringing together set designers, engineers, architects and storytellers to collaborate on a single task. Disney found breakthroughs came from bringing together people with diverse perspectives or divergent experiences. Then even though they held opposing opinions, he could keep them together, maintaining passion for a common cause.

BUILD CRASH TEAMS

Disney and Edison both understood that when divergent ideas converge, they create a new idea. Similarly, digital marketing requires the crashing together of varied expertise for higher levels of system integration. It requires a united force of creative minds, media experts and analytics experts. They all need to talk with one another and, in real time, integrate ad-tracking pixels and meta data from corporate CRM and accounting systems. Many brand managers have been limited by fragmented departments, fractured agency relationships and political blockades within an organization.

Because of the common practice of separating their traditional media department from their digital media department, 66% of marketers are not using data from digital advertising to inform traditional media, including TV, radio and print. But it will no longer be possible to separate digital from traditional media as these two disciplines become co-dependent forces. Integration will become crucial to making it all work together as budgets shift toward digital over time. True integration requires leadership and accountability from the highest levels of the organization.[22]

Hopefully, you have a full-service advertising agency. If not, the first step toward integration is to put digital media and traditional media under the management of one media director. Second, if your media team is separate from your creative team, you have a lot more work to do. Integrating separate firms isn't easy when they are accustomed to working independently. For that reason, most digital agencies are terrible at making great creative content, and most creative agencies are terrible at digital analytics, so pick your poison. You will need to prioritize your goals to develop a united team, but keep it lean and agile for change. This is where you will have to "throttle your *Sunflower*."

A PICTURE OF INTEGRATION

What does integration look like? It will take a concerted effort for both your internal team and your advertising agency. Your team will need to establish the foundational components of an integrated analytics engine, as well as interpret data and translate it into consumer profiles to be used in direction for creative content. In an industry fragmented by niche branding agencies and digital firms, specialization has become the enemy of integration. Industry leaders are breaking the silos between traditional and digital media for three reasons:

Team alignment: All media solutions involve digital now. With the emergence of digital radio and digital TV, many of the creative assets are shared between media. Breaking it up among specialty agencies creates confusion and team conflict. Integration and centralized planning end the fight over who "owns" digital content in your marketing mix.

Budget alignment: As budgets shift from traditional to digital, clients need an unbiased voice to trust when assessing options and recommending proper weights. Consider human nature: If we continue to break up media into buckets of digital and non-digital solutions, the various departments will continue to fight over politics and power, rather than what is best for the brand.

Content alignment: We will only optimize our impact as we unite the "branding agency" with our "digital agency." This is the best way to eliminate costly redundancy and conflicting creative messages to improve advertising productivity. It used to be possible to coordinate a strong creative team with a separate but strong media team. New media platforms cannot be developed without the involvement of the creative team, so these teams must be brought together under one lead digital strategist.

Worst of all mistakes would be to hire one agency for the strategy and a different agency to execute the creative. We know better than that now. Remember, the consumer brain doesn't respond to analytical stimulus. It responds to creative stimulus. If your strategic team makes the error of testing ideas without a creative presentation that simulates the real world, you will most definitely get a false positive result, as we did for CHI St. Vincent before we tested creative concepts.

Furthermore, if your strategy team is not creative or innovative in their ideation process, you will never get an innovative hypothesis to test. As we say in research, "One bad idea tested against another bad idea gives us the best bad idea."

Another thing: Don't get enamored by the colossal size of an agency or proprietary platforms. The playing field has flattened. A digital trading desk is best managed by a single person with a small support staff. Like managing an Excel spreadsheet, nobody sells the power of Microsoft Excel anymore. It's about the user and the facilitating integrated working conditions for the various unrelated skill sets. Today's crash teams will look a lot smaller than the assembly line models used in the past. They will reflect Edison's model in Menlo Park and Disney's model of Imagineers.

If fewer than a dozen scrappy guys can design Disneyland, your crash team can build a platform for change with even less.

Thomas Edison always limited his innovation teams to 10 or 20 people at most. No matter how big his factory eventually became, he insisted that he never again was as productive as when the original "muckers" of Menlo Park produced more than 400 patents from only a handful of hard-working machinists, craftsmen, scientists and laborers.

Remember, the *Sunflower* only had room for 20 people. This presents a good rule of thumb for a crash team. So, "throttle your *Sunflower*."

Platforms are also important, but don't get carried away with software systems either. Digital media and CRM planners all use the same systems now. The hidden secret is that each agency brands them differently. Whether they use Salesforce or HealthGrades as their CRM platform, whether they use Google DoubleClick Bid Manager or Trade Desk as their media buying platform, they all support the same channels. CRM platforms all offer email analytics. Programmatic platforms all buy space on Google, YouTube and Facebook. And, with modern exchanges, all have the same buying power now. Gone are the days of the big agency software systems. They will never be able to keep up with the artificial-intelligence models being built into Salesforce's new Einstein platform. They call it "artificial intelligence for everyone," and that's just one option of many to come.[23]

Look for a strong core creative content team with proven analytics reporting. If anything, the larger agencies are like the larger ships off the coast of Japan. They can be slowed down by their weight. They become encumbered by their holding companies, confined by dated platforms they built to compete with much more powerful systems that have become available to everyone. Without a need to justify past investments and platforms, modern mad men can work in small groups that can stay nimble amidst the changes. These are the firms that will navigate emerging brands into leadership positions without warning.

The advantage of integration will be a common measurement for evaluation. We cannot continue to depend on impression counts to determine media effectiveness. What matters more than impressions is sales, and digital integration can measure sales. How else will we keep the media honest? It wasn't long ago that the *Wall Street Journal* reported Facebook was caught overestimating video viewing time by 80%. That means advertisers were paying Facebook for 10 minutes of video, but only getting two minutes viewed by consumers.[24]

Digital is not alone in ongoing erroneous reporting. Many traditional TV rating systems are equally flawed. In fact, the latest numbers show that for every 10 minutes of video advertisers pay for on traditional TV, less than one minute ever gained the attention of a consumer. Even less was remembered. This is why a level playing field and sophisticated auditing systems are critical to any media buying platform.

In the past, we didn't hold TV accountable for specific results. We just knew it worked. In fact, we still do. Our team can show study after study of brands that use TV to grow awareness, preference and sales. In case after case, brands that use TV increase awareness more than via any other media. In case after case, direct response sales more than double when accompanied by TV, but we can't put a finger on exactly how, who or when the impact of TV was made on the consumer.

In digital media, we have more data, so it's being held to a higher standard. Immediacy is the new rule being held up against digital, while traditional TV and radio still get a pass. How do we equalize this disparity? How do we narrow this gap?

We each need to measure our own campaigns. We each need to create test cases of our own. Now that we can measure costs per acquisition, we can provide real time reports on what advertisements are working on which audiences and at what times. This is not a software platform you can buy. This kind of reporting will require a common "project cheerleader" who will be responsible for CRM to digital media buying and traditional media buying, as well as internal purchasing and accounting systems.

The maps built to develop such a network can be perplexing and overwhelming. But, don't fall into the trap of doing nothing for the sake of not knowing where to start. Start something. Start something now. Make it little at first. Start with a small, integrated team with small, measurable initiatives. Then it will have a fighting chance to grow.

RIDE THE 80/20 INNOVATION CYCLE

During a lull in film production, Walt Disney would often become worried about how to fund the creative staff. Due to stress, his doctor actually advised Disney to pick up a hobby. Disney decided to work on miniature trains. He loved to get his hands dirty. He built everything himself. His passion for small trains led to bigger and bigger trains. In order to find a lot big enough for his next train, he decided to design a theme park.

As a busy manager of the business and an onlooker to his brother's distraction with trains, Walt's brother Roy didn't want anyone to use Disney Brothers film funds on Walt's next hairbrained idea, so he forced Walt to form a new company so that he could keep tinkering around without risking harm to the foundational movie franchise. Roy offered Walt $10,000 when Walt began his dream for Disneyland. They formed Walter E Disney Enterprises (WED) to allow Walt to have his own sandbox to play in.

But by the time he formed WED, Walt was not just playing anymore. He deeply believed that he could save the film company by establishing another source of work to keep the creative team busy. Plus, he decided, it would be fun.[25]

Don't think innovation is only for big companies with lots of resources. Don't tell yourself you don't have a big enough marketing budget to add innovation to your media mix. Our study of the greatest innovations show that the opposite is true.

As with Disney, there is no need to put at risk the core business model if it is currently healthy and financially sound. Start small.

Clayton Christensen is a leading thinker on practical business innovation models. From his study of hundreds of companies disrupted by innovation, he has discovered that to remain sustainable, innovation must be balanced against the core competency of your industry.[26]

So, don't cancel the TV campaign. Take a breath. Don't dump your whole marketing budget into an experimental digital venture. That would be the wrong conclusion from our findings. As marketers, we cannot afford to risk current brand equity in favor of a future that is not sustainable yet. However, we all know innovation must be a way of life in these changing times. So, what is the proper balance when we go to throttle our *Sunflower*?

In our study of innovation, we have discovered there is an 80/20 rule at work among successful business and marketing leaders.[27] We must take into account the reality that all innovation presents risk. Just as a financial advisor recommends to keep your high-risk, high-reward stock investments capped below 20% of your total portfolio, a marketing investor should follow suit.

Some innovation is ahead of the curve, and other innovation is behind the curve. Even if you have the perfect idea for the future, but your timing isn't right, you may fail. This is why innovation brings such scrutiny. And, scrutiny of marketing innovation is never scarce. If innovative marketing gets a win, the team doesn't get much recognition for the success. After all, isn't successful marketing the job of the marketing department? However, if innovation fails, the target is placed directly on the team that caused the failure. For this reason, many marketing departments become innovation-averse.

This means we must build in a certain tolerance to allow for error, without putting the core business model at risk.

Experts in innovation have come to understand that innovation is a balance. In his study of the performance of hundreds of companies over two decades, Jim Collins learned that key innovators always "preserve the core" while maintaining a culture to "stimulate progress." His model uses the yin and yang symbol to illustrate the tension between the two key forces in a healthy business.

His study of businesses that sustain change concluded that a company should never let the core competency become an anchor to innovation. Yet, we should never let the core business model be put at risk during the innovation window. This model toward innovation is captured in his famous statement, "Avoid the tyranny of the 'OR.'"

We must always look at our marketing model in two parts. The core business must be maintained to sustain the current business challenges, while the future progress of the business entirely depends on innovation that will deliver very little revenue to the bottom line for what could be years.

These opposing forces present a constant tension among leadership. Visionary leaders love to explore the new ideas that will bring the company into the future. Operational leaders drive the focus on maintaining stability by emphasizing current market demands for product delivery. Who is right? Who is the better leader? If an answer were that simple, everyone would be great leaders. The reality is that proven leaders have been found to be experts at managing the tension, rather than eliminating it. More art than science, this requires a thoughtful balance.

If you ever have been surfing before, you know that there are those who are better at balance than others. You can't take a class on it that will help. You just have to go out there, face that wave and get pummeled over and over. The last time I went surfing, the pros told me to relax when a big wave hits me. How strange. I thought to myself, "How am I supposed to relax, when I'm about to die?" Then, I got it. Fear is the problem. It sucks the life out of the surfer.

Fear sucks the life out of a brand manager or a marketing director, too. Eventually, you will hit the wall. You will face your own innovator's dilemma. Fear will tell you to stay down. Anxiety over past failure can make you think you will never come up again. That is normal in surfing. It's a normal tension in business innovation, as well. Don't fight it. Just get used to it.

Consider the tension that existed between Apple's founders, Steve Jobs and Steve Wozniak. Not unlike the relationship between Walt Disney and his brother Roy, Jobs was the visionary leader who was always focused on the next thing, while Wozniak was focused on actually making and finishing what they had started together. In fact, "Woz," as Jobs called him, was not excited about the distraction that the Mac represented to the core business of Apple. At the time, revenue was almost entirely driven by the Apple II, but Jobs was spending most of it on the Mac. This created famous tension between these two icons of Silicon Valley. Perhaps this tension wasn't the problem at all. Could this tension have been core to Apple's success?[28]

History has proven that the Apple II funded the Mac and the legacy of the most celebrated brand in modern history. This dynamic between the "business visionary" and the "business operator" must be understood in terms of resource allocation. In order to reliably operationalize innovation, our first instinct is to explore a pie chart to graph resource allocation toward a specialized group or innovation lab. However, that model of resource allocation assumes that we should divide the focus of the core business. Innovation experts agree that we should never divide the core business focus, but rather we should leverage it.

Instead of a pie chart, our team prefers to use the bicycle image representing two wheels as a way to describe the unity of two pie charts working together. This keeps the innovation unit separate from the core business unit. However, we don't use the image of a modern day Schwinn or Huffy bicycle. That would assume innovation should get equal resource allocation as the core business gets. Imagine the one wheel much bigger than the other, as in the 1800s bicycle called a "High Wheeler."

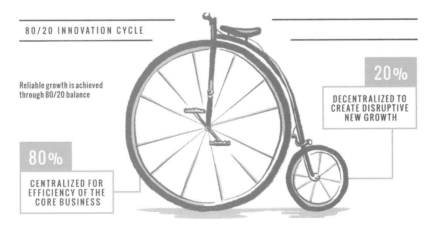

80/20 INNOVATION CYCLE

Reliable growth is achieved through 80/20 balance

20%
DECENTRALIZED TO
CREATE DISRUPTIVE
NEW GROWTH

80%
CENTRALIZED FOR
EFFICIENCY OF THE
CORE BUSINESS

This "Innovation Cycle" presents the larger wheel or larger part of the pie chart as the core competency of the business or marketing strategy. The smaller wheel or part of the pie chart represents the initiatives that are focused on the future of the business or marketing strategy. As a rule of thumb, we use the

80/20 rule. As long as 80% of the marketing budget is spent on tried-and-true models of marketing, you can expect to get 80% of the results that are necessary to grow and maintain the business. That leaves up to 20% of the marketing budget for innovation and exploration of new media options. The worst-case scenario is that 20% of the marketing budget is lost, but the best-case scenario is that the 20% accomplishes more than the 80%.

Often this gamble isn't a gamble at all. The one proven concept in marketing history is that lack of innovation has been the death of many businesses. The reason we use the 80/20 rule is that over-innovation has also been the death of many businesses. Never bet the farm on a single long shot. This is how innovators lose. While the core business has a rigid approach, the crash team should have more freedom to explore. At the peak of Thomas Edison's innovative run, one new recruit stopped him to ask about the rules at the Invention Factory. Edison simply replied, "There ain't no rules around here. We're trying to accomplish something."

However you approach innovation, what is most important is that you can maintain a sustainable model for innovation. *How* you do it is as important as *that* you do it. Great innovators would rarely say, "Innovate or die." That statement adds more rules and puts too much stress on an unknown future. Worse yet, it would put fear into the core business team. A great innovator would prefer the phrase, "Innovate to live." This puts innovation in the context of balance versus a desperate, last-ditch maneuver of a dying brand.

As a business owner, I understand how innovating while maintaining a strong core marketing model can be like changing a tire on a car while driving 100 miles per hour — although, that analogy isn't very helpful. Jim Collins' analogy using firepower seems to get the point across much more efficiently.

In his more recent book, *Great by Choice*, Collins uses the analogy that we should save our "gun powder" on innovation by using various amounts of it in the battle for the future. In this analogy, corporate leaders should fire small gun shots to understand the trajectory of a sustainable concept, followed by the cannon.[29] The cannon should only be fired at an innovative concept after an idea has been fully vetted and determined as predictable. This is why we should always focus on extensive testing and research for any creative approach.

CREATE YOUR OWN CASE STUDIES

With all of the benefits available from new technology and big data, it would seem that industry-wide integration would happen quickly. You would think case data would be available to students of marketing. However, this is not our reality. Many marketers are still manually making media choices based on instinct and old models of mass media impression counts, rather than measured results. In a survey conducted by SocialCode, a group of 80 CMOs admitted to no use or limited use of big data in 2016.[30] In a supporting study by Iron Mountain and PwC, only 4% of the businesses said they were able to extract full value from the data they already have.[31]

The problem of big data integration is similar to the problem faced by Katada, who was trying to figure out how to get the citizens of Japan to run from a tsunami. The people all understood the threat of the tsunami. They all understood the importance of high ground. But, nobody wanted to be the first to run. Looking for somebody to lead, they were left to stand there and stare at the ocean as an imperceptible 500 mile per hour seismic wave came rushing toward the shoreline. They were overconfident in their walls and their old maps that showed the pathways of tsunami of the past.

Don't fall in the same trap. Don't get caught up on using last year's media maps and don't become paralyzed looking for case studies about the future. Data doesn't come from the future. Data comes from the past. This is why data is not very helpful for innovation. The scientific method prefers the use of hypothesis instead. If we wait for the collection of data, we will never even begin the process of innovation; we could only hope for incremental improvement, at best.

There is no big data warehouse that stores the world's data. Amazon won't give you their data, and Google wouldn't dream of giving away their proprietary knowledge. In some industries, including health care and banking, it's illegal to share consumer data, so there will never be a common Big Data repository. Therefore, each brand is on its own in this regard. The data will come from your own digital media activity, so just start doing something and measuring your results. At first, it will feel like Ray Bradbury's analogy of jumping with a plan to "unfold your wings as you fall," but Big Data starts by building your own small data.

Simply start heading for high ground. Nobody wants to admit they don't have all the answers, but somebody will eventually need to step out and take a risk. As we often say in digital advertising, "Every C-suite executive wants to see something new, and three examples of how it worked before." Of course, we use this phrase in jest, but the reason we all laugh is because we all relate. The executive who will rise above the others will be the one who takes the risk and leads as a first mover.

66 The right audience is more important than a big audience.

In an article published by Adobe's CMO, former brand manager of Procter & Gamble's Tide, Todd Morris said many marketers "think they're using data, but they're really at step one of a 10-step process."[32] He explained that in the early '90s, P&G held a belief that mass marketing and owning large segments of consumers was critical to their success. However, new data analytics have proven this theory wrong. In fact, he now tells us that 80% of all sales from new consumer package goods come from 2.5% of all shoppers. We are now finding that the right audience is more important than a big audience. Over time, and with careful testing, Big Data is the secret to identifying these hyper-targeted audiences and their "look-alikes" with great accuracy.

This is probably why P&G moved toward a highly targeted digital-first strategy as early as 2013. The brand publicly committed to spending 35% or more of their $7.2 billion in marketing outlays that year on targeted digital media, with a long-term goal of 70% going to programmatic media. Less than two years following this strategy, the company said it would cut back because, P&G's Morris, "We targeted too much, and we went too narrow, and now we're looking at: What is the best way to get the most reach but also the right precision?"[33]

P&G quickly learned that targeted media is also expensive media, and offers fewer options for the emotional impact delivered from sight, sound and motion. During the course of tracking their results, P&G began moderating their buy to bring more traditional television back into their media mix.

Although P&G has stumbled as an early mover — in fact, adding to the woes that the retail titan has been facing in its sluggish core business — the digital leader has voiced no regrets for moving ahead of the market. As they say, "It's impossible to steer a boat that's not moving at all." Now P&G is miles ahead of its competitors in understanding this new wave of consumerism.

For the early first movers, digital marketing is no longer the test.

For some, digital carries the core business model. Although P&G has not yet found its sweet spot in the digital arena, other digital-savvy brands including Amazon have already refined their consumer pathway down to the purchase. This ongoing analysis has led Amazon to increase its digital spend to 91% of its $1.5 billion in marketing investments. Most of this will be allocated toward digital search strategies. This does not include the estimated $3 billion Amazon spends on branded entertainment, in the form of music and featured original movies and TV shows from Amazon Studios. This effectively makes branded entertainment two-thirds of Amazon's marketing budget.[34]

AMAZON MARKETING MIX

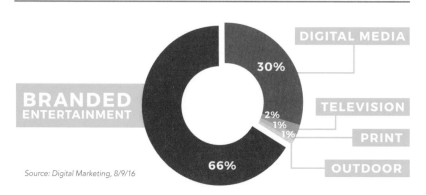

Source: Digital Marketing, 8/9/16

This commitment by Amazon is telling. Keep in mind, Amazon has the best analytics on effective advertising in the industry, yet the brand is all but absent from traditional media. When was the last time you saw a TV commercial for Amazon.com?

To give some perspective where advertising is headed, below are the total advertising expenditures by media, showing that digital tied with TV as the No. 1 medium as ranked by spending in 2016, and projections show digital continuing to increase annually toward almost half of all media spending by 2020. Keep in mind, digital video is becoming the new TV branding medium of choice, representing more than 20% of all digital spending, and growing faster than all other categories.[35]

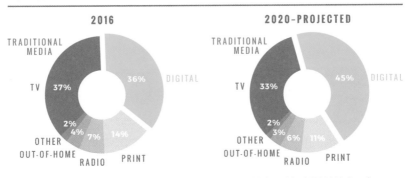

2016

2020-PROJECTED

TRADITIONAL
MEDIA

TV 37%

DIGITAL 36%

2%
4% 7% 14%

OTHER
OUT-OF-HOME
RADIO PRINT

TRADITIONAL
MEDIA

TV 33%

DIGITAL 45%

2%
3% 6% 11%

OTHER
OUT-OF-HOME
RADIO PRINT

eMarketer, March 2016, U.S. Spending report

THE NEW DIGITAL FUNNEL

Here's an example of the type of case studies that are emerging from the industry. These new digital analytics are actually causing marketing teams to update the consumer funnel.

The CRN consumer funnel is slightly different than a branding funnel. It measures specific conversion points from the mass-reach media through behaviorally targeted media. On the next page is a marketing funnel modeled from a study by the Boston Consulting Group to illustrate a consumer purchasing journey for a real-world test that was performed in the consumer packaged goods (CPG) industry.[36]

As the consumer moves closer to the conversion point, the conversion rate is higher, but sales are attributed to various points throughout the pathway.

In the updated marketing funnel on the next page provided by the Boston Consulting Group, we can demonstrate the specific points of conversion where consumers engaged the CPG brands that were in the study. Each number directly correlated to a communication point in the marketing funnel. For example, mass media at the top of the funnel tracked 30 direct sales while behavioral analytics measured 280 direct sales.

Don't think you can use this chart to analyze and plan your next digital media campaign. After Google and BCG finished this analysis, they were intent about the following disclaimer: "The timing of the techniques along the purchasing journey in this chart is one example; it can differ by campaign. The number in each circle is the indexed number of users who made a purchase, averaged across test campaigns in the study. The data is based on an 'equal attribution' methodology in which equal credit went to each targeting technique used during a consumer's path to conversion."

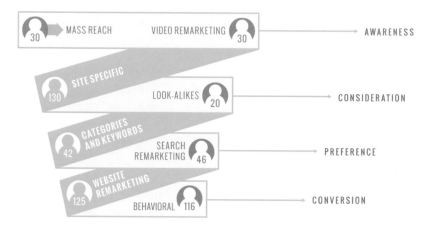

Of course, the data can tempt us to gear up for increased keywords, search, website remarketing and behavioral retargeting, but that was the mistake P&G made. As P&G learned the hard way, the bottom of the funnel is merely the end of the pathway. In essence, that type of thinking would be akin to the previous generation saying, "We get most of our results from our 800 number, so let's invest in more 800 numbers." As my director of media platforms likes to say, adding more digital search marketing would be like adding more tellers at a bank or more cashiers at a grocery store. They simply take the order that branding inspired.

Let's not allow data to make us dumb, and let's not allow calculators to make marketing decisions for us.

It's important to note that this report is the same kind of data P&G used to make the wrong decisions that it finally reversed by 2017. It's always tempting to remove branding when direct marketing becomes traceable and proven. However, direct marketing and digital analytics alone don't take into account the importance of emotional connections or branding at the top of the funnel.

Since a "share of heart" analysis was not performed in this study, we cannot conclude the importance of the mass-reach branding media and video remarketing in the early stages of the consumer pathway. Think about it this way: Even love at first sight rarely leads to a trackable marriage proposal in that very moment. We realized that we needed to account for time and repeat connections with our consumers. So, we built our own test to track the impact of branding in digital marketing.

SHARE OF HEART ANALYSIS

In 2016 and 2017, we performed a new analysis[37] of the consumer pathway for retail brands. By separating two markets, offering branding supported by direct response marketing in one market and only direct response marketing in the other, we learned the answer to advertising's most elusive question. Which half of our advertising works?

Interestingly, the markets that invested in branding media at the top of the funnel experienced 2.4 times more sales in the bottom of the funnel. In other words, if the consumer experienced no emotional connection through a branded story, the exact same direct response media and messaging produced less than half the results as it did in the markets where branding media was present.

No, branding is not the half of advertising that we don't understand. New analytics are revealing neither half of the advertising budget has been wasted. In fact, building a strong emotional connection through mass branding media is critical to your direct response effectiveness.

Let's apply these findings to the new digital funnel. Since the we know the lower-funnel media produced 790 conversions in our model, we can create a "share of heart proxy" for the impact of branding. Using our findings that top funnel awareness generates 2.4 times the response at the bottom of the funnel, we can estimate that the branding provided by mass media and video remarketing at the top of the funnel produced an estimated 461 of those conversions. Redistributing these brand-induced conversions evenly to the top of the funnel, we can attribute 671 conversions, or approximately two-thirds of all sales conversions to branding.

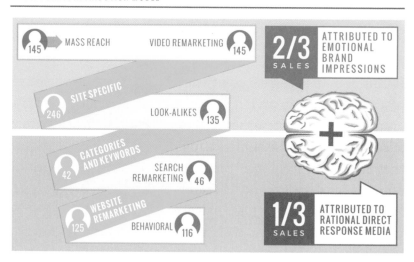

FULL FUNNEL ATTRIBUTION MODEL

From our calculations and "share of heart" metrics, we were able to build a full funnel report. We attributed approximately two-thirds of sales to emotional brand impressions, and one-third of sales were attributed to rational call-to-action or promotion, through direct response media.

This confirms our earlier findings that emotional appeals drive preference, while cognitive appeals close the gap by driving action. Because the actual conversions for most of these sales were tracked at the bottom of the funnel, we can conclude that either end of the funnel cannot exist without the other.

Brands including P&G have learned this phenomenon the hard way, so you don't have to. Although this benchmark can be helpful, this model represents early findings in a single industry study. It's clear that each campaign we track will require human intervention to both question and understand the metrics, and this spotty science will remain yet an art for some time ahead.

KEY PRINCIPLE NO. 3:

LEADERS DON'T HESITATE

For his most important lesson of all, Katada encouraged children to avoid hesitation, saying, "In general, people don't evacuate even though they know they should. It's natural to be reluctant to escape when no one else is escaping. So I told the students that they must be brave and be the first ones to evacuate. If you do, others will follow you and you can save their lives, too," he said. "And that is exactly what happened."

For black wave surfers, this means taking our brands out to sea. Our final marketing principle for the age of digital consumerism can be summarized in one picture of a boat cresting on the edge of a 50-foot wave ...

 ## THROTTLE YOUR SUNFLOWER

It would seem safer to stay on shore or even run for the hills during a tsunami, but thanks to one brave soul who ran to his boat and faced the tumult head on, his whole community was saved.

Likewise, our study found that companies who played it safe and focused strictly on their core competencies always failed to make the transition in times of innovation. Conversely, companies that create a sustainable balance toward innovation, gradually adding new competencies, have been proven to create new markets and grow at a healthy rate — especially during times of great disruption.

We have discovered several best practices for being an innovator that will prepare us for this new age of consumerism:

Have the Faith of a Child: Great innovators will not need pedigree or titles, but must possess a passionate belief in a better future without regard for fear or pride. Great leaders prepare for failure, but they don't expect it. When things go wrong, they won't give up. They will allow sufficient time for failure and second or third attempts at the goal.

Build Crash Teams: Innovators will break out a separate, smaller team to develop the new innovation. As the project cheerleader, you will need to build and align a diverse set of media skills, technology expertise and creativity tightly working together toward a common goal.

Ride the 80/20 Innovation Cycle: Innovators will build small case studies and trials before risking the core business on a new idea. By remaining sustainable, innovators will survive to celebrate failures, because of the lessons they bring.

Create Your Own Case Studies: The secret to Big Data is that you have to build your own. Because data comes from the past, we all need to start now, so we can build a platform to sustain the change that's surely coming.

Back to the observation established at the beginning of our journey: "I know at least half of my advertising budget works; I just don't know which half." This is certainly not a new dilemma. Most people attribute this quote to Henry Ford, so it's clear that this is a challenge which has plagued the industry since before our modern concept of media was invented. We believe it's critical to revisit this question annually for the brands we serve.

Under the shadow of the black wave, we determined to finally ask ourselves the question: Is advertising broken? Or, is it merely changed? So, we evaluated the impact of digital marketing against the old broadcast media models. Tests were performed by Daniel Brian Advertising with a national retail chain that will remain unnamed for the sake of confidentiality. The test included more than 500 store units distributed throughout the USA. The study was conducted over the course of six years in the real world, during the peak of the social media revolution: 2010 through 2016

It was a natural test because the chain was broken into four groups, based on voluntary inclusion into the corporate marketing campaign. By opting in or opting out of the various parts of the campaign, our retailers provided us with a clear picture of the various media options.

The first group, which we called "broadcast stores," included broadcast TV and radio. The second group, called "digital-only stores," included digital only; and the third group, called "digital + broadcast," included TV, radio and digital marketing. The final group was called "non-participating stores" because they did not opt in to any of the advertising for their markets. This acted as our natural control group.

The results of this real world test were as follows:

Broadcast stores vs. non-participating stores: Broadcast stores that supported media costs with 5% or more of their total revenue toward TV and radio experienced between 10% and 15% higher total sales increases each year. Spending nearly $1 per person in the target market per year over six years, the broadcast stores achieved an 86% awareness level. That statistically placed them tied for No. 1 in awareness for the category. The non-broadcast stores experienced no significant change in sales or awareness.

Digital + Broadcast vs. Digital-only stores: All participating digital stores received on average a 188% return on investment, after expenses and directly related to their digital spend. But the results were much higher for stores that added broadcast TV and radio. Stores that ran an integrated campaign, including both digital and broadcast media, were able to get 140% higher conversion rates on the digital call-to-action than those who ran digital media only.

Digital + Broadcast vs. non-participating stores: The stores that did not participate in the advertising campaign experienced a 1% drop in sales, matching industry trends, while the stores that participated in the full digital and broadcast campaigns experienced an 8% annual increase in year-over-year sales.

The effectiveness of digital media was unmistakable. One digital blitz among the participating stores more than doubled total sales to more than 200% over normal sales levels for the duration of the event.

Of note, some of the participating stores increased the price of their primary product by 17% over the price of the non-participating stores and sales actually went up 4.37% for those locations.

In summary, participating stores experienced both better

margins and higher sales volumes, just by adding the corporate advertising campaign to their mix.[353]

Concerning the traditional media versus digital media question: We did not find any evidence to support an "either/or" position. Both clearly worked best when used together. Although digital represented nearly 25% of the budget by 2017, an annual study will be needed to determine the future weight to distribute, based on the specific objectives of the brand.

These are early metrics in the study of an evolving digital environment. Yes, advertising works. Advertising isn't broken. It's merely changing, and we need to change our model to adapt to it.

KEY PRINCIPLES FOR SURFING A TSUNAMI

History is full of stories of people who have run from a tsunami. Captains of great ships have powered through a tsunami, but could it be possible to surf a tsunami? Countless tsunami researchers have told surfers it's impossible to even consider such a feat. But they forgot to tell Chris Nel.

Nel was surfing off the coast of Samoa with some friends, when an 8.3- magnitude quake launched a shockwave in his direction. Being from New Zealand where they feel quakes all the time, he said, "I didn't really think too much of it, so I went for a wave and caught a few." Then as he recounted, "All of a sudden the water went real weird." Nel said, "We started moving real quick, getting sucked out to sea … The reef completely dried up. It looked like a volcanic riverbed — it was just gone."

Nel and his four friends pointed their surfboards out and headed to the deep water, rather than heading for shore. Then it happened for the first time in recorded history: Five surfers faced the waves of their lifetime for 45 minutes, timing the surges and surfing the tsunami, while the remainder of the surfers and villagers by the shore were washed into the jungle. Nel described surfing and surviving the tsunami as a "pretty full-on experience."[38]

We don't need to fear the drying up of traditional advertising models. We don't have to run away from the black wave threatening to decimate the media industry. But what new innovation will defy this media maelstrom? How will we go about inventing it? And, who is qualified to invent such disruptive technology?

Those of us who steward advertising investments have not only the opportunity but the responsibility to drive marketing innovation. If not us, then who? The shift toward new media technology is a chance to reinvent advertising and help our brands survive, and even thrive in the face of the wave of disruption emerging from consumer-driven media.

If we are going to reinvent advertising, where will we start? Like all forms of creativity, invention starts with a blank page. We fill it with ideas that come from random connections all around us.

It's all about our attitude. We must tap into our basic human instinct to make things better. We must have profound faith in a greater purpose. The seeds of innovation grow in the fertile ground of innocent minds, not bound by the word "can't." Inventions exude from childlike faith that is set free to imagine fantastic possibilities.

Entertainers, marketers and media innovators have already proven that they will find a way to bring consumers what they don't even know they want or need. As new media tools continue to emerge, wildly creative people will manifest a future that we cannot fully predict. However this future unfolds, there is one thing we can depend on. With all of this new capability, the media is not likely to stay the same.

Followers of these trends may survive the shift, but not if they are living in denial or far behind. Those followers are the ones who will be crushed by the force of this consumer movement. The Black Wave riders will find a way to create this future by leading, not following. These pioneers will position their brands to win new levels of market share that the world has never seen. There is still room for your brand to participate in this movement. In fact, this movement has barely started.

Start small, but look at every opportunity. You will find inspiration in your next social media campaign. You could build your platform by looking at your loyalty app in a new way. You could build a crash team by introducing your digital analytics team to your creative team. There are so many places to start, and so many questions to ask, and we have the time to address all of the challenges, but only if we start now. In fact, these challenges are common to us all, and nobody has it all figured out yet. Just stay curious, innovative and don't play it too safe.

What is most important is that we get out of the mindset that advertising is a formula consisting of interruptive media space that will always be there for us to purchase. As more and more consumers opt out of that definition of advertising in their lives, we must reinvent our approach. We must go back to the original definition of advertising. The word was invented by a storyteller for the purpose of storytelling — long before digital media existed.

Today's media environment presents a new canvas for the marketing artist, so we need to understand the new palette of tools available to us. These tools bring the power to connect with consumers at a deeper level than ever before. For this reason, it's important that we understand and stay true to our core purpose and values. Programmatic media doesn't have purpose. Data analytics don't have values. People do. We cannot depend on machines to do this work for us. We must go back to the principles that made advertising great in the first place, and get busy.

Most important, let's learn the lessons that only children can teach us. The Miracle of Kamaishi was the result of Toshitaka Katada embedding three concepts into the minds of the survivors:

First, follow principles, not pathways. Don't put too much faith in outdated assumptions. The past models might not work, so question next year's plan if it doesn't inspire a passion for innovation. Like Katada, we must flip Maslow's pyramid in our brand management model and turn followers into leaders. Not to serve ourselves. Greater results have been proven in serving others.

Second, lead with an innovative attitude. As the old platforms of media fail us, we must overcome our fear of being a first-mover onto new platforms. Our teams need to learn to act as leaders and inventors rather than wait to follow other market forces. Be resourceful. Find a rooftop and shout from it, if necessary, but focus on a platform that will bring authentic value to those you serve.

And finally, don't hesitate. In the words of Katada, "It's natural to be reluctant. ... So I told the students that they must be brave and be the first ones. ... If you do, others will follow you and you can save their lives, too. ... And that is exactly what happened."

There is a wave of change upon us. Some will run from it. Some will go out to sea. Yet, an amazing few will become bold enough to run toward it and surf the tsunami. We will thrive after this great shift is over. At least some of us will, as long as we actively prepare for it. And as long as we actually do something.

Only one question remains for us to decide before we go forward. How will your brand participate in this new wave? As the wildly successful advertising spokesman and former Chrysler CEO Lee Iacocca once said, "Lead, follow or get out of the way."

NOTES

INTRODUCTION: The Third Wave: Lessons from the Tsunami that rocked the world

1) The 2011 tsunami was a well-known natural disaster, talked about countless times in varying media venues. In order to paint a complete picture, a combination of sources helped develop the story of the tsunami that rocked the world on that fateful day in March.

    Oskin, Becky. "Japan Earthquake & Tsunami of 2011: Facts and information." LiveScience. Purch, 7 May 2015. http://www.livescience.com/39110-japan-2011-earthquake-tsunami-facts.html. Accessed on 10 Nov. 2016.

    "How the Japan Earthquake Shortened Days on Earth." Space.com. Purch, 3 Mar. 2011, http://www.space.com/11115-japan-earthquake-shortened-earth-days.html. Accessed on 10. Nov. 2016.

    Onishi, Norimitsu. "Japan Revives a Sea Barrier That Failed to Hold." The New York Times. The New York Times Company, 2 Nov. 2011. mobile.nytimes.com/2011/11/03/world/asia/japan-revives-a-sea-barrier-that-failed-to-hold.html?_r=0. Accessed on 10 Nov. 2016.

2) "The Miracle of Kamaishi," as it came to be known, was written about in the aftermath of the tsunami in many ways. Toshitaka Katada's principles set the standard for tsunami evacuations in the following years. Several sources were consulted in order to describe the pre- and post-tsunami landscape and the Miracle of Kamaishi.

    "Miracles of Kamaishi as a result of following 'Three principles of evacuation' Students all safe thanks to disaster reduction education." Translated by SEEDS Asia, SEEDS Asia. MSN Sankei News, 13 Apr. 2011, http://www.seedsasia.org/hp/EJET/k_8.pdf. Accessed on 11 Nov. 2016.

    Thompson, Christopher S. "The Study of Hope in Kamaishi." Social Science Japan Journal, vol. 13, no. 2, 2010, pp. 241–247. www.jstor.org/stable/40961266.

    Kamiya, Setsuko. "Tsunami Hero Continuing Disaster Education Efforts". The Japan Times. The Japan Times LTD, 30 May 2013. http://www.japantimes.co.jp/news/2013/05/30/ national/tsunami-hero-continuing-disaster-education-efforts/#.WCXmRcf5zox11. Accessed on 11 Nov. 2016.

    "Disaster Management Education in Kamaishi." Consulate-General of Japan in Atlanta. http://www.atlanta.us.emb-japan.go.jp/hts5.html. Accessed on 11 Nov. 2016.

    Katada, Toshitaka. "No miracle that 99.8% of the schoolkids survived." WEDGE Infinity. Wedge, 2011. http://wedge.ismedia.jp/articles/-/1334. Accessed on 11 Nov. 2016.

    Sekine, Ryohei. "The 2011 East Japan Earthquake Bulletin of the Tohoku Geographical Association." The 2011 East Japan Earthquake Bulletin of the Tohoku Geographical Association. The Tohoku Geographical Association, 13 Jun. 2011. http://tohokugeo.jp/articles/e-contents22.html. Accessed on 11 Nov. 2016

    "The 'Miracle of Kamaishi': How 3,000 Students Survived March 11." Japan for Sustainability. Creative Commons, Sept. 2013. http://www.japanfs.org/en/news/archives/news_id034287.html. Accessed on 11 Nov. 2016.

    Osamu, Sawaji. "Education and Disaster Reduction." The Japan Journal, Feb. 2012, pp. 6-10.

3) Koizumi, Miyagi Prefecture. "The Great Wall of Japan." economist.com, 14 June 2014. Accessed 11 Nov. 2016. http://www.economist.com/news/asia/21604200-tsunami-protectionor-boondoggle-builders-great-wall-japan

4) Katada, Toshitaka. "No miracle that 99.8% of the schoolkids survived." WEDGE Infinity. Wedge, 2011. http://wedge.ismedia.jp/articles/-/1334. Accessed on 11. Nov. 2016.

5) See "Miracle of Kaimishi," 2.

6) "Three Principles of Evacuation": MSN Sankei News, 13 April 2013 http://www.seedsasia.org/hp/EJET/k_8.pdf Accessed on 11 Nov. 2016

7) ComScore, GoldSpot Media & DoubleClick, 2014 http://blog.hubspot.com/marketing/horrifying-display-advertising-stats

8) "I know at least half of my advertising budget works, I just don't know which half.": This is a quote commonly attributed to several people, including Henry Ford and John Wanamaker.

9) The legend of Billy Durant and GM:

Gustin, Lawrence R. "Billy Durant's Version of How He Founded General Motors." Generations of GM History. GM Heritage Center, 1973. https://history.gmheritagecenter.com/wiki/index.php/Billy_Durant's_Version_of_How_He_Founded_General_Motors. Accessed on Nov. 11, 2016.

Davidson, Joshua. "Durant, William Crapo." Generations of GM History. GM Heritage Center, 15 Dec. 2007. https://history.gmheritagecenter.com/wiki/index.php/Durant,_William_Crapo. Accessed on Nov. 11, 2016.

General Motors Heritage Center: history.gmheritagecenter.com/wiki/index.php/Durant,_William_Crapo

Adler, Dennis. Packard. Motorbooks International, 2004.

CHAPTER 1: The Participation Age: The next age of enlightenment

1) "Category Creation Basics: Building Your Breakthrough Innovation Model." The Cambridge Group. Nielsen, 2013. http://executive-insights.thecambridgegroup.com/v2/category-creation-basics-building-your-breakthrough-innovation-model.php. Accessed 14 Nov. 2016.

2) Rules of Three: Wolchover, Natalie. "Physicists Prove Surprising Rule of Threes." Quanta Magazine, 27 May, 2014.https://www.wired.com/2014/05/physicists-rule-of-threes-efimov-trimers/

3) Fullard-Leo, Betty. "Tsunamis, The Big Waves." Coffee Times. LBD Coffee, 2006. http://www.coffeetimes.com/tsunamis.htm. Accessed 14 Nov. 2016.

4) J. P. Eaton, D. H. Richter and W. U. Ault "The tsunami of May 23, 1960 on the island of Hawaii."http://www.bssaonline.org/content/51/2/135.abstract

5) Borromean rings: "Hint of Universal Behavior seen in Exotic 3-Atom States." Joint Quantum Institute. Joint Quantum Institute, 23 Sept. 2011. http://jqi.umd.edu/news/hints-universal-behavior-seen-exotic-3-atom-states. Accessed 14 Nov. 2016.

6) Heidrick, Bill. "Hebrew Gematria: Values from 1 – 9." Bill Heidrick's Cross References. www.billheidrick.com/works/hgm1/hg0001.htm. Accessed 14 Nov. 2016.

7) Movements and ages are subjective in some ways. I came to this conclusion through my ownknowledge, and the distinctions made by others.

"Industrial Revolution." History Channel. A&E Television Network, http://www.history.com/topics/industrial-revolution. Accessed 14 Nov. 2016

Rouse, Margaret and Linda Tucci. "Information Age." Tech Target. TechTarget. http://searchcio.techtarget.com/definition/Information-Age Accessed on 14 Nov. 2016.

8) Graham, Jefferson. "Turkey coup attempt, brought to you live via stream on Facebook: Periscope." USA Today. Gannett Satellite Information Network, 16 Jul.

2016. http://www.usatoday.com/story/tech/news/2016/07/16/turkey-coup-at-tempt-livestream-facebook-live-periscope/87168060/. Accessed on 14 Nov. 2016.

9) Full Henry Ford quote: "I will build a motor car for the great multitude...construct-ed of the best materials, by the best men to be hired, after the simplest designs that modern engineering can devise...so low in price that no man making a good salary will be unable to own one-and enjoy with his family the blessing of hours of pleasure in God's great open spaces."

Burlingame, "Henry Ford", p. 62. The precise year in which Ford issued the "multitude" statement is not known. Earliest source 6/6/13 Ford Times.

www.thehenryford.org/collections-and-research/digital-resources/popular-topics/henry-ford-quotes/

10) Sekine, Ryohei. "Did the People Practice 'Tsunami Tedenko?' http://tohokugeo.jp/articles/e-contents22.html

11) See "Miracle of Kaimishi," 2.

12) Newman, Jared. "Nearly 1 in 4 millennials have cut the cord or never had cable." TechHive. IDG Consumers & SMB, 15 Oct. 2014. http://www.techhive.com/article/2833829/nearly-1-in-4-millennials-have-cut-the-cord-or-never-had-cable.html. Accessed on 14 Nov. 2016.

13) Chaffey, Dave. "Mobile Marketing Statistics compilation." Smart Insights. Smart Insights (Marketing Intelligence) Ltd., www.smartinsights.com/mobile-marketing/mobile-marketing-analytics/mobile-marketing-statistics/. Accessed 14 Nov. 2016.

14) Kharif, Olga and Leslie Patton. "Starbucks Takes Its Pioneering Mobile-Phone App to Grande Level." Bloomberg Technology. Bloomberg L.P., 30 Mar. 2016. https://www.bloomberg.com/news/articles/2016-03-30/starbucks-takes-its-pioneering-mobile-phone-app-to-grande-level. Accessed 14 Nov. 2016.

15) Chandler, Adam. "Why is Chick-fil-A's App Number One in the App Store?" The Atlantic. The Atlantic Monthly Group, 4 Jun. 2016. http://www.theatlantic.com/business/archive/2016/06/chick-fil-a-app/485654/Accessed 14 Nov. 2016.

16) Taylor, Kate. "The biggest change in fast food isn't about food – and it should terrify the chains that can't keep up." Business Insider. Business Insider Inc., 1 May 2016. http://www.businessinsider.com/mobile-orderings-major-fast-food-impact-2016-4. Accessed 14 Nov. 2016.

Kieleer, Ashlee. "More Restaurants Push Order-Ahead Apps, But Customers Worry About Cold Food." Consumerist. Consumer Media LLC, 13 Sept. 2016. https://consumerist.com/2016/09/13/more-restaurants-push-order-ahead-apps-but-cus-tomers-worry-about-cold-food/. Accessed 14 Nov. 2016.

17) Hynum, Rick. "The 2016 Pizza Power Report: A state-of-the-industry analysis." PMQ Pizza Magazine. PMQ, Dec. 2016. http://www.pmq.com/December-2015/The-2016-Pizza-Power-Report-A-state-of-the-industry-analysis/. Accessed 14 Nov. 2016.

18) Swinderman, Amy. "Quicken Loans launches Rocket Mortgage." inman. inman, 25 Nov. 2015. http://www.inman.com/2015/11/25/quicken-loans-launches-rock-et-mortgage/. Accessed on 15 Nov. 2016.

19) Schultz, Cory. "Kaiser Permanente launches comprehensive patient app My Health Manager app for iOS." iMedicalApps, 18 May 2012. http://www.imedicalapps.com/2012/05/kaiser-permanente-launches-health-manager-app-itunes/. Accessed on 15 Nov. 2016.

20) Cendrowski, Scott. "Nike's new marketing mojo." FORTUNE. Time. 13 Feb. 2012. http://fortune.com/2012/02/13/nikes-new-marketing-mojo/ Accessed 15 Nov. 2016.

21) Shaw, Lucas and Michaela Ross. "Netflix's $5 Billion Budget Is Setting Off an Arms Race in Cable." Bloomberg Technology. Bloomberg LP, 2 Mar. 2016. https://www.bloomberg.com/news/articles/2016-03-02/media-companies-try-to-spend-their-way-out-of-cable-tv-crunch. Accessed 15 Nov. 2016.

Bookman, Samantha. "A closer look at the billions of dollars Netflix, Amazon and Hulu are spending on original content" http://www.fiercecable.com/special-report/a-closer-look-at-billions-dollars-netflix-amazon-and-hulu-are-spending-original Accessed 15 Nov. 2016

22) Cook, James. "Analysts estimate that Amazon has up to 69 million Prime subscribers" Business Insider, 2 June 2016. http://www.businessinsider.com/analysts-estimate-that-amazon-has-up-to-69-million-prime-subscribers-2016-6 Accessed 15 Nov. 2016

23) Meola, Andrew. "Traditional pay-TV loses even more ground to cord cutters". Business Insider, 16 Mar. 2016 http://www.businessinsider.com/cable-tv-curbs-subscriber-losses-but-cord-cutters-continue-to-grow-2016-3 Accessed 15 Nov. 2016

24) Onishi, Norimitsu. "Japan Revives a Sea Barrier That Failed to Hold." The New York Times. The New York Times Company, 2 Nov. 2011.http://mobile.nytimes.com/2011/11/03/world/asia/japan-revives-a-sea-barrier-that-failed-to-hold.html?_r=0. Accessed on 10 Nov. 2016.

25) Kotler, Philip, Hermawan Kartajaya, and Iwan Setiawan. Marketing 3.0: From Products to Customers to the Human Spirit. Hoboken, NJ: Wiley, 2010. Print.

26) Gazzaniga, Michael S. Who's In Charge? Free Will and the Science of the Brain. New York: Ecco, 2011. Print.

27) Maslow, A.H. (1943). "A theory of human motivation." Psychological Review. 50 (4): 370–96.

28) Wingfield-Hayes, Rupert. "Why does Japan have such a high suicide rate?" BBC News, 3 July 2015 http://www.bbc.com/news/world-33362387 Accessed 10 Jan. 2017

Min-sik, Yoon. "South Korea still has top OECD suicide rate." Korea Herald, 30 Aug. 2015 http://www.koreaherald.com/view.php?ud=20150830000310 Accessed 10 Jan. 2017

29) "Suicide Rates By Country." http://www.worldatlas.com/articles/countries-with-the-most-suicides-in-the-world.html. Accessed 10 Jan. 2017

Tavernise, Sabrina. "U.S. Suicide Rate Surges to a 30-Year High." The New York Times, 22 April 2016. www.nytimes.com/2016/04/22/health/us-suicide-rate-surges-to-a-30-year-high.html Accessed 10 Jan. 2017

30) Zak, Paul. "The Neuroscience of Trust." Harvard Business Review. Jan.-Feb. 2017 Issue.

31) Akerlof, George A., and Rachel E. Kranton. "Economics and Identity." The Quarterly Journal of Economics 116.3 (2000): Web. 11 Nov. 2016.

32) Facebook. 2004. https://www.facebook.com/pg/facebook/about/. Accessed 17 Nov. 2016.

33) Amazon. 1994. https://www.facebook.com/pg/Amazon/about/. Accessed 17 Nov. 2016.

34) Stout, Lynn A. The Shareholder Value Myth: How Putting Shareholders First Harms Investors, Corporations, and the Public. San Francisco: Berrett-Koehler, 2012. Print.

CHAPTER 2: Principles Before Pathways: How purpose-driven brands win

1) Kawasaki Ari is a real person, yet I have taken liberties with some of the quotes in order to move the story forward. Much of the news stories already consulted were used in this story as well, including the following article about the preparedness of the students.

Kamiya, Setsuko. "Students credit survival to disaster preparedness drills." The Japan Times. The Japan Times LTD, 4 Jun. 2011. http://www.japantimes.co.jp/news/2011/06/04/ national/students-credit-survival-to-disaster-prepared-ness-drills/#.WCxtnMf5z-Y. Accessed 16 Nov. 2016.

2) "The 2011 Japan Tsunami – Survivors Tell Their Stories." http://wol.jw.org/en/wol/d/r1/lp-e/102011452. Accessed 16 Nov. 2016.

3) Rebick, Stephanie. "World Peace Through International Trade and Travel." Grand Hotel World Peace Through International Trade and Travel Comments. 13 July 2011. Web. 18 Nov. 2016.

4) Wharton, Annabel Jane. Building the Cold War: Hilton International hotels and modern architecture. Chicago: U of Chicago, 2001. Print.

5) "Henry Ford." Entrepreneur. Entrepreneur Media, inc., n.d. https://www.entrepreneur.com/article/197524. Accessed 16 Nov. 2016.

6) Steve Jobs and Apple:

Ashcroft, Sean. "How Steve Jobs' vision changed the world." Macworld. IDG, 6 Oct. 2011. http://www.macworld.co.uk/news/mac/how-steve-jobs-vision-changed-world-3308914/. Accessed 16 Nov. 2016.

Farfan, Barbara. "What is Apple's Mission Statement?" the balance. About Inc., 18 Sept. 2016. https://www.thebalance.com/apple-mission-statement-4068547. Accessed 16 Nov. 2016.

7) Osman, Maddy. "Connecting Emotions with Brand Loyalty." Mabbly. 16 Aug. 2016. https://www.mabbly.com/call-beep-no-snap-me/. Accessed 16 Nov. 2016.

8) Traverse Bay Strategy Group, 2015.

9) Traverse Bay Strategy Group & Daniel Brian Advertising. CHI St. Vincent research. 2015-2016.

10) Jonathan W. Schooler, verbal overshadowing described in Blink by Malcolm Gladwell.

11) Gallup, Inc. "Behavioral Economics." Gallup.com. Web. 18 Nov. 2016.

12) "Imagination Is More Important Than Knowledge." Quote Investigator. 1 Jan. 2013. http://quoteinvestigator.com/2013/01/01/einstein-imagination/. Accessed 16 Nov. 2016.

13) Einstein, Albert. "The World As I See It." https://www.aip.org/history/exhibits/einstein/essay.htm

14) "Chrysler Eminem Super Bowl Commercial – Imported From Detroit." YouTube, Uploaded by Chrysler, 5 Feb. 2011, https://www.youtube.com/watch?v=SKL254Y_jtc.

15) Buss, Dale. "Chrysler's Eminem Spot Has Lit a Fire in Detroit." brandchannel. Interbrand, 8 Feb. 2011. http://brandchannel.com/2011/02/08/chryslers-eminem-spot-has-lit-a-fire-in-detroit/. Accessed 17 Nov. 2016.

16) Los Angeles Times Blog. 6 Feb. 2011.latimesblogs.latimes.com/showtracker/2011/02/super-bowl-ad-tracker-chrysler-eminem-proclaim-detroit-is-still-alive.html

17) Nudd, Tim. "Chrysler's 'Born of Fire' Wins Emmy for Best Commercial." ADWEEK. Adweek, 13 Sept. 2011. http://www.adweek.com/adfreak/chryslers-born-fire-wins-emmy-best-commercial-134823. Accessed 16 Nov. 2016.

18) Gladwell, Malcolm. Blink: The Power of Thinking without Thinking. New York: Little, Brown, 2005. Print.

19) Brennan, Bridget. "Top 10 Things Everyone Should Know About Women Consumers." Forbes. Forbes Media, 21 Jan. 2015. http://www.forbes.com/sites/bridgetbrennan/2015/01/21/ top-10-things-everyone-should-know-about-women-consumers/#34a5d94d2897. Accessed 17 Nov. 2016.

20) Carter, Brandon. "Millennial Loyalty Statistics: The Ultimate Collection." Access. Access Development, 18 Aug. 2016. http://blog.accessdevelopment.com/millennials-loyalty-statistics. Accessed 17 Nov. 2016.

21) For more, visit WarbyParker.com.

22) For more, visit TOMSshoes.com.

23) Cone Communications/Ebiquity Global CSR Study. 2015. www.conecomm.com/ 2015-cone-communications-ebiquity-global-csr-study-pdf. Accessed 17 Nov. 2016.

24) "Doing Well by Doing Good." Nielsen. 2014. www.nielsen.com/us/en/insights/ reports/2014/doing-well-by-doing-good.html. Accessed 17 Nov. 2016.

25) Cone Communications Digital Activism Study. 2014. www.conecomm.com/ research-blog/2014-cone-communications-digital-activism-study. Accessed 17 Nov. 2016.

26) Petruno, Tom. "Beyond profits: Millennials embrace investing for social good." Los Angeles Times. The Los Angeles Times, 7 Dec. 2014. http://www.latimes.com/ business/la-fi-socially-conscious-investing-20141207-story.html. Accessed 17 Nov. 2016.

27) "What We Give." TOMS. TOMS Shoes, LLC., http://www.toms.com/what-we-give-shoes. Accessed 17 Nov. 2016.

28) O'Connor, Clare. "Bain Deal Makes TOMS Shoe Founder Blake Mycoskie A $300 Million Man." Forbes. Forbes Media LLC., 20 Aug. 2014. http://www.forbes.com/ sites/clareoconnor /2014/08/20/bain-deal-makes-toms-shoes-founder-blake-my-coskie-a-300-million-man/#2308a7813875. Accessed 17 Nov. 2016.

29) Traverse Bay Strategy Group and Daniel Brian Advertising. Banking Research. "Aspirationals." 2016.

30) Hungry Howie's:

"2014 Top 100 Pizza Companies List." Pizza Today. Emerald Expositions, LLC., 17 Nov. 2014. http://www.pizzatoday.com/departments/features/2014-top-100-piz-za-companies/. Accessed 17 Nov. 2016.

"Love, Hope, and Pizza." The Shorty Awards. Sawhorse Media, http://shortyawards. com/ 7th/love-hope-pizza. Accessed 17 Nov. 2016.

31) Traverse Bay Strategy Group and Daniel Brian Advertising. 2015.

32) Information is based on the average cost of mammogram screenings for uninsured patients as $102 reported by Blue Cross Blue Shield of North Carolina. And based on American Cancer Society statistic that breast cancer is detected in 5 out of every 1,000 women who receive a mammogram, with a 5-year survival rate for 90% of those whose breast cancer is detected early. The Love, Hope & Pizza™ campaign raised $1.5 million, enough to provide 1,471 mammograms for uninsured women.

33) "Book Notes: An Interview With Seth Godin." Interview by Michael Hyatt. Web. www.michaelhyatt.com/book-notes-an-interview-with-seth-godin.html. Accessed 17 Nov. 2016.

CHAPTER 3: North Star Values: Your compass in the maelstrom of social conflict

1) 1936, Tagline "A Gift of Pleasure," Albert Lasker, owner, Lord & Thomas ad agency (Chicago) with George Washington Hill of American Tobacco Co.

2) 1952, Camel, R.J. Reynolds Tobacco Company, William Esty Company (ad agency), "More Doctors" campaign.

3) Weiner, Matthew. "Smoke Gets In Your Eyes"; Mad Men TV series; dir. Taylor, Alan; Episode 1, Season 1; originally aired 19 July 2007; AMC.

4) Swinland, Andrew. "Corporate social responsibility is millenni-al's new religion." Crain's, 25 March 2014. Accessed 11 Nov. 2016. www.chicagobusiness.com/article/20140325/OPINION/140329895/ corporate-social-responsibility-is-millennials-new-religion

5) "Religion: Gallup Historical Trends." www.gallup.com. Gallup, Inc. 29 Aug. 2015. Accessed 11 Nov. 2016. http://www.gallup.com/poll/1690/religion.aspx

6) Ibid., 79

7) "Theory of Mind." Goldman, Alvin. In Margolis, Eric, Richard Samuels, and Stephen P. Stich. The Oxford handbook of philosophy of cognitive science. New York: Oxford U Press, 2012. Print.

8) Gazzaniga, Michael S., The Ethical Brain. Dana Press, 2005.

Gazzaniga, Michael, Tales from Both Sides of the Brain: A Life in Neuroscience. HarperCollins, 2015.

9) Ritz-Carlton Gold Standards. http://www.ritzcarlton.com/en/about/gold-standards

10) Davidson, Kate, "Cullen/Frost CEO Looks to the Past." American Banker, 30 Nov. 2011, Accessed 11 Nov. 2016. www.americanbanker.com/specialreports/176_13/best-in-banking-community-banker-of-the-year-evans-1044478-1.html

11) Frost Bank Values Manifesto. https://thefinancialbrand.com/14141/frost-bank-core-values-manifesto-microsite/

12) "Noam Chomsky on Public Relations Industry – Principles, Mechanisms Extent." YouTube, 13 Nov. 2015. Accessed 11 Nov. 2016. https://www.youtube.com/watch?v=mLkEF8l3q1s

13) New York Times, third-quarter spending, April 21, 2016, and Digital Contact, 2016.

14) "Which three Presidential candidates are dominating the talk on social media? Digital Contact.20 Aug. 2015. http://digitalcontact.co.uk/blog/three-presidential-candidates-dominate/

15) Aron, Hillel. "Hey, What's Up with that L.A. Times Poll Showing Donald Trump Winning?" LA Weekly, 7 Oct. 2016. Accessed 11 Nov. 2016. http://www.laweekly.com/news/hey-whats-up-with-that-la-times-poll-showing-donald-trump-winning-7470190

16) Meckler, Laura. "Exit Polls 2016: Voters Show a Deep Hunger for Change." Wall Street Journal. 9 Nov. 2016. www.wsj.com/articles/exit-polls-2016-voters-back-more-liberal-immigration-policy-oppose-border-wall-1478646147?mg=id-wsj

17) Ingram, Matthew. "Here's Why the Media Failed to Predict a Donald Trump Victory." Fortune. 9 Nov. 2016. http://fortune.com/2016/11/09/media-trump-failure/

Sakuma, Amanda. "Trump Did Better With Blacks, Hispanics Than Romney in '12: Exit Polls," NBC News. 9 Nov. 2016.http://www.nbcnews.com/storyline/2016-election-day/trump-did-better-blacks-hispanics-romney-12-exit-polls-n681386

Rose, Lacey. "TV Networks, Studios Shifting Program Strategies in the Trump Age: 'Are We Telling the Right Stories?'" Hollywood Reporter. 16 Dec. 2016. www.hollywoodreporter.com/news/tv-networks-studios-shifting-program-strategies-trump-age-are-we-telling-right-stories-956768

18) De Tocqueville, Alexis, Introductory Chapter, "Democracy in America." Saunders and Otley (London), 1835-1840.

19) Vibes, John. "Snowden on Trump: Stop Putting So Much Faith and Fear In Presidents—We Must Be The Change." The Free Thought Project. 16 Nov. 2016. thefreethoughtproject.com/snowden-trump-stop-putting-presidents/

20) Cooper, Mariah, "Oregon bakery that refused lesbian customers shuts down." WashingtonBlade, 5 Oct. 2016. Accessed 11 Nov. 2016. http://www.washingtonblade.com//10/05/oregon-bakery-refused-lesbian-customers-shuts/

21) Shepherd, Eric. "Viral post by 'hero dad' about Target's bathroom policy is a parenting FAIL." 25 Apr. 2016. aporia.bangordailynews.com/2016/04/25/equality/viral-post-by-hero-dad-about-targets-bathroom-policy-is-a-parenting-fail/

22) Kangadis, Nick, "Target Stock Drops Amid Transgender Bathroom 'Inclusivity' Controversy." mrctv.org, 29 April 2016. Accessed 11 Nov. 2016. http://www.mrctv.org/blog/target-stock-drops-amid-transgender-bathroom-inclusivity-controversy

Vander, Alex. "Target loses $1.5 billion as boycott reaches 1 million." uspolitics. news, 29 April 2016. Accessed 11 Nov. 2016. www.uspolitics.news/2016/04/29/ news/2016-elections/target-loses-1-5-billion-as-boycott-reaches-1-million/2885

Smith, Lisa. "Target CEO Ignores Boycott, Claims Sales are Dropping for Unbelievable Reason." rightwingnews.com, 21 May 2016. Accessed 11 Nov. 2016.

rightwingnews.com/economy/target-ceo-ignores-boycott-claims-sales-dropping-unbelievable-reason/

Peterson, Hayley. "The Target boycott is costing more than anyone expected." businessinsider.com, 24 Aug. 2016. Accessed 11 Nov. 2016. http://www.businessinsider. com/target-boycott-costs-20-million-2016-8

23) "Kroger store's explanation of unisex bathroom goes viral." wgntv.com, 28 March 2016. Accessed 11 Nov. 2016. http://wgntv.com/2016/03/28/ kroger-stores-explanation-of-unisex-bathroom-goes-viral/

24) "Values." TheKrogerCo.com. Accessed 11 Nov. 2016. http://www.thekrogerco.com/ about-kroger/values

25) Margolin, Emma. "Target to Spend $20 Million on Single-Stall Bathrooms." nbcnews.com, 18 Aug. 2016. Accessed 11 Nov. 2016. www.nbcnews.com/feature/ nbc-out/target-spend-20-million-single-stall-bathrooms-n633801

26) Reiman, Samuel. "Watch stunt man's blind backflip over a moving Formula E race car." foxsports.com, 18 April 2016. Accessed 11 Nov. 2016. http://www.foxsports. com/motor/story/video-stunt-backflip-formula-e-041816

27) Red Bull Stratos Supersonic Jump. www.redbullstratos.com.

28) Porter, Tom. "Red Bull Under Fire Over Seventh Death at Tyrol Stunt Event." ibtimes.co.uk, 5 May 2013. Accessed 11 Nov. 2016. www.ibtimes.co.uk/ red-bull-stunt-marketing-extreme-sports-death-464619

29) Red Bull Media House Company Page. www.redbullmediahouse.com/company. html

30) KiteForum.com. https://www.kiteforum.com/viewtopic.php?t=2311335&p=187436

Ian Young is considered the pioneer or kite surfing in Australia. Born in Asbury, New South Wales, in 1960, he taught himself how to kite surf and then opened Australia's first kite surfing school in 1998. Young has won numerous kite surfing competitive awards and has served as an official at competitions. He helped found the Australian Kite Surfing Association in 1999.

http://members.iinet.com.au/~ianyoung/profile_kite.html

31) Traverse Bay Strategy Group. Banking Study, 2016.

32) "Whole Foods Market® Makes Fortune's 'Change the World' List, a Ranking of 'Companies that are Doing Well by Doing Good.'" businesswire.com, 20 Aug. 2015. Accessed 11 Nov. 2016. http://www.businesswire.com/news/ home/20150820005926/en/Foods-Market®-Fortunes-'Change-World'-List-Ranking

33) Grisales, Claudia. "Whole Foods' shares fall on earnings miss." statesman. com, 4 Nov. 2016. Accessed 11 Nov. 2016. www.statesman.com/business/ whole-foods-shares-fall-earnings-miss/Spzkz9uXaTMoyhYj8Q1CI

"4th Quarter Results Script." investor.wholefoodsmarket.com, 4 Nov. 2015. Accessed 11 Nov. 2016. http://investor.wholefoodsmarket.com/investors/events-and-presentations/event-details/2015/4th-Quarter-Results/default.aspx

34) "John Oliver Whole Food's Overcharge." The Connector uploaded to youtube. com on 9 Aug.2015. Accessed 11 Nov. 2016. https://www.youtube.com/ watch?v=JwJ0Vj3cxyQ

35) Panera Bread's "Live Consciously, Eat Deliciously" platform launched in late February 2012 after nearly a year of testing and research. The goal of the platform is to focus on the brand's philosophy of making a positive impact in their community instead of focusing on their products.

The St. Louis–based eatery sponsors Panera Cares cafés where customers are charged based on what they can afford to pay. Panera Bread has formed a partnership with Feeding America to support the nonprofit's food banks.

36) Ibid, Akerlof & Kranton (39)

37) Subaru Commercial "I'm Sorry." youtube.com, published 29 Aug. 2016. Accessed 11 Nov. 2016. https://www.youtube.com/watch?v=nRkOc-uxbu0

38) Proverb 17:28, The Holy Bible, English Standard Version.

39) Raman, Manikandan. "Chipotle Goes on the Attack with New Video, 'A Love Story.'" bezinga.com, 6 July 2016. Accessed 11 Nov. 2016. http://www.benzinga.com/news/16/07/8188790/chipotle-goes-on-the-attack-with-new-video-a-love-story

40) Strom, Stephanie. "Chipotle Food-Safety Issues Drag Down Profits." nytimes.com, 2 Feb. 2016. Accessed 11 Nov. 2016. http://www.nytimes.com/2016/02/03/business/chipotle-food-safety-illness-investigation-earnings.html?_r=0

CHAPTER 4: Life After TV Advertising: How branded storytelling will evolve

1) Koizumi, Miyagi Prefecture. "The Great Wall of Japan." economist.com, 14 June 2014. Accessed 11 Nov. 2016. http://www.economist.com/news/asia/21604200-tsunami-protectionor-boondoggle-builders-great-wall-japan

2) Ibid., Oskin (1)

3) Kleinman, Alexis. 2 Apr. 2013. www.hungtonpost.com/2013/04/02/cable-cuers-internet_n_3000576. html, Belkin and Harris Interactive Study.

4) Hollywood Reporter. 18 Apr. 2016. www.hollywoodreporter.com/news/netflix-passes-80-million-subscribers-885121

5) Meola, Andrew. "Traditional pay-TV loses even more ground to cord cutters." businessinsider.com, 16 March 2016. Accessed 11 Nov. 2016. http://www.businessinsider.com/cable-tv-curbs-subscriber-losses-but-cord-cutters-continue-to-grow-2016-3

6) Horowitz Research. "TV Trends: Millennials Stream More than Half of Their TV and are More Likely to Turn to Netflix for TV than a Live Broadcast." bulldogreporter.com, 6 May 2016. Accessed 11 Nov. 2016. https://www.bulldogreporter.com/tv-trends-millennials-stream-more-than-half-of-their-tv-and-are-more-likely-to-turn-to-netflix-for-tv-than-a-live-broadcast/

7) Boorstin, Julia. "TV industry on the brink of a cord-citing storm: Analyst." cnbc.com, 17 May 2016. Accessed 11 Nov. 2016. http://www.cnbc.com/2016/05/17/tv-industry-on-the-brink-of-a-cord-cutting-storm-analyst.html

8) Morgan Stanley analyst Benjamin Swinburne, 2013. www.businessinsider.com/brutal-50-decline-in-tv-viewership-shows-why-your-cable-bill-is-so-high-2013-1#ixzz2x1f8pWFv

9) The story of Hiro has been adapted from an article in GQ Magazine: Paterniti, Michael, and Yuko Shimizu. "Hiromitsu Shinkawa and the Japan Tsunami Rescue Story." GQ. 2016. Web. 19 Nov. 2016.

10) Teacher, Jordan. "The State of Content Marketing Heading Into 2015." contently.com, 3 Dec. 2014. Accessed 11 Nov. 2016. contently.com/strategist/2014/12/03/the-state-of-content-marketing-heading-into-2015/

11) Zimmerman, Megan. "Storytelling Can Improve Health." blog.centerforinnovation.mayo.edu, 9 Oct. 2016. Accessed 11 Nov. 2016. http://blog.centerforinnovation.mayo.edu/2015/10/09/storytelling-positively-impacting-lives-and-healthcare/

"Homer's Colonoscopy." Public service announcement for Stand Up to Cancer. Aired 5 Sept. 2008. youtube.com, uploaded 7 Dec. 2009. https://www.youtube.com/watch?v=CIbHiWvRl6M

12) 1984 Kellogg's Frosted Flakes Tony The Tiger Rapids Commercial. youtube. com, published 23 Nov. 2014. Accessed 11 Nov. 2016. https://www.youtube.com/ watch?v=nucoClXiaac

Keebler Elves Rich'n Chips Commercial - 1980s Vintage Advertisement. youtube. com, published 30 May 2014. https://www.youtube.com/watch?v=9zBwXop5fAk

Marlboro TV commercial 1960s. youtube.com, published 9 July 2014. Accessed 11 Nov. 2016. https://www.youtube.com/watch?v=1TUQoP-QkpQ

13) Patel, Ushma. "Hassan brings real life into the lab to examine cognitive processing." princeton.edu, 5 Dec. 2011. Accessed 11 Nov. 2016. www.princeton.edu/main/ news/archive/S32/27/76E76/index.xml?section=science

14) Gardner, Gail. "How Steve Wynn Used Storytelling to Build Company Culture." growmap.com, 28 Oct. 2016. Accessed 11 Nov. 2016. http://growmap.com/ steve-wynn-storytelling/

15) goodreads. Maya Angelou quotes. goodreads.com. Accessed 11 Nov. 2016. https:// www.goodreads.com/author/quotes/3503.Maya_Angelou

16) Connor, Jay. "The Pixar Pitch! Telling Your Story Crisply and with Clarity in order to Compel Action." workingdifferently.com, 25 March 2013. Accessed 11 Nov. 2016. http://www.workingdifferently.org/working-differently-blog/the-pixar-pitch-telling-your-story-crisply-and-with-clarity-in-order-to-compel-action

17) Coats, Emma. (@lawnrocket) "Pixar's Rules of Storytelling." PBJPublishing.com. pixar-animation.weebly.com. Accessed 11 Nov. 2016. http://pixar-animation. weebly.com/pixars-rules.html

18) Transformers. Director: Michael Bay. Screenplay: Roberto Orci, Alex Kurtzman. Story: John Rogers, Roberto Orci, Alex Kurtzman. Production: Hasbro Studios diBonaventura Pictures. Distributed by DreamWorks Pictures. Release date: 3 July 2007 (USA).

19) "GM cuts back marketing budget for 2009, hurts AutoBots' feelings." egmcartech. com, 27 Feb. 2007. Accessed 11 Nov. 2016. http://www.egmcartech.com/2009/02/27/ gm-cuts-back-marketing-budget-for-2009-hurts-autobots-feelings/

20) Garrett, Mike (words), Chen, Larry (images). "Boosted Bandit: A '70s Icon Reinvented." speedhunters.com, 24 April 2015. Accessed 11 Nov. 2016. http://www. speedhunters.com/2015/04/boosted-bandit-a-70s-icon-reinvented/

21) McKnight, Brent. "The Ridiculous Number of Cars Burt Reynolds Burned Through Filming Smokey and the Bandit." cinemablend.com. Accessed 11 Nov. 2016. http:// www.cinemablend.com/new/Ridiculous-Number-Cars-Burt-Reynolds-Burned-Through-Filming-Smokey-Bandit-79437.html

22) Henry Ford Health System. Minds of Medicine. 2005—Present.

23) For further reading on the idea of "closure": Buckarova, Mariana Ph.D. "Why We Need Closure." psychologytoday.com, 17 Sept. 2016. Accessed 11 Nov. 2016. https://www.psychologytoday.com/blog/romantically-attached/201609/ why-we-need-closure

24) The Sixth Sense. Director: M. Night Shyamalan. Screenplay: M. Night Shyamalan. Production: Hollywood Pictures, Spyglass Entertainment, The Kennedy/Marshall Company, Barry Mendel Productions. Release date: 6 Aug. 1999 (USA). imdb.com. Accessed 11 Nov. 2016. http://www.imdb.com/title/tt0167404/?ref_=nv_sr_1

25) Ogilvy, David. "Confessions of an Advertising Man." Atheneum. Publication Date: August 1963.

26) Wieden+Kennedy. "I'm On a Horse," Old Spice Commercial. youtube.com, uploaded 10 May 2010 by commerciallydazzling. Accessed 11 Nov. 2016. https://www. youtube.com/watch?v=VX5auoLOJp8

27) "Case Study: Old Spice Response Campaign." D&AD. D&AD, http://www.dandad. org/en/d-ad-old-spice-case-study-insights/. Accessed 17 Nov. 2016.

28) For more on the Triune Brain Theory:

MacLean, Paul. "Brain evolution relating to family, play, and the separation call." Archives of General Psychiatry. 1985.

MacLean, Paul. The triune brain in evolution: role in paleocerebral functions. New York: Plenum Press. 1990.

Nomura T, Kawaguchi M, Ono K, Murakami Y. 2013. Reptiles: A New Model for Brain Evo-Devo Research.

29) See Malcolm Gladwell's Blink (Little, Brown and Company, New York 2005) p. 119-122.

30) Scheve, Tom. "How many muscles does it take to smile?" 2 June 2009. HowStuffWorks.com. science.howstuffworks.com/life/inside-the-mind/emotions/muscles-smile.htm

31) Hormby, Tom. "Think Different: The Ad Campaign that Restored Apple's Reputation." Low End Mac. 10 Aug. 2013. http://lowendmac.com/2013/think-different-ad-campaign-restored-apples-reputation/. Accessed 18 Nov. 2016.

32) Olson, Parmy. "BlackBerry's Famous Last Words At 2007 iPhone Launch: 'We'll Be Fine'" Forbes. Forbes Magazine, 26 May 2015. www.forbes.com/sites/parmyolson/2015/05/26/blackberry-iphone-book/#1d75980a4547

33) Taylor, William C. Simply Brilliant: How Great Organizations Do Ordinary Things in Extraordinary Ways. Portfolio, 20 Sept. 2016.

34) "Richard Branson: The P.T. Barnum of British Business." Entrepreneur. Entrepreneur Media Inc., 10 Oct. 2008. https://www.entrepreneur.com/article/197616. Accessed 18 Nov. 2016.

Varadian, Kevin. "Virgin America. The Best Airline. Ever." LinkedIn. LinkedIn Corporation, 14 Nov. 2014. https://www.linkedin.com/pulse/20141114034144-23168-virgin-america-the-best-airline-ever. Accessed 18 Nov. 2016.

35) Ross, Randy Dr. and David Salyers. Remarkable!: Maximizing Results through Value Creation. Baker Books, 9 Feb, 2016

36) Facebook views ranked by Facebook reports compiled by Daniel Brian Advertising analytics, 2016.

37) Grider, Geoffrey. "Chick-Fil-A Passes McDonald's For First Time In 25 Years In This Category."Now The End Begins. 10 Sept. 2014. www.nowtheendbegins.com/chick-fil-passes-mcdonalds-first-time-25-years-category/

38) Tice, Carol. "7 Fast-Food Restaurant Chains That Rake In $2M+ Per Store." Forbes. Forbes Media, 14 Aug. 2014. www.forbes.com/sites/caroltice/2014/08/14/7-fast-food-restaurantchains-that-rake-in-2m-per-store/#4aac1489ce5a. Accessed 18 Nov. 2016.

Beard, Ross. "How Chick-Fil-A Creates A Memorable Experience (And Grows Revenue By 13% Annually)." Client Heartbeat. Client Heartbeat, 19 Nov. 2014. http://blog.clientheartbeat.com/chick-fil-a-customer-experience/. Accessed 17 Nov. 2016.

39) Daniel Brian Advertising bank study. 2016.

40) Daniel Brian Advertising. 2016.

41) Gerber Products Company. 2013.

42) "Customers Reward Outstanding Service by Spending More and Spreading the Word to Friends and Family." American Express. American Express Company, n.d. http://about.americanexpress.com/news/pr/2014/outstanding-service-spend-more-spread-word.aspx. Accessed 18 Nov. 2016.

43) Freeman, Debbie. "New Customer-Rage Study out for Holiday Shopping Season." W.P. Carey School of Business. Arizona State University, 16 Nov. 2013. https://wpcarey.asu.edu/ news-releases/2013-11-26/new-customer-rage-study-out-holiday-shopping-season. Accessed 18 Nov. 2016.

Fainberg, Sasha. "Apologies Lead to Customer Satisfaction." SMARI. SMARI, 18 Jun. 2015. http://www.smari.com/apologies-customer-satisfaction/. Accessed 18 Nov. 2016.

44) Brown, Brandon. "How brands like GoPro & Red Bull turned the marketing message, and medium, into revenue streams." Group Y.

45) Gillum, Scott. Forbes. Forbes Magazine, 7 Jan. 2013. Web. 20 Nov. 2016. www.forbes.com/sites/gyro/2013/01/07/the-disappearing-sales-process

46) Bianchini, Daniel. "10 Stats to Justify SEO." Search Engine Journal, 19 Nov. 2011. Web. 20 Nov. 2016. www.searchenginejournal.com/10-stats-to-justify-seo/36762/

CHAPTER 5: Don't Just Buy the Media, Be The Media: Tectonic shifts in the way brands engage consumers

1) "The 2011 Japan Tsunami Was Caused By Largest Fault Slip Ever Recorded." nationalgeographic.com. 2013. Web. 18 Nov. 2016.

"How Shifting Plates Caused The Japan Earthquake - Interactive Feature." Nytimes.com. 2016. Web. 18 Nov. 2016.

Marder, Jenny. "Japan's Earthquake And Tsunami: How They Happened". PBS NewsHour. 2011. Web. 18 Nov. 2016.

2) Daniel Brian Advertising. 2015.

3) "98% of Push Notifications & Text Messages are Opened." iminmarketer.com. Accessed 20 Nov.2016. http://iminmarketer.com/98-of-push-notifications-text-messages-are-opened/

4) Reece, Fischer. "Walt Disney: The Early Years." plosion.com, 2004. www.plosin.com/beatbegins/projects/fischer.html Accessed 20 Nov. 2016.

5) Fabrikant, Geraldine. "Walt Disney to Acquire ABC in $19 Billion Deal to Build a Giant for Entertainment." The New York Times. The New York Times, 31 July 1995. Web. 15 Jan. 2017.

6) "Who Knows?" Surfline. http://www.surfline.com/community/whoknows/whoknows.cfm?id=1132. Accessed 20 Nov. 2016.

7) Lawrence, Alex. "Five Customer Retention Tips for Entrepreneurs." Forbes. 1 Nov. 2012. www.forbes.com/sites/alexlawrence/2012/11/01/five-customer-retention-tips-for-entrepreneurs/#3bc9fb5417b0Accessed 20 Nov. 2016.

8) Dilger, Daniel Eran. "Apple Inc. gears up to distribute $3.2 billion in dividends to shareholders" Apple Insider. 11 Aug. 2016. http://appleinsider.com/articles/16/08/09/apple-inc-gears-up-to-distribute-32-billion-in-dividends-to-shareholders- Accessed 20 Nov. 2016

9) Covert, Adrian. "A decade of iTunes singles killed the music industry." 25 Apr. 2015. money.cnn.com/2013/04/25/technology/itunes-music-decline/ Accessed 20 Nov. 2016

10) Costello, Sam. "How Many iPhones Have Been Sold Worldwide?" lifewire.com, 3 Nov. 2016. https://www.lifewire.com/how-many-iphones-have-been-sold-1999500 Accessed 20 Nov. 2016.

11) Kapner, Suzanne. "Amazon Struts Its Fashion Sense, Challenging Traditional Stores." Wall Street Journal. wsj.com, 6 April 2016. Accessed 20 Nov. 2016. http://www.wsj.com/articles/amazon-struts-its-fashion-sense-challenging-traditional-stores-1459965440

12) Chowdhry, Amit. Amazon Testing Same Day Delivery. 8 Apr. 2016. www.forbes.com/sites/amitchowdhry/2016/04/08/amazon-adds-11-more-cities-to-same-day-delivery-service/#7a9985b03b92 Accessed 20 Nov. 2016.

13) Nike Mission Statement. Nike.com. help-us.nikeinc.com/app/answers/detail/a_id/113/~/nike-mission-statement Accessed 20 Nov. 2016.

14) BizBash 2016: www.bizbash.com/event-innovators-2016-top-10-innovative-brands/new-york/story/32138#.WDHTkmUSB5E

BizBash 2015: www.bizbash.com/event-innovators-2015-top-10-innovative-brands/new-york/story/30679/#.WDHTz2USB5E

BizBash 2014: www.bizbash.com/event-innovators-2014-top-10-innovative-brands/new-york/story/28724/#.WDHULWUSB5E

FastCompany 2014: www.fastcompany.com/most-innovative-companies/2014

FastCompany 2013: www.fastcompany.com/most-innovative-companies/2013

15) Fleming, Kristen. "Why Thousands of People are Running with Kevin Hart." 27 Oct. 2015. nypost.com/2015/10/27/why-thousands-of-people-are-running-with-kevin-hart/

16) Petersen, Kelly. "28M-strong mobile community gives Nike competitive edge." Carnival.io, accessed 20 Nov. 2016. insights.carnival.io/28m-strong-mobile-community-gives-nike-competitive-edge

17) Plaft, Fred. "Why Marketers Need to Reorganize Around the Most Powerful Behavior Principle of All: Utility." Ad Age, 15 April 2013. Accessed 20 Nov. 2016. adage.com/article/guest-columnists/utility-powerful-behavior-principle/240860/

18) Reddit. "No Stupid Questions." Web Forum. Accessed 20 Nov. 2016. www.reddit.com/r/NoStupidQuestions/comments/36yt7a/what_happens_to_a_submarine_during_a_tsunami/

19) "Lessons from the Leading Edge of Customer Experience Management." White Paper. Harvard Business Review. 2014. Harvard Business School Publishing. Accessed 20 Nov. 2016. www.sas.com/content/dam/SAS/en_us/doc/whitepaper2/hbr-leading-edge-customer-experience-mgmt-107061.pdf

20) Sculley, John (CMO Humana) and Broussard, Bruce (CE Humana). "It's Time to Disrupt the $3 Trillion Healthcare Industry." Forbes, 16 Nov. 2016. Accessed 20 Nov. 2016. http://www.forbes.com/sites/sciencebiz/2016/11/16/its-time-to-disrupt-the-3-trillion-healthcare-industry/#46b506d22534

21) Sullivan, Mark. VB News. 26 July 2014. "Health Trends." inventivhealth.com, 2015. Accessed 20 Nov. 2016. page 14. inventivhealth.com/pdf/2015HealthTrends_GSW.pdf

22) Pai, Aditi. "Report: 4.9M members use Kaiser's line health management platform." mobihealthnews.com, 30 July 2015. Accessed 20 Nov. 2016. www.mobihealthnews.com/45726/report-4-9m-members-use-kaisers-online-health-management-platform

23) Comstock, Jonah. "Mayo Clinic study finds app reduces cardiac readmissions by 40 percent." mobihealthnews.com, 1 April 2014. Accessed 20 Nov. 2016. www.mobihealthnews.com/31580/mayo-clinic-study-finds-app-reduces-cardiac-readmissions-by-40-percent

24) Plaft, Fred. "Why Marketers Need to Reorganize Around the Most Powerful Behavior Principle of All: Utility." Ad Age. 15 April 2013. Accessed 20 Nov. 2016. adage.com/article/guest-columnists/utility-powerful-behavior-principle/240860/

25) IBM is No. 47 on Fortune's 2016 "Change the World List." Fortune. Accessed 20 Nov. 2016. beta.fortune.com/change-the-world/ibm-47

26) Marinier, Michael. "IBM Watson and Metropolitan Health Transform African Health Care." IBM developerWorks, 21 May 2015. Accessed 20 Nov. 2016. www.ibm.com/developerworks/community/blogs/dfa2dc54-5a14-4cf8-91e0-978bfd59d0d4/entry/ibm_watson_and_metropolitan_health_transform_african_health_care?lang=en

27) Sterling, Greg. "Report: 60% of Internet Access is Mostly Mobile." Marketing Land. 19 Feb. 2014. marketingland.com/outside-us-60-percent-internet-access-mostly-mobile-74498

28) Daniel Brian Advertising. Study with Flagstar Bank. 2016.

29) Daniel Brian Advertising. Study with Flagstar Bank. 2016.

30) Ziobro, Paul and Ng, Serena. "Wal-Mart Ratchets Up Pressure on Suppliers to Cut Prices." The Wall Street Journal. 31 March 2015. Accessed 20 Nov. 2016. www.wsj.com/articles/wal-mart-ratchets-up-pressure-on-suppliers-to-cut-prices-1427845404

31) McCormack, David. "Netflix now accounts for 35% of peak internet traffic — more than double nearest rival YouTube." dailymail.com, 20 Nov. 2014. Accessed 20 Nov. 2016. www.dailymail.co.uk/news/article-2843225/Netflix-accounts-35-peak-internet-traffic-double-nearest-rival-YouTube.html

Amazon annual sales in 2015: $107B. statistic.com, accessed 20 Nov. 2016. www.statista.com/statistics/266282/annual-net-revenue-of-amazoncom/

https://www.statista.com/statistics/272545/annual-revenue-of-netflix/

32) Goenka, Himanshu. "Jeff Bezos Says Amazon (AMZN) To Invest $3 Billion More In India." International Business Times. 2016. Web. 20 Nov. 2016.

Kline, Daniel B. "Amazon Prime Members Spend Almost Twice as Much as Non-Members." The Motley Fool. 23 June 2014. Web. 20 Nov. 2016.

33) Ibid. Morgan Stanley (128).

34) Miller, Mark J. "Red Bull TV is Coming to Linear TV—and Virtual Reality." brandchannel.com, 17 April 2015. Accessed 19 Nov. 2016. http://brandchannel.com/2015/04/17/red-bull-tv-041715/

35) Christensen, Clayton M. and Raynor, Michael E. (authors). The Innovator's Solution. Harvard Business School Publishing Corporation, 2003.

36) Duggan, Maeve. "Gaming and Gamers." pewinternet.org, 15 Dec. 2015. Accessed 19 Nov. 2016. www.pewinternet.org/2015/12/15/who-plays-video-games-and-identifies-as-a-gamer/

37) "The Global Games Market 2016 | Per Region & Segment | Newzoo." Newzoo. Web. 20 Nov. 2016. newzoo.com/insights/articles global-games-market-reaches-99-6-billion-2016-mobile-generating-37/

38) "59% of Americans Play Video Games, 51% Of Households Own Two Consoles on Average, Report Finds." dualshockers.com, accessed 19 Nov. 2016. www.dualshockers.com/2014/04/28/59-of-americans-play-video-games-51-of-households-own-two-consoles-on-average-report-finds/

39) Hideyuki, Sano (Reuters). "Nintendo's market cap doubles to $42 billion since Pokemon GO launch." yahoo.com, 19 July 2016. Accessed 19 Nov. 2016. www.yahoo.com/news/nintendos-market-cap-doubles-42-billion-since-pokemon-072709283--finance.html

40) Perez, Sarah. "Pokémon Go tops Twitter's daily users, sees more engagement than Facebook." techcrunch.com, 13 July 2016. Accessed 19 Nov. 2016. techcrunch.com/2016/07/13/pokemon-go-tops-twitters-daily-users-sees-more-engagement-than-facebook/

41) Smith, Craig. "75 Incredible Pokemon Go Statistics (November 2016)." expandedramblings.com, 15 Nov. 2016. expandedramblings.com/index.php/pokemon-go-statistics/

42) Schiavo, Amanda. " 'Pokemon Go' Helping Small Business Owner Boost Sales." thestreet.com, 13 July 2016. www.thestreet.com/story/13638437/1/lsquo-pok-ea-cute-mon-go-rsquo-helping-small-business-owner-boost-sales.html

Chapter 6: Big Data Surfing: Riding a Tsunami of media innovation

1) Jeff Clark stories:

Jeff Clark (surfer). en.wikipedia.org. Accessed 19 Nov. 2016. en.wikipedia.org/wiki/Jeff_Clark_(surfer)

"Titans of Mavericks: History." titansofmavericks.com. Accessed 19 Nov. 2016. http://titansofmavericks.com/history/

"Back in the Big Waves." rebuildjeffclark.blogspot.com, 9 Nov. 2009. Accessed 19 Nov 2016. http://rebuildjeffclark.blogspot.com/2009/11/back-in-big-waves.html

2) Haro, Alexander. "Disruptors: The History Behind the Invention of Tow Surfing." theinteria.com, 8 Nov. 2015. Accessed 19 Nov. 2016. www.theinertia.com/surf/disruptors-the-history-behind-the-invention-of-tow-surfing/

3) "Garrett McNamara breaks world record surfing 100 foot wave!" youtube.com. Published 29 Jan 2013 by CleanTVcom. Accessed 19 Nov. 2016. www.youtube.com/watch?v=LM2u3NknU4Q

"Hawaiian surfer Garrett McNamara rides monster waves off Nazare, Portugal." telegraph.co.uk, accessed 19 Nov. 2016. www.telegraph.co.uk/sport/picturegalleries/9837058/Hawaiian-surfer-Garrett-McNamara-rides-monster-waves-off-Nazare-Portugal.html

4) Verne, Jules. Twenty Thousand Leagues Under the Sea. 1870.

5) Wall, Mike. Space Station's 3D Printer Makes Wrench From 'Beamed Up' Design. Space.com. 23 Dec. 2014. www.space.com/28095-3d-printer-space-station-ratchet-wrench.html

6) Marketing Charts, June 14, 2016. http://www.marketingcharts.com/research/

"For the First Time, More than Half of American Will Watch Streaming TV." emarketer.com, 3 Feb. 2016. Accessed 19 Nov. 2016. www.emarketer.com/Article/First-Time-More-Than-Half-of-Americans-Will-Watch-Streaming-TV/1013543

7) Digital TV, Movie Streaming Reaches a Tipping Point. eMarketer. 2 Apr. 2013. www.emarketer.com/Article/Digital-TV-Movie-Streaming-Reaches-Tipping-Point/1009775

8) Bruell, Alexandra. Programmatic TV to Account for $10 billion of TV Budgets by 2019. 28 May 2015. adage.com/article/agency-news/programmatic-tv-climb-10-billion-global-tv-budgets-2019/298786/

9) Berman, Dan, and Adam Wollner. "Websites Are Already Selling Out of Ad Inventory for 2016." National Journal. Web. 20 Nov. 2016. www.nationaljournal.com/s/72369/websites-are-already-selling-out-ad-inventory-2016

10) Higginbotham, Stacey. Inside Facebook's Biggest Artificial Intelligence Project Ever. Fortune. fortune.com/facebook-machine-learning/

11) Hetzner, Christiaan & Wolde, Haro Ten. Putting Cars In Video Games Is Now A $2.8 Billion Industry. The Huffington Post. www.huffingtonpost.com/2013/08/22/car-in-video-games_n_3793607.html

"Product Placement in Movie Industry." pwc.com, 2012. Accessed 19 Nov. 2016. www.pwc.com/it/it/publications/assets/docs/product-placement-movie.pdf

"The Economics of Product Placements." priceonomics.com, 4 Dec. 2013. Accessed 19 Nov, 2016. priceonomics.com/the-economics-of-product-placements/

12) Amit, Seth. "Nielsen Simulmedia - The Data-Driven Future of Video Advertising - Whitepaper." slideshare.net, 4 March 2014. Accessed 19 Nov. 2016. www.slideshare.net/aseth/nielsen-simulmedia-future-of-video-advertising-whitepaper

13) MyersBizNet Media and Marketing Investment Data and Forecasts, January 30, 2013. eMarketer. March 2016 shows $9.84 billion in digital video, plus Marketing Charts shows $5.4 billion in online TV networks like Hulu.

14) "More people watched the Super Bowl online than ever before." steakhouse.net, accessed 19 Nov. 2016. www.stephouse.net/2016/03/more-people-watched-the-super-bowl-online-than-ever-before/

15) House of Cards, created by Beau Willmon. Adaptation of the BBC's mini-series of the same name. Based on a novel by Michael Dobbs (Chivers, North America, 1989). Premiered 27 Feb 2015 on Netflix.

Orange is the New Black, created by Jenji Kohan. Produced by Tilted Productions in association with Lionsgate Television. Based on Piper Kerman's memoir Orange is the New Black: My Year in a Women's Prison (Spiegel & Grau, 2010, USA). Premiered on 11 July 2013 on Netflix.

Stranger Things, created by the Duffer Brothers (Matt Duffer and Ross Duffer). Produced by Shawn Levy. Premiered 15 July 2016 on Netflix.

16) Yee, Nick. "As Gamers Age, the Appeal of Competition Drops the Most. Strategy is the Most Age-Stable Motivation." quanticfoundry.com, 10 Feb. 2016. Accessed 19 Nov. 2016. quanticfoundry.com/2016/02/10/gamer-generation/

Gaudiosi, John. "'Fallout 4' $750 million game launch leaves 'Call of Duty' in the dust." fortune.com, 16 Nov. 2015. Accessed 18 Nov. 2016. fortune.com/2015/11/16/fallout4-is-quiet-best-seller/

North, Dale. "155m Americans play video games, and 80% of households own a gaming device." venturebeat.com, 14 April 2015. Accessed 18 Nov. 2016. venturebeat.com/2015/04/14/155-million-americans-play-video-games-and-4-out-of-5-households-own-a-gaming-device/

17) Campbell, Colin. "Here's how many people are playing games in America." polygon.com, 14 April 2015. Accessed 18 Nov. 2016. www.polygon.com/2015/4/14/8415611/gaming-stats-2015

18) Everson, Bryan. "Pokemon Go Takes Area, World By Storm. Rochester & Rochester Hills Gazette. 21 July 2016. www.gazettemediagroup.com/uploads/1/3/3/1/13313629/rrhg7-21-16.pdf

19) The story of Susumu Sugawara: Hancocks, Paula. "Defiant Japanese boat captain rode out tsunami." cnn.com, 3 April 2011. Accessed 18 Nov. 2016. www.cnn.com/2011/WORLD/asiapcf/04/03/japan.tsunami.captain/

20) Harlan, Josh. "Meet the 'Muckers' Behind Edison's Great inventions." modernnotion.com, 15 May 2015. Accessed 18 Nov. 2016. modernnotion.com/meet-the-muckers-behind-edisons-great-inventions/

21) Gennawey, Sam. The Disneyland Story: The Unofficial Guide to the Evolution of Walt Disney's Dream. Birmingham, AL: Keen Communications, LLC, 2014. Print.

22) "CMOs Hungry for More Consumer Insights from Digital Advertising, According to The CMO Club and SocialCode Report." socialcode.com, 3 Dec. 2015. Accessed 18 Nov. 2016. socialcode.com/thought-leadership/press-center/press-releases/cmos-hungry-for-more-consumer-insights-from-digital-advertising-according-to-the-cmo-club-and-socialcode-report/

23) Sinai, Jim. "Introducing Salesforce Einstein — AI for Everyone." salesforce.com, 19 Sept. 2016. Accessed 18 Nov. 2016. www.salesforce.com/blog/2016/09/introducing-salesforce-einstein.html

24) Vranica, Suzanne and Marshall, Jack. "Facebook Overestimated Key Video Metric for Two Years." wsj.com, 22 Sept. 2016. Accessed 18 Nov. 2016. www.wsj.com/articles/facebook-overestimated-key-video-metric-for-two-years-1474586951

25) Ibid, Gennawey (229).

26) Christensen, Clayton. The Innovator's Dilemma: When New Technologies Cause Great Firms to Fail. Harvard Business Review Press. 1997.

27) Collins, James C. Good to Great: Why Some Companies Make the Leap...and Others Don't." William Collins, Publisher. USA. 16 Oct. 2001.

Collins, James C. and Hansen, Morten T. Great by Choice: Uncertainty, Chaos and Luck — Why Some Thrive Despite Them All. HarperCollins, New York, NY. 11 Oct. 2011.

Collins, James C. and Porras, Jerry I. Built to Last: Successful Habits of Visionary Companies. HarperBusiness, an imprint of HarperCollins Publishers, USA. 1994.

28) Wu, Tim. "The Apple Two." slate.com, 6 April 2010. Accessed 18 Nov. 2016. www.slate.com/articles/technology/technology/2010/04/the_apple_two.html

29) Collins, James C. and Hansen, Morten T. Great by Choice. HarperCollins (New York, NY), 11 Oct. 2011. p. 74-77.

30) Ibid. Social Code (230).

31) "First-Ever Information Value Index from PwC and Iron Mountain." ironmountain.com, 2015. Accessed 18 Nov. 2016. www.ironmountain.com/Knowledge-Center/Reference-Library/View-by-Document-Type/Infographics/I/Information-Value-Index.aspx

32) Washerman, Todd. "Despite the Hype, Marketers Still Are Mostly Fumbling Around with Data." cmo.com, 9 Mar 2016. Accessed 18 Nov. 2016. www.cmo.com/features/articles/2016/1/27/despite-the-hype-marketers-still-are-mostly-fumbling-around-with-data.html#gs.null

33) Dan, Avi. "Why P&G Is Quickly Shifting to a Digital-First Approach to Building Brands." forbes.com, 12 March 2015. Assessed 18 Nov. 2016. www.forbes.com/sites/avidan/2015/03/12/why-pg-is-quickly-shifting-to-a-digital-first-approach-to-building-brands/#4b7285b12753

Neff, Jack. "P&G's Pritchard on Where Marketing, Media and Metrics are Going." adage.com, 16 March 2015. Accessed 18 Nov. 2016. adage.com/article/cmo-strategy/p-g-s-pritchard-marketing-metrics/297592/

Neff, Jack. "Procter & Gamble Aims to Buy 70% of Digital Ads Programmatically." adage.com, 4 June 2014. Accessed 18 Nov. 2016. adage.com/article/digital/procter-gamble-buy-70-digital-ads-programmatically/293553/

Terqlep, Sharon and Seetharaman, Deepa. "P&G to Scale Back Targeted Facebook Ads." wsj.com, 17 Aug. 2016. Accessed 18 Nov. 2016. www.wsj.com/articles/p-g-to-scale-back-targeted-facebook-ads-1470760949

34) "How Much Does Amazon Spend on Digital Marketing?" spinutech.com, 9 Aug. 2016. Accessed 18 Nov. 2016. www.spinutech.com/blog/digital-marketing/how-much-does-amazon-spend-on-digital-marketing/

35) Marketing Charts, June 14, 2016 adds $5.4 billion to this 20% figure by counting Hulu and streaming TV as separate from the general digital category.

"US Spending on Paid Media Expected to Climb 5.1% in 2016." emarketer.com, 25 March 2016. Accessed 18 Nov. 2016. www.emarketer.com/Article/US-Spending-on-Paid-Media-Expected-Climb-51-2016/1013739

"Digital Ad Spend Could Eclipse TV By 2017, Cowen Says; Facebook, LinkedIn PTs Raised." Street Insider. 12 Jan. 2015. www.streetinsider.comAnalyst+Comments-Digital+Ad+Spend+Could+Eclipse+TV+By+2017,+Cowen+Says%3B+Facebook+(F-B),+LinkedIn+(LNKD)+PTs+Raised/10155305.html

Cowen and Company, "Programmatic Spotlight: Ad Buyer Survey IV & Criteo Implications, Jan 25, 2016

36) Google and Boston Consulting Group Case Study. slideshare.com, 8 March 2016. Accessed 18 Nov. 2016. www.slideshare.net/IAB_Europe/google-and-boston-consulting-group-case-study

37) Daniel Brian Advertising. 2015-2016.

38) "Kiwi surfer rides out tsunami." tvnz.co.nz, 3 Oct. 2009. Accessed 11 Nov. 2016. tvnz.co.nz/content/3046293/2591764/video.xhtml

DANIEL COBB
CEO/Chief Strategy Officer
Daniel Brian Advertising

For almost 30 years, Daniel has had the pleasure of advising and working with some of the world's most remarkable and fastest-growing brands, including Disney, Warner Bros., Domino's Pizza, Hungry Howie's Pizza, Chick-fil-A, Sony, General Motors, Microsoft, Henry Ford Health System, Valley Children's Healthcare, Blue Cross Blue Shield, SSM Health, Flagstar Bank and Citizens Bank, among others.

With a corporate purpose of "Better Brands for a Better Human Condition," Daniel believes success is a science that follows a worthy contribution to society, rather than the clever use of social manipulation.

Frustrated with the limitations of traditional advertising, Daniel built DBA with the intent to reinvent the marketing industry. Today, DBA is a leading agency, serving some of the fastest-growing businesses in health care, retail, food, finance and branded entertainment marketing.

RECOGNITIONS:

21 Emmy Awards, plus advertising and Web awards, including Caddy, D Awards, Target, Global and Telly, Corp! Magazine's "Entrepreneur of Distinction" and Future 50 of Detroit.

CONTACT

www.linkedin.com/in/danielbrian

Speaking engagements or RFPs:
info@danielbrian.com

Personal notes:
dcobb@danielbrian.com

Daniel Brian Advertising
222 S. Main
Rochester, MI 48307
248.601.5201
danielbrian.com